Healthcare Knowledge Management Primer

Quality care of patients requires evaluating large amounts of data at the right time and place and in the correct context. With the advent of electronic health records, data warehouses now provide information at the point of care and facilitate a continuous learning environment in which lessons learned can provide updates to clinical, administrative, and financial processes. Given the advancement of the information tools and techniques of today's knowledge economy, utilizing these resources is imperative for effective healthcare. Thus, the principles of Knowledge Management (KM) are now essential for quality healthcare management.

The *Healthcare Knowledge Management Primer* explores and explains essential KM principles in healthcare settings in an introductory and easy to understand fashion. This concise book is ideal for both students and professionals who need to learn more about key aspects of the KM field as it pertains to effecting superior healthcare delivery. It provides readers with an understanding of approaches to KM by examining the purpose and nature of its key components and demystifies the KM field by explaining in an accessible manner the key concepts of KM tools, strategies and techniques, and their benefits to contemporary healthcare organizations.

Nilmini Wickramasinghe is Associate Professor at the Stuart School of Business, Illinois Institute of Technology, and Co-director of the IIT Center for the Management of Medical Technology, Chicago, U.S.

Rajeev K. Bali is a Reader in Healthcare Knowledge Management at Coventry University. He heads the Knowledge Management for Healthcare (KARMAH) research subgroup (part of the Biomedical Computing and Engineering Technologies (BIOCORE) Applied Research Group) based in the Health Design and Technology Institute (HDTI).

Brian Lehaney is Professor of Systems Management in Coventry University's Faculty of Engineering and Computing.

Jonathan L. Schaffer is Managing Director of the Information Technology Division of the e-Cleveland Clinic as well as an active surgical member of the Department of Orthopaedic Surgery, Cleveland Clinic, U.S.

M. Chris Gibbons is Associate Director of the Johns Hopkins Urban Health Institute (UHI), Director of the Center for Community HEALTH (CCH) and Assistant Professor of Public Health and Medicine at Johns Hopkins Medical Institutions, Baltimore, U.S.

Routledge Series in Information Systems

Edited by Steve Clarke (Hull University Business School, U.K.),
M. Adam Mahmood (University of Texas at El Paso, U.S.A.), and
Morten Thanning Vendelø (Copenhagen Business School, Denmark)

The overall aim of the series is to provide a range of text books for advanced undergraduate and postgraduate study and to satisfy the advanced undergraduate and postgraduate markets, with a focus on key areas of those curricula.

The key to success lies in delivering the correct balance between organizational, managerial, technological, theoretical and practical aspects. In particular, the interaction between, and interdependence of, these often different perspectives is an important theme. All texts demonstrate a "theory into practice" perspective, whereby the relevant theory is discussed only in so far as it contributes to the applied nature of the domain. The objective here is to offer a balanced approach to theory and practice.

Information Systems is a rapidly developing and changing domain, and any book series needs to reflect current developments. It is also a global domain, and a specific aim of this series, as reflected in the international composition of the editorial team, is to reflect its global nature. The purpose is to combine state-of-the-art topics with global perspectives.

Information Systems Strategic Management 2nd edition

An Integrated Approach
Steve Clarke

Managing Information and Knowledge in Organizations: A Literacy Approach
Alistair Mutch

Knowledge Management Primer
Rajeev K. Bali, Nilmini Wickramasinghe, Brian Lehaney

Healthcare Knowledge Management Primer
Nilmini Wickramasinghe, Rajeev K. Bali, Brian Lehaney, Jonathan L. Schaffer, M. Chris Gibbons

Healthcare Knowledge Management Primer

Nilmini Wickramasinghe
Rajeev K. Bali
Brian Lehaney
Jonathan L. Schaffer
M. Chris Gibbons

Routledge
Taylor & Francis Group

NEW YORK AND LONDON

First published 2009
by Routledge
270 Madison Ave, New York NY 10016

Simultaneously published in the U.K.
by Routledge
2 Park Square, Milton Park, Abingdon, Oxon, OX14 4RN

Routledge is an imprint of the Taylor & Francis Group, an informa business

Transferred to Digital Printing 2011

Typeset in Perpetua and Bell Gothic by
Florence Production Ltd., Stoodleigh, Devon

Library of Congress Cataloging in Publication Data
Healthcare Knowledge Management Primer/
　　Nilmini Wickramasinghe . . . [et al.].
　　　　p. cm. — (Routledge series in information systems)
　　　Includes bibliographical references and index.
　　1. Medical informatics.　2. Knowledge management.
　　I. Wickramasinghe, Nilmini.　II. Series: Routledge series in information
systems. [DNLM:　1. Medical Informatics.　2. Information
Management.]
　　W 26.5 H43463 2009]
　　R858.H3465 2009
　　651.5′04261—dc22　　　　　　　　　　　　　　　2008047985

ISBN10: 0–415–99443–8 (hbk)
ISBN10: 0–415–99444–6 (pbk)
ISBN10: 0–203–87983–X (ebk)

ISBN13: 978–0–415–99443–9 (hbk)
ISBN13: 978–0–415–99444–6 (pbk)
ISBN13: 978–0–203–87983–2 (ebk)

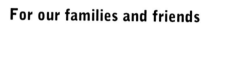

BERNARD WOOLLEY:
"But you only need to know things on a need to know basis."

SIR HUMPHREY APPLEBY:
"I need to know everything! How else can I judge
whether or not I need to know it?"

Yes, Prime Minister (Man Overboard),
written by Jonathan Lynn and Sir Antony Jay

Contents

List of Figures   xi
List of Tables   xii
Preface   xiii
Acknowledgments   xviii
Foreword by Sir Muir Gray   xx

1   What is Knowledge Management?   1
Introduction   1
Knowledge Management (KM)   1
How Did Knowledge Management Come About?   2
Key Concepts   3
Data, Information, Knowledge and Wisdom   4
The Knowledge Spiral   5
Case Exercise: The Knowledge Spiral   7
Key Role of Data and Information in Healthcare   8
Data Mining   9
Data Mining as an Enabler for Realizing the Knowledge Spiral   9
Application of Knowledge Management and Data Mining to Healthcare—A Clinical
   Example   10
Conclusions   11
Summary   11
Review Questions   11
Discussion Questions   12
Case Exercise: From Data to Decisions in a Radiology Department   12
Further Reading   20
References   21

2   Knowledge Strategies and Knowledge Capture   **23**

Introduction   23

Capturing Knowledge   24

Organizing Knowledge: A Strategic View   25

Intelligence Gathering   26

Measuring   27

Knowledge Representation   28

Knowledge Engineering and the Semantic Web   29

Case Exercise: NHS Direct   30

Conclusions and Summary   35

Review Questions   35

Discussion Questions   36

Case Exercise: Operating Room Optimization   36

Further Reading   39

References   39

3   Knowledge Tools and Techniques   **41**

Introduction   41

Taxonomies and Ontologies   41

Data Mining Tools and Techniques   43

Steps in Data Mining   43

Case Exercise: KM and Personal Health Records—A Malaysian Perspective   45

Business Intelligence and Analytics   50

Communities of Practice   50

Storytelling and the Power of Narrative   52

Have You Heard the One About . . . ?   53

Social Networks (and Social Networking Sites)   56

Social Networking (Internet-based)   56

Intellectual Capital   57

Knowledge Assets   57

Knowledge Nuggets   57

Conclusions   57

Summary   57

Review Questions   58

Discussion Questions   58

Case Exercise: Increasing Breast Cancer Screening Attendance in the U.K.   58

Further Reading   63

References   63

4   Knowledge Management: A Systems View   **65**

Introduction   65

General Systems and Hard Systems Thinking   66

Soft Systems Thinking   68

Case Exercise: Louisiana Mass Immunization Exercise (2007)   72

Case Exercise: Intervention in an Outpatient's Department   79
Critical Systems Thinking   81
Conclusions and Summary   83
Review Questions   84
Discussion Questions   84
Case Exercise: Empowering Patients: Immunizations and Knowledge-based
   Personal Health Records   84
Further Reading   88
References   88

5 Knowledge: The Organization, Culture and Learning   90
Introduction   90
The Learning Organization   90
The Importance of Organizational Culture   92
Organizational Culture   94
Case Exercise: KM in AMERA (The Africa Middle East Refugee Association
   in Cairo)   100
Socio-Technical Issues   103
Evolution of Knowledge Management Systems   109
"Double Loop" Learning   110
Case Exercise: A Knowledge-based Healthcare Resource Balancing System   113
Trends in Healthcare   117
Conceptualizing Knowledge Within Healthcare   117
Worked Example: Personalized Healthcare   118
Conclusions   121
Summary   121
Review Questions   121
Discussion Questions   121
Case Exercise: KM for Urban Health   122
Further Reading   131
References   131

6 Applying Knowledge   135
Introduction   135
Creating Value from Knowledge   135
The Intelligence Continuum   137
Clinical Example: Operating Room   140
Case Exercise: Substance Abuse Patient   141
Networkcentric Healthcare Operations   143
ICT Use in Healthcare Networkcentric Operations   145
The Health Insurance, Portability and Accountability Act (HIPAA)   148
Information Producers, Consumers and Information Flows Within the
   Healthcare System   149
Information Integrity and Quality (I*IQ)   150
Information Integrity   150

CONTENTS

Healthcare Quality Aims — 150

Populomics — 151

Transdisciplinarity and the Role of Health Information Technology — 153

Populomics and Knowledge Management — 154

Summary and Conclusions — 156

Review Questions — 156

Discussion Questions — 156

Case Exercise: KM and the Sociobiologic Integrative Model (SBIM) — 156

Further Reading — 162

References — 163

Appendix A (Integrative Case Exercise) — 166
Crane Care Trust, U.K.

Appendix B (Integrative Case Exercise) — 176
NHS Maternity Services, U.K.

Epilogue — 185

Glossary — 186

Notes — 192

Index — 194

Figures

1.1	Knowledge: Intersection of People, Process and Technology	2
1.2	The "Traditional" View of Data—Information—Knowledge—Wisdom	6
1.3	Sense-making and Knowledge (from Snowden)	6
3.1	Essential Aspects of Data Mining	44
3.2	KARMAH "Starwheel"	51
3.3	Simple Social Network	56
4.1	A grid of Social Theory	70
5.1	Levels of Mental Programming	93
5.2	Culture as both an Input and an Output	97
5.3	The Cultural Onion	98
5.4	Culture—The Organization and the External Environment	104
5.5	The Cultural Web	105
5.6	Activities and Framework for an Organization's IS Requirements	107
5.7	The Integration of MIS and Management	108
5.8	Knowledge: Intersection of People, Process and Technology	109
5.9	Single, Double and Triple Loop Learning	112
5.10	The "Carpet Tile" Conceptualization	119
5.11	Mapping the Carpet Tile onto the "Healthcare Cube"	120
6.1	Boyd's OODA Loop	136
6.2	AQV Möbius	137
6.3	Generic Healthcare Information System with Healthcare Challenges	138
6.4	The Intelligence Continuum™	139
6.5	The Key Steps of Knowledge Management	140
6.6	Three Interconnecting Domains for Networkcentric Healthcare	145
6.7	Networkcentric Information/Knowledge Grid System	146
6.8	"Knowledge Node" (e.g. Healthcare-IT System) Mapping onto Grid Architecture	146
6.9	The HIPAA Triangle	148
6.10	Depicting "Populomics"	152
6.11	The Link between "Populomics" and Knowledge Management	155
6.12	Knowledge as a Unifier	155

Tables

1.1	Key KM Concepts	4
1.2	Data Mining as an Enabler of the Knowledge Spiral	10
2.1	Sample Intelligence Gathering Questions	27
3.1	Example of the Dewey Decimal System	42
3.2	The KARMAH Research Group's Spread of Competencies	52
3.3	Difference Between Story and Narrative	53
4.1	Knowledge Constituitive Interests, SSM and Knowledge Management	78
4.2	Sources of Motivation	82
4.3	Sources of Power	82
4.4	Sources of Knowledge	83
4.5	Sources of Legitimation	83
5.1	Levels of Learning According to David Skyrme Associates (2008)	91
5.2	Kroeber and Kluckhohn's Cultural Traits	94
5.3	Robbins' Ten Characteristics	95

Preface

In the 21st century, knowledge is the key element to improving health.
In the same way that people need clean, clear water,
they have a right to clean, clear knowledge.

Sir Muir Gray

THE REASON FOR THIS BOOK

Knowledge Management (KM) is an approach that is very much in vogue, despite immense confusion over its contents and efficacy. Many healthcare managers (and indeed academics) remain skeptical over its numerous merits despite not fully understanding the field.

Quality care of patients requires the evaluation of considerable amounts of data at the right time and right place and in the correct context. These clinical, administrative and operational sources of data are typically kept in separate and disparate operational repositories. With the advent of the electronic health record, these data warehouses will provide data and information at the point of care and provide for a continuous learning environment in which lessons learned can provide updates to clinical, administrative and financial processes.

What becomes critical in such a context is the identification of relevant data, pertinent information and germane knowledge to support rapid and superior healthcare decision making. Given the advancement of the information tools and techniques of today's knowledge economy, it is imperative that these tools and techniques be appropriately utilized to enable and facilitate the identification and evaluation of these knowledge assets. To do this effectively and efficiently it is imperative that healthcare incorporates the principles of KM.

The motivation for this book was simple—to produce a text that introduces the multi-faceted aspects of contemporary KM in a simple way. This book aims to explore the area of KM from the "bottom up" in order to facilitate and/or reinforce understanding of key concepts. We believe that there are numerous KM texts, which either deal with the subject at too high a level—thus skirting over first principles—or are so tangential to the subject as to be irrelevant. The plethora of books currently available on the subject largely fail to do this and assume an in-depth understanding of KM before describing potential and actual healthcare and clinical applications.

This book therefore deals with the very essence of KM and describes component parts in a simple and easy to understand manner. The three essential components of KM (namely people, process and technology) are presented and explored in a clear manner.

Our combined extensive experience in both the academic, business and medical worlds allows us to discuss concepts that are both academically-grounded and credible, while remaining vocationally and clinically relevant and applicable.

AIMS OF THE BOOK

The general aim of the book is to provide a theoretically and empirically grounded approach to KM. The discipline of KM is rapidly becoming established as an essential course or module in the Higher Education sector around the world. Such courses and modules may be at either undergraduate or postgraduate level. Research students, perhaps with no formal KM training, require essential skills in order to pursue their studies. Similarly, managers at all levels in healthcare institutions often find the KM subject area to be both intriguing and confusing.

Moreover, given that healthcare professionals are busy saving lives, what is essential for them is to have a book that provides the essence of KM for superior healthcare delivery. This will enable them to grasp the key points quickly and more importantly be able to implement effective KM strategies and techniques into healthcare operations.

Examples of such strategies and techniques include:

a) Diagnosing complex diseases and then deciding upon an appropriate treatment strategy, the healthcare professional must sort though multi-spectral data and various information sources. By incorporating the various tools of KM, e.g. sorting and searching tools as well as decision-making tools, it is possible to search large databases and electronic repositories to access the relevant information and pertinent data required to make a more informed and thus better decision after careful evaluation of critical knowledge.

b) A computerized medical record represents a document that provides the user, typically a healthcare professional, with specific and important information pertaining to a patient from which (s)he can then make further healthcare treatment recommendations. By incorporating various KM tools and techniques (including drill down, connectivity to a healthcare portal as well as searching), it is possible to transform a relatively static computerized medical record into an intelligent knowledge repository from which the healthcare provider can make better decisions pertaining to treatment issues.

c) Developing appropriate utilization usage criteria which impact on reimbursement for healthcare funds and healthcare professionals, it is necessary to process large amounts of disparate data and analyze trends and so forth. In order to develop accurate utilization levels, it is of paramount importance that the tools and techniques offered by KM offers are employed.

This book will explore and explain the nature of essential KM components skills in an introductory and easy to understand way. Accessibility and usability in this manner would be of use to both novice and amateur students and professionals wishing to learn more about the KM field.

The book would provide readers with an understanding of approaches to KM by examining the purpose and nature of its key components. The rationale of the text is to demystify the KM field by explaining in an accessible manner the key concepts of KM tools, strategies and techniques, and their benefits to contemporary healthcare organizations.

The text will demonstrate how, with practice and understanding, students can apply its key precepts. Generally, each chapter is followed by a suitable case exercise (with questions), from which readers can apply the key principles from the chapter.

WHO SHOULD USE THIS BOOK?

The book is targeted at students and novice healthcare practitioners new to the area of KM. As mentioned, KM has evolved from existing disciplines such as organizational behavior, ICT and human factors—some understanding and appreciation of these areas would be beneficial. The main academic audience is perhaps MBA (Master of Business Administration) Healthcare students, but it is also aimed at supporting final year undergraduate studies in, for example, business studies and information science, post-experience courses (e.g. NVQ (National Vocational Qualification), DMS (Diploma in Management Studies)), and other Masters courses (information management (IM), and other courses where IM forms a key part). For MBA, this is a core subject, while for undergraduate, other post-experience, and other Masters courses, it is more likely to be a supporting text. The main vocational audience would include managers and practitioners working in the healthcare information management fields wanting to learn more about how KM could bring about organizational benefits.

STRUCTURE AND DISTINCTIVE FEATURES OF THE BOOK

The layout followed is standard for the Routledge Information Systems Series. The aim of this, together with the supplied instructor's manual, is to provide a basis for courses of academic study at the levels identified within its target audience:

- Case examples are provided.
- Each chapter concludes with a Review and Discussion questions.
- Case exercises are provided for each chapter.
- Further reading is suggested at the end of each chapter.

Issues in KM are fully integrated with current thinking in organizational theory; in particular, we focus on design or planning aspects as well as the more human-centric and participative approaches (which in themselves are very similar to the IS 'soft' or human-centered methods). This book aims to do justice to all strategic developments seen to be of relevance to the KM arena, ranging from the planned and political to the totally participative and emancipatory. To achieve this, key approaches to KM are addressed and related to organizations, allowing the emergence of a synthesized approach to KM strategy which is firmly grounded on current thinking.

USE OF THE BOOK FOR TEACHING

In terms of specific pedagogical features:

- Each chapter begins with learning objectives. Chapters are summarized, and key words and phrases listed. Questions for review and questions for discussion are given towards the end of each chapter.
- Suggested further reading, with a guide as to the relevance of the reading suggested, and references appear at the end of each chapter.
- Case exercises and questions to be addressed by the cases are given. Generally the plan is to provide one per chapter, but some chapters may not lend themselves to the use of case material.
- A glossary is provided at the end of the book.

    A full instructor's guide is provided on the World Wide Web.

- An instructor's manual is provided containing study guides (with lecture plans and overhead transparencies), worked examples, answers to review questions and discussion questions, and suggested approaches to case exercises. The instructor's manual also gives:

    - Suggested assignment questions not given in the main text.
    - Suggested schemes of work are provided.

- The instructor's guide is split into the same chapters as the book, and for each chapter:

    - a lecture plan is given;
    - key issues are identified for the lectures, together with overhead projector slides;
    - answers to review questions, discussion questions and case exercises are provided; and
    - suggestions for assignments are given.

Nilmini Wickramasinghe
Center for the Management of
Medical Technology (CMMT)
Stuart School of Business
Illinois Institute of Technology
CHICAGO
U.S.
nilmini@stuart.iit.edu

Rajeev K. Bali
Knowledge Management for Healthcare
(KARMAH) research subgroup
Biomedical Computing and
Engineering Technologies (BIOCORE)
Applied Research Group
Health Design and Technology Institute (HDTI)
Coventry University
COVENTRY
U.K.
r.bali@ieee.org

Brian Lehaney
Department of Engineering and
Knowledge Management
Coventry University
COVENTRY
U.K.
b.lehaney@coventry.ac.uk

Jonathan L. Schaffer
Advanced Operative Technology Group
Orthopedic Research Center
Cleveland Clinic
CLEVELAND, OH
U.S.
schaffj@ccf.org

M. Chris Gibbons
Johns Hopkins Urban Health Institute (UHI) and
Center for Community HEALTH (CCH) and
Assistant Professor of Public Health and Medicine
Johns Hopkins Medical Institutions
BALTIMORE, MD
U.S.
mgibbon1@jhmi.edu

August 2008

Acknowledgments

Many thanks to Prof. Steve Clarke (Series Editor) for green-lighting the project and for his insightful comments and support during the project period. Particular thanks are reserved for Nancy Hale (Editor) and Felisa Salvago-Keyes (Editorial Assistant) at Routledge in New York for their support and enthusiasm, as well as all the other members of the Routledge editorial team for their invaluable assistance in helping this book to take shape.

We acknowledge our respective universities for affording us the time to work on this project as well as our numerous friends and colleagues for their varied and stimulating discussions and interactions; the "social network" aspect of KM was indeed in force.

Many of the schematics included in this text were very kindly supplied to us by Doctrina Applied Research and Consulting LLC (www.consultdoctrina.com) and we are grateful to all involved for their excellent contributions.

Several cases appear courtesy of the Knowledge Management for Healthcare (KARMAH) research subgroup (operating under the Biomedical Computing and Engineering Technologies (BIOCORE) Applied Research Group) at Coventry University (U.K.) (www.coventry.ac.uk/karmah/) and we would like to thank the following PhD students involved: Vikram Baskaran (Increasing Breast Cancer Screening attendance in the U.K.), Mohd Abdul Khanapi Ghani (KM and Malaysian Personal Health Records) and Aapo Immonen (Knowledge-based healthcare resource balancing system). Thanks also to Ranveer Nagra for use of her postgraduate case exercise on NHS Direct.

Some of the vignettes and cases appear courtesy of several clinicians, allied healthcare professionals and industry practitioners and we are grateful to the following for their contributions:

- Dr Thomas Goodfellow (Consultant Radiologist, University Hospitals Coventry and Warwickshire NHS Trust (UHCW), Coventry, U.K.)
- Michael L. Popovich (CEO) and the team at Scientific Technologies Corporation, U.S.): Robert Conn, Project Manager (STC, U.S.), Dr Jeffery J. Aramini (Public/Animal Health Epidemiologist, Director of Canadian Operations, STC Canada), Michael Garcia (Vice President/COO, STC, U.S.)
- Frank J. Welch, MD (Medical Director, Pandemic Preparedness Louisiana Office of Public Health, U.S.)

- Sushil Patria (PRIMIS+ Service, U.K.)
- Kim Davis (NHS Maternity Services, U.K.)
- David Johnston (Director, Applied Network Solutions Ltd, U.K.) with special thanks to Barbara Harrell-Bond OBE, chairman of AMERA, for giving her permission to produce the AMERA case exercise
- Viktor E. Krebs MD, Ted M. Omilanowski PA-C and Second Lt J.H. James Choi USAFR, MSC at the Advanced Operative Technology Group, Orthopaedic Research Center, Cleveland Clinic, U.S.

Our gratitude also to Sir Muir Gray DSc, MD, FRCPSGlas, FCLIP (Director of the U.K.'s National Health Service (NHS) National Knowledge Service and Chief Knowledge Officer to the NHS) for writing such a fine foreword and for his insights into the world of KM.

We reserve special thanks to Jonathan Lynn and Sir Antony Jay for their kind permission to reproduce lines from *Yes, Prime Minister* (from the chapter/episode entitled *Man Overboard*).

Foreword

Knowledge is the enemy of disease; the application of what we know will have a bigger impact on health and disease than any drug or technology likely to be developed in the next decade. In many ways, knowledge is like water. People need clean, clear, knowledge just as they need clean, clear, water. However, again like water, very few people are in the position of being able to have access to clean clear knowledge; it has to be supplied through the organized efforts of society and the provision of clean clear knowledge is therefore a public health service, a core service for any individual or organization that seeks to improve the health of individual patients or populations.

Knowledge can be divided into tacit and explicit, and one management task is to convert tacit to explicit. Explicit knowledge can be divided into generalizable and particular. Generalizable knowledge may be derived from research, sometimes called evidence, or from the analysis of data, or from experience, but it is clear that simply allowing this knowledge to lie inside journals will not deliver it where and when it is needed. Just as water has to be collected in reservoirs and filtered and piped, so knowledge has to be collected, filtered and piped, and the internet, of course, is the piping system. However, knowledge has to be delivered not only to the door of the hospital but to the bedside and the consulting room, and the generalizable knowledge has to be linked to the particular knowledge about "this patient." This final step in the flow of knowledge is perhaps the most difficult and requires not only an understanding of epidemiology but also an understanding of information technology (IT).

This book reviews a wide range of different aspects of knowledge management and is as important as a classic textbook on pharmacology or surgery. In the twentieth century, priority was given to pharmaceutical and clinical technology; in the twenty-first century, IT will have the same impact, if not greater. To realize its potential, however, it has to be managed very carefully and this book describes how this can be done.

Sir Muir Gray, CBE
Director, National Knowledge Service
Chief Knowledge Officer to the NHS
September 2008

Chapter 1

What is Knowledge Management?

INTRODUCTION

Significant quantities of data and information permeate the healthcare industry. However, the healthcare industry has not fully embraced key business management processes (such as KM) or techniques (such as data mining) to capitalize on realizing the full value of this data/information resource. The inherent limitations of organizational structures in healthcare, coupled with the demographic, financial and technical challenges of integrating patient care inhibit the introduction of these management processes.

However, KM and data mining are of tremendous value to healthcare, particularly in enabling and facilitating superior clinical practice and administrative management. Given the current challenges facing healthcare globally, many are confident that the tools, techniques, technologies and tactics of KM hold the key to effecting the healthcare value proposition. So this chapter presents the fundamentals of KM and how KM might benefit superior healthcare operations. Further, clinical examples help to illustrate how the value proposition can be achieved in a clinical setting.

KNOWLEDGE MANAGEMENT (KM)

Central to KM is organizational knowledge, which exists at the confluence of people, process and technology (see Figure 1.1).

KM is an emerging management approach that is aimed at solving the current business challenges to increase efficiency and efficacy of core business processes while simultaneously incorporating continuous innovation. Specifically, KM through the use of various tools, processes and techniques combines germane organizational data, information and knowledge to create business value and enable an organization to capitalize on its intangible and human assets so that it can effectively achieve its primary business goals as well as maximize its core business competencies (Davenport and Prusak, 1998; Swan et al., 1999). The premise for the need for KM is based on a paradigm shift in the business environment where knowledge is central to organizational performance (Drucker, 1993).

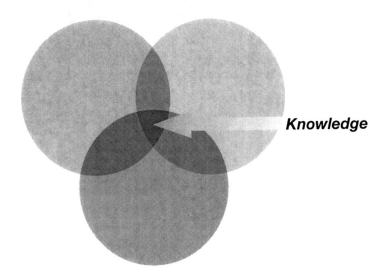

Figure 1.1 *Knowledge: Intersection of People, Process and Technology.*
Reproduced with kind permission of Doctrina Applied Research and Consulting LLC—www.consultdoctrina.com

In today's context of escalating costs in healthcare, managed care, regulations and a technology and health information savvy patient, the healthcare industry can no longer be complacent regarding embracing key processes and techniques to enable better, more effective and efficient practice management. We believe such an environment is appropriate for the adoption of a KM perspective and key tools and technologies such as data mining.

HOW DID KNOWLEDGE MANAGEMENT COME ABOUT?

There are few who would argue that the current business environment is global as well as complex and dynamic. To survive in such an environment requires the attainment of a competitive advantage. Such a competitive advantage must be sustainable, i.e. difficult for competitors to imitate.

Sustainable competitive advantage is dependent on building and exploiting an organization's core competencies (Prahalad and Hamel, 1990). In order to sustain competitive advantage, resources that are idiosyncratic (and thus scarce), and hence difficult to transfer or replicate are of paramount importance (Grant, 1991). A knowledge-based view of the firm identifies knowledge as the organizational asset that enables sustainable competitive advantage, especially in hyper competitive environments (Davenport and Prusak, 1998; Alavi, 1999; Zack,1999). This is attributed to the fact that barriers exist regarding the transfer and replication of knowledge (Alavi, 2000); thus making knowledge and KM of strategic significance (Kanter, 1999).

Since the late 1980s, organizations have embraced technology at an exponential rate. This rapid rate of adoption and diffusion of ICTs (information and communication technologies), coupled with the ever increasing data stored in databases or information that is being continually exchanged throughout networks, necessitates organizations to develop and embrace appropriate tools, tactics, techniques and technologies to facilitate prudent management of these raw knowledge assets; i.e. adopt KM.

Finally, during the late 1990s many organizations, especially in the U.S., have been experiencing significant downsizing and the reduction of senior employees. These employees over time have gained much experience and expertise and, as they leave their respective organizations, this expertise leaves too. In an attempt to stem the loss of expertise and vital know-how, organizations needed to embrace KM.

Taking together the need for a sustainable competitive advantage, the need to manage terabytes of data and information, and the need to retain vital expertise and knowledge residing in experts' heads, organizations throughout the world are turning to KM solutions.

KEY CONCEPTS

In order to understand what KM is, it is essential to understand several key concepts. Since, KM addresses the generation, representation, storage, transfer and transformation of knowledge (Hedlund, 1990), the knowledge architecture is designed to capture knowledge and thereby enable KM processes to take place. Underlying the knowledge architecture is the recognition of the binary nature of knowledge; namely its objective and subjective components. Knowledge can exist as an object, in essentially two forms, explicit or factual knowledge, which is typically written or documented knowledge, and tacit or "know how," which typically resides in people's heads (Polanyi, 1958, 1966). It is well established that while both types of knowledge are important, tacit knowledge, as it is intangible, is more difficult to identify and thus manage (Nonaka, 1991, 1994).

Further, objective knowledge, be it tacit or explicit, can be located at various levels; e.g. the individual, group or organization (Hedlund, 1994). Of equal importance, though perhaps less well defined, knowledge also has a subjective component and can be viewed as an ongoing phenomenon, being shaped by social practices of communities (Boland and Tenkasi, 1995).

The objective elements of knowledge can be thought of as primarily having an impact on process. Underpinning such a perspective is a Lockean/Leibnitzian standpoint (Malhotra, 2000; Wickramasinghe and von Lubitz, 2007) where knowledge leads to greater effectiveness and efficiency. In contrast, the subjective elements of knowledge typically impact innovation by supporting divergent or multiple meanings consistent with Hegelian/Kantian modes of inquiry (ibid) essential for brainstorming or idea generation and social discourse. Both effective and efficient processes, as well as the function of supporting and fostering innovation, are key concerns of KM in theory. These issues are critical if a sustainable competitive advantage is to be attained as well as maximization of an organization's tangible and intangible assets.

The knowledge architecture recognizes these two different, yet key aspects of knowledge and provides the blueprints for an all-encompassing KMS (Wickramasinghe and von Lubitz, 2007). By so doing, the knowledge architecture is defining a KMS that supports both objective and subjective attributes of knowledge. The pivotal function underlined by the knowledge architecture is the flow of knowledge. The flow of knowledge is fundamentally enabled (or not) by the KMS.

In addition, it is possible to change from one type of knowledge to another type of knowledge and this too must be captured in the knowledge architecture. Specifically, as proposed by

Nonaka (1994), there exist four possible transformations: 1) combination—where new explicit knowledge is created from existing bodies of explicit knowledge, 2) externalization—where new explicit knowledge is created from tacit knowledge, 3) internalization—where new tacit knowledge is created from explicit knowledge and 4) socialization—where new tacit knowledge is created from existing tacit knowledge. The continuous change and enriching process of the extant knowledge base is known as the knowledge spiral (Nonaka, 1994).

Once the knowledge architecture has been developed, it is then necessary to consider the knowledge infrastructure. The knowledge infrastructure consists of technology components and people that together make up the knowledge sharing system, and hence it is a socio-technical system (Wickramasinghe and von Lubitz, 2007). Table 1.1 provides a succinct definition of these key concepts relating to KM.

DATA, INFORMATION, KNOWLEDGE AND WISDOM

Data is a series of discrete events, observations, measurements or facts that can take the form of numbers, words, sounds and/or images. Most useful organizational data is in the form of transaction records, stored in databases and generated through various business processes and activities. Today organizations generate large amounts of multi-spectral data. Given its discrete form, data in itself may not be very useful and thus it is often termed a raw knowledge asset. When data is processed, and organized into a context, it becomes information.

Table 1.1 *Key KM Concepts*

Concept	Definition
Tacit knowledge	Knowledge that resides in peoples' heads , "know how"
Explicit knowledge	Knowledge that is written down as facts, "know what"
Knowledge architecture	The blueprints for identifying where subjective and objective knowledge and/or tacit and explicit knowledge reside in an organization
Knowledge infrastructure	The design of the socio-technical requirements for ensuring appropriate KM, i.e. the design of the necessary people and technology requirements for facilitating KM in a specific organization
Objective perspective of knowledge	Following the Lokean/Leibnitzian forms of inquiry, such knowledge facilitates greater effectiveness and efficiency
Subjective perspective of knowledge	Following the Hegalian/Kantian schools of inquiry, such knowledge facilitates sense making and innovation
Knowledge spiral	The transformation of one type of knowledge to another
Socialization	The transformation of tacit knowledge into new tacit knowledge
Internalization	The transformation of explicit knowledge into new tacit knowledge
Externalization	The transformation of tacit knowledge into new explicit knowledge
Combination	The transformation of explicit knowledge into new explicit knowledge

Information is data that has been arranged into a meaningful pattern and thus has a recognizable shape, i.e. data that has been endowed with relevance and purpose. An example is a report created from intelligent database queries. ICTs (information and communication technology) not only enhance the communication capabilities with data but also facilitate the transferring and processing of this data into information.

According to Webster's Dictionary, knowledge is the fact or condition of knowing something with familiarity gained through experience or association. Another useful way to understand knowledge is to define it as contextualized information. The literature is peppered with numerous definitions of knowledge. However, a frequently referenced definition is that given by Davenport and Prusak (1998: 5):

> Knowledge is a fluid mix of framed experiences, values, contextual information, and expert insights that provides a framework for evaluating and incorporating new experiences and information. It originates and is applied in the minds of knowers. In organizations, it is often embedded not only in documents or repositories but also in organizational routine, processes, practices and norms.

It is important to note that this definition is both broad and recognizes that knowledge is indeed not a homogenous construct.

It is widely agreed that beyond knowledge lies wisdom (Wickramasinghe and von Lubitz, 2007). Wisdom is essentially a process by which we are able to discern, or judge, between right and wrong, good and bad. In essence, it embodies more of an understanding of fundamental principles embodied within the knowledge that are essentially the basis for the knowledge being what it is.

What is particularly interesting to researchers is the transformation from data to information to knowledge and even wisdom. Figure 1.2 depicts the generally accepted relationship between data, information, knowledge and wisdom.

However, several researchers have suggested other ideas, among them Snowden's (2005) notion that the effective transition to knowledge should also include an element of sense-making (i.e. how can we make sense of the world so we can act in it?). Sense-making is associated with the work of Weick (1995) and Dervin (1998). Figure 1.3 shows how sense-making can be integrated into the "move" towards knowledge.

The conventional (or traditionally accepted) view of data, information and knowledge (a suitable example of which is Figure 1.2) suggests that there is a hierarchical relationship between these items. Other schematics depict this linkage as a pyramid (with wisdom taking pride of place at the top). This can be confusing if one accepts that one is automatically "better" or more useful than the item underneath. Making sense of information (via sense-making as in Figure 1.3) can be of great assistance.

THE KNOWLEDGE SPIRAL

Knowledge is not static; rather it can be changed and evolves during the life of an organization as it does during the life and care processes of a patient. Hence, it is possible to change the form of knowledge; i.e. turn existing tacit knowledge (or experiential "know how") into new

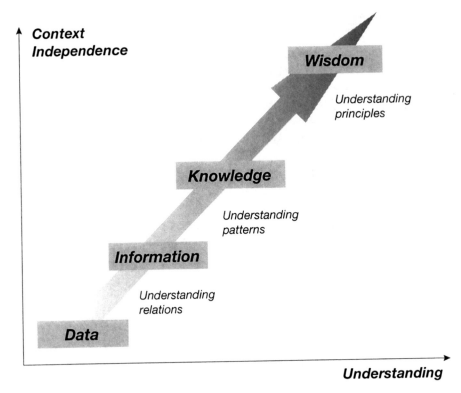

Figure 1.2 *The "Traditional" View of Data—Information—Knowledge—Wisdom.*

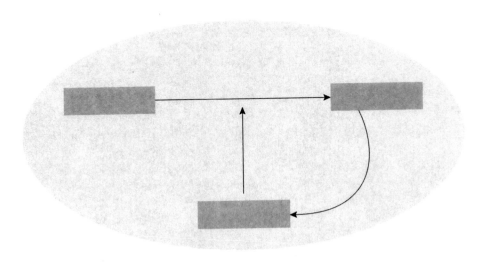

Figure 1.3 *Sense-making and Knowledge.*

Source: Snowden (2005)

explicit knowledge (or factual "know what") and existing explicit knowledge into new tacit knowledge (Wickramasinghe and Mills, 2001). This process of changing the form of knowledge is known as the knowledge spiral in which, according to Nonaka (1994):

1 Tacit to tacit knowledge transfer usually occurs through apprenticeship type relations where the teacher or master passes on the skill to the apprentice.

CASE EXERCISE: THE KNOWLEDGE SPIRAL

The following case exercise discusses the use of ICT in which clinical consultations can be provided through the use of web-based technologies and electronic medical records systems. The figure below depicts the typical pathway that a patient experiences from the time that they have symptoms to the time that they seek treatment for those symptoms, are provided with a diagnosis and treatment regimens are recommended. Given the significant impact of some of these diagnoses on the patient, the desire to seek a second opinion from a leading clinical institution and a leading clinical expert is common.

Clearly the use of ICT can be the enabler for the generation and capture of the data, information and knowledge. For each diagnosis, specific clinical knowledge needs to be shared and provided to the clinician rendering the second opinion. It is reasonable to expect that the second opinion cannot be rendered until the data set upon which the first is based has been provided to that clinician providing the second opinion. The exchange of tacit knowledge and the generation of further tacit and explicit knowledge through data mining and KM provide additional knowledge both to the clinician rendering the second opinion as well as the clinician who provided the first opinion. The knowledge spiral provides a model of this entire process and helps the clinicians improve the care processes for future patients.

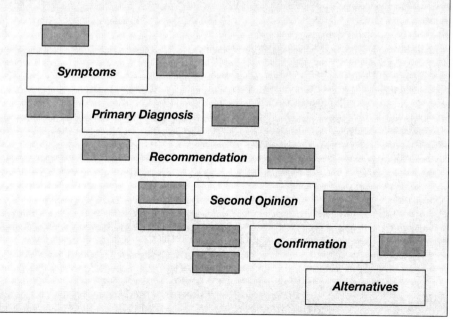

2 Explicit to explicit knowledge transfer usually occurs via formal learning of facts.
3 Tacit to explicit knowledge transfer usually occurs when there is an articulation of nuances; for example, if a renowned surgeon is questioned as to why he does a particular procedure in a certain manner, by his articulation of the steps his tacit knowledge becomes everyone's explicit knowledge.
4 Explicit to tacit knowledge transfer usually occurs as new explicit knowledge is internalized; it can then be used to broaden, reframe and extend one's tacit knowledge.

These transformations are often referred to as the modes of socialization, externalization, internalization and combination respectively (Becerra-Fernandez and Sabherwal, 2001). Integral to this changing of knowledge through the knowledge spiral is that new knowledge is created (Nonaka, 1994) and this can bring many benefits to organizations. In the case of transferring tacit knowledge to explicit knowledge, for example, an organization is able to capture the expertise of particular individuals; hence, this adds not only to the organizational memory but also enables single loop and double loop organizational learning to take place (Huber, 1984). In healthcare, this may translate, for example, to the developing of better and more appropriate clinical protocols for patient care and clinical practice management.

KEY ROLE OF DATA AND INFORMATION IN HEALTHCARE

The proliferation of databases in every quadrant of healthcare practice and research is evident in the large number of isolated claims databases, registries, electronic medical record data warehouses, disease surveillance systems, and other ad hoc research database systems. Not only does the number of databases grow daily, but even more importantly, so does the amount of data within them. Pattern-identification tasks such as detecting associations between certain risk factors and outcomes, ascertaining trends in healthcare utilization, or discovering new models of disease in populations of individuals rapidly become daunting even to the most experienced healthcare researcher or manager (Holmes *et al.*, 2002).

Yet these tasks may hold the answers to many clinical issues such as treatment protocols or the identification across geographic areas of newly emerging pathogens and thus are important. Add to all of this the daily volumes of data generated and then accumulated from a healthcare organization administrative system, clearly then, the gap between data collection and data comprehension and analysis becomes even more problematic. IT tools coupled with new business approaches such as data mining and KM should be embraced in an attempt to address such healthcare woes (McGee, 1997; Berinato, 2002).

Due to the immense size of the data sets, computerized techniques are essential to helping physicians as well as administrators address these issues. Of particular relevance are the relatively young and growing fields of data mining, knowledge discovery and KM. Data mining is closely associated with databases and shares some common ground with statistics—both strive toward discovering structure in data. However, while statistical analysis starts with some kind of hypothesis about the data, data mining does not. Furthermore, data mining is much more suited to deal with heterogeneous databases, data sets and data fields, which are typical of medical databases. Data mining also draws heavily from many other disciplines, most notably machine learning, artificial intelligence and database technology.

DATA MINING

Data mining is the non-trivial process of identifying valid, novel, potentially useful and ultimately understandable patterns from data (Krysztof, 2001). Clinicians accomplish these tasks daily in their care of patients using their own "personal CPU"; however, the enormous amounts and divergent sources of information coupled with time constraints limit any clinician's ability to fully examine all issues. Data mining algorithms are used on databases for model building, or for finding patterns in data. When these patterns are new, useful and understandable, we say that this is knowledge discovery. How to manage such discovered knowledge and other organizational knowledge is the realm of KM.

Data mining is a step in the broader context of the knowledge discovery process that transforms data into knowledge (Fayyad *et al.*, 1996). It is essential to emphasize here the importance of the interaction with the medical professionals and administrators who always play a crucial and indispensable role in a knowledge discovery process. This is particularly true when we take into consideration features that are specific to the medical databases. More and more medical procedures employ imaging as a preferred diagnosing tool. Thus, there is a need to develop methods for efficient mining in databases of images and associated clinical data, which is inherently more difficult than mining in numerical databases.

Other significant features include but are not limited to security and confidentiality concerns and the fact that the physician's interpretation of images, signals or other clinical data, is written in unstructured English—which is also very difficult to mine (McGee, 1997). Some important data issues in which data mining is most useful in helping organizations wrestle with include: huge volumes of data, dynamic data, incomplete data, imprecise data, noisy data, missing attribute values, redundant data and inconsistent data. Furthermore, data mining offers a wide variety of models to capture the characteristics of data and to help knowledge discovery; including summarization, clustering/segmentation, regression, classification, neural networks, rough sets, association analysis, sequence analysis, prediction, exploratory analysis and visualization.

DATA MINING AS AN ENABLER FOR REALIZING THE KNOWLEDGE SPIRAL

One of the key strengths of data mining as a tool for facilitating knowledge discovery, and thereby its benefit to healthcare, is concerned with its ability to enable the realization of the knowledge spiral. Furthermore, data mining supports both the subjective and objective components of knowledge. We depict this in Table 1.2.

Key to the power of data mining is that with the one technology we have the potential to address all four aspects of the knowledge spiral (i.e. turn existing tacit knowledge into new explicit knowledge and existing explicit knowledge into new tacit knowledge); and hence supporting all possible transformations of knowledge and thereby expanding the existing knowledge base of the organization. The implications for this technique are tremendous, especially when we factor in the high volumes of data and information in today's healthcare organizations.

APPLICATION OF KNOWLEDGE MANAGEMENT AND DATA MINING TO HEALTHCARE—A CLINICAL EXAMPLE

Advancing age can lead to the degeneration of a patient's knee and hip joints that often requires the reconstruction of the joint. Coupled with the aging of populations, these devices are being implanted in increasingly larger numbers. These reconstructions entail a major surgical procedure in which the degenerative joint surfaces are removed and replaced with a combination of metal and plastic components. There are a multitude of variables in these reconstructions from the patient characteristics and healthcare status to the implant design and implantation methodologies.

The surgeon's explicit knowledge determines the "best" implant design and implantation methodologies that are used for each particular patient. The examination of the clinical results leads to the explicit knowledge that determines if those choices are appropriate for each patient population. However, the examination of the results of these interventions has been limited at the very least to just a few of the thousands of clinical data points and rarely to more than one surgeon or one clinical site.

Moreover, at each clinical site, the data of interest is often housed in divergent databases from administrative, clinical, financial, imaging and laboratory sources. The complete and accurate examination of the clinical results of joint replacement requires an examination of each of these data sets for the relationships that may exist within and across databases. Post-operative and regular radiographs of these implanted devices are used by clinicians to determine if the implant methodologies, such as device alignment and bone–implant interface, are appropriate.

Migration of the implant within the host bone or wearing of the plastic component can be visualized on the radiographs and is indicative of impending failure of the component. Combinations of the various data sources will lead to the development of exploratory and predictive data mining, which will in turn assist with the handling of failures and complications and offer the clinicians the opportunity to develop solutions to problems as or even before the problems develop into patient symptoms.

Table 1.2 *Data Mining as an Enabler of the Knowledge Spiral*

To From	Explicit	Tacit
Explicit	Performing exploratory data mining, such as summarization and visualization, it is possible to upgrade, expand, and/or revise current facts and protocols.	By assimilating and internalizing knowledge discovered through data mining, physicians can turn this explicit knowledge into tacit knowledge which they can apply to treating new patients.
Tacit	Interpretation of findings from data mining helps the revealing of tacit knowledge, which can then be articulated and stored as explicit cases in the case repository.	Interpreting treatment patterns for example for hip disease discovered through data mining enables interaction among physicians – hence making it possible to stimulate and grow their own tacit knowledge.

Each entry explains how data mining enables the knowledge transfer from the type of knowledge in the cell row to the type of knowledge in the cell column.

The predictive models derived from the data mining will assist the clinician in the determination of the best device and best implantation method to use for specific situations. The knowledge transformations from explicit and tacit knowledge to each of the forms depicted in Table 1.2 will assist in the search for clinical perfection and ultimately lead to improved clinical outcomes and increased healthcare value.

CONCLUSIONS

This chapter has set out to define what KM is as well as highlighting the significance and key role for KM and data mining in healthcare. This has been accomplished by discussing some of the major challenges facing healthcare today. Next, KM and in particular the integral role of the knowledge spiral was discussed. Then data mining was introduced in order to demonstrate that data mining enables the realization of the knowledge spiral.

The power of data mining partially lies in the fact that it can realize the transformations of knowledge in the knowledge spiral. This was further illustrated with a clinical application that underscores various opportunities for enabling increased healthcare value by incorporating developments not only in predictive and exploratory data mining but also in embracing KM perspectives.

On the completion of this chapter the reader should now be able to define clearly and succinctly what KM is and what it is not, and why it is considered critical for facilitating superior healthcare delivery.

SUMMARY

- KM is not just project management.

- KM is not just a fad.

- KM is not just data mining.

- KM is not Business Process Reengineering (BPR).

- KM is comprised of a set of tools, techniques, tactics and technologies aimed at maximizing an organization's intangible assets through the extraction of relevant data, pertinent information and germane knowledge to facilitate superior decision making so that an organization attains and maintains a sustainable competitive advantage.

REVIEW QUESTIONS

1 What is KM?

2 Why is KM necessary for current businesses?

3 What is the knowledge spiral and four transformations of knowledge?

4 What is a sustainable competitive advantage?

5 What are the myths of KM?

DISCUSSION QUESTIONS

1 Do you think tacit knowledge or explicit knowledge is more important for healthcare and why?

2 Do you think the need for a sustainable competitive advantage, the need to manage terabytes of data and information or the need to retain key expertise plays the most important part in the development and embracing of KM by healthcare organizations?

CASE EXERCISE: FROM DATA TO DECISIONS IN A RADIOLOGY DEPARTMENT[2]

by T.Goodfellow, Consultant Radiologist

Background

In the U.K., the National Health Service (NHS) is the "public face" of the publicly funded healthcare system. The organizations within it provide the majority of healthcare in the U.K. (general practitioners, Accident and Emergency Departments, long-term healthcare and dentistry). Founded in 1948, they have become an integral part of British society, culture and everyday life. Private healthcare has continued in parallel to the NHS, largely paid for by private insurance, but still generally used by a small percentage of the population (and generally as a top-up to NHS services). NHS services are largely free at the point of delivery and are paid for by way of taxation. The NHS's budget for 2005–2006 is over £80 billion and the Service employs over 1 million people and is ranked as one of the largest employers in the world. Healthcare in the U.K. has been the subject of global focus given the radical and far-reaching Connecting for Health (CfH) change program currently taking place (Hendy et al., 2005; Cross, 2006).

The University Hospitals Coventry and Warwickshire NHS Trust (Trust being a term generally interchangeable for "hospital" and a statutory body responsible for delivering better healthcare and health improvements to its local area) is a newly built "super hospital" (replacing an older hospital on virtually the same site). The Trust possesses clean, modern facilities, which rival the best private hospitals. With 250 top specialists in heart care, stroke, joint replacements, diabetes and cancer care, the 1,250 bed hospital has low waiting times for operations and appointments and has twenty-seven operating theatres.

The Department of Radiology carries out diagnostic imaging, which is fundamental to the delivery of healthcare. It is therefore central in enabling the Trust to carry out its primary business and deliver key objectives. With the recent moves (July 2006) into the new hospital (one from the old hospital, the other from a hospital in Coventry City Centre), the Department of Radiology is presented with an almost unique opportunity to introduce fundamental changes in working practices. This is due to the coming together (at the same time) of the implementation of a hospital-wide Picture Archiving and Communication System (PACS) and the move to a film-less environment, voice-activated (voice recognition) reporting, extensive state of the art equipment and the consolidation of the majority of the department on one site in the new hospital.

PACS

Picture Archive and Communications System (PACS) is a filmless system currently being adopted by many radiology departments as it enables numerous benefits over conventional X-ray systems—such as the capture of diagnostic images in a digital form (Reed et al., 1996a,b; Smith et al., 1999). In due course this will be extended to all types of diagnostic images in addition to radiology through-out the Trust. PACS replaces hard-copy based means of managing medical images (such as those stored on film, e.g. X-rays) and would expand on such conventional systems by providing capabilities revolving around off-site viewing and reporting and the prospect of tele-diagnosis. It would enable practitioners at various physical locations (Aas, 2005) to peruse the same information simultaneously (teleradiology). Given the decreasing price of digital storage, PACS systems provide a cost and space advantage over traditional film archives.

PACS was partially installed within the Trust in February 2006, leading up to a full implementation in the new hospital in July 2006, which was fully filmless. Role-out started in January 2006 in The Hospital of St. Cross, Rugby (a small satellite of the Trust). This was initially by the implementation of a new Radiology Information System (RIS) to replace the outdated previous system. This was crucial to making the PACS work, ensuring that the system integrated with other IT systems in the Trust. This was followed by full PACS implementation in Rugby, and a further limited roll-out within the old hospital, prior to the move in July 2006, to help introduce the PACS culture to all staff and deliver appropriate training.

Digital Radiography

The conventional X-ray rooms in the new department will use mainly Digital Radiography (DR) equipment as opposed to the more usual Computed Radiography (CR). DR allows the capture of the image directly onto the system without the need for X-ray cassettes (as in CR) that then need to be processed separately. Because DR systems are much more rapid to use, in theory they allow a much faster throughput in the X-ray room, and consequent increased productivity, although this depends to a large extent on the case-mix being put through that room. This will require a re-assessment of the staffing requirements of the department to ensure that radiographic staff are fully used in X-raying patients supported by an appropriate number of radiographic aides to assist and change patients in readiness for their examination.

Benefits Realization

The benefits realization of PACS and DR will be a key element of the department. Through CfH, the Department of Health is investing a huge amount of money in IT within the NHS, of which PACS forms a significant part. It is essential, therefore, to show that this investment brings with it an increase in both efficiency and productivity. This should be clearly demonstrable and quantifiable, and should be used to support the business planning of the Trust, and indeed ultimately of the whole NHS. When the use of DR equipment is also added into the equation then the possible benefits become very significant. It is likely that once the PACS is used to its fullest extent (which will take some time due to the inevitable learning process), it could result in an improved productivity of up to 40 percent. This is based on the experience of other medical institutions, particularly in the U.S.

However, to achieve this in UHCW will require a huge cultural change and detailed management and monitoring. The new hospital is the largest in Europe and although PACS has been introduced into other large hospitals throughout the world, these have generally been into existing radiology departments. This allows the PACS to run in parallel with the old system allowing a backup until the PACS has achieved stability both in terms of functionality and clinical usage. However, UHCW is almost certainly unique in the U.K., and possibly in Europe, in the particular combination of timing and events. Other than the rather limited roll-out in the past few months, the new hospital systems went live from day one.

Voice Activated Reporting (VAR)

VAR is currently being implemented in the radiology department, and it is planned that its use will extend once the full ramifications of the move have been resolved. This technology allows the reporting radiologist to report directly onto the RIS and immediately verify the report. This is then available to the clinicians and may be viewed alongside the images. After a short learning process this becomes a highly efficient way of reporting. In the majority of cases it obviates the need for a transcription process, and eliminates the (often significant) delays inherent in this. It is accepted that not all radiologists many be initially comfortable with using VAR; however they should be strongly encouraged to use this whenever practical. This will bring immediate benefits in report turnaround time for the majority of examinations. There will also be significant savings in both clerical and radiologist time.

Single Site Working

The previous situation with radiologists working on multiple sites created significant and largely unsolvable inefficiencies. The benefits of consolidating the department onto one site cannot be overemphasized. Although there will still be a small satellite unit at St. Cross (Rugby), this is now connected to the main department through PACS and is, in consequence, functionally part of the main department.

KEY OBJECTIVES

In order to get the maximum benefits out of the new hospital and PACS, it was essential that working practices were changed and redesigned to reflect the new environment. The main key factors already outlined presented the opportunity to completely re-appraise the way in which radiologists worked. This was carried out in light of the requirements of the clinical needs of the patients and the referring

Ingenious Med
emory atlanta sports
Atl gastroenterology associ.
Himformatics LLC
Intown womens health
    associates, LLC

channeled into this. These requirements included

ns;

ncy (A&E) trauma images;

d Emergency Department (ED) images during

facilitate diagnosis and prompt discharge);

tigations for patients in the ED (ultrasound, CT,

isease and allow discharge;

TU), High Dependency Unit (HDU)and neonatal

itions by primary care (ultrasound, CT, MRI);

- prompt reporting of all non-urgent examinations (e.g. GP referrals);
- prompt access to image-guided interventions;
- improved access and short waiting times for non-urgent OP/GP examinations (CT, MRI, ultrasound, angiography and so forth);
- a "duty" radiologist immediately available for consultation and advice; and
- radiological input to cancer Multi Disciplinary Teams (MDTs);
- increased joint clinico-radiology meetings;
- increased radiology teaching for students and non-radiology clinicians.

Over the last few years the department has made significant progress in delivering some of these objectives. However, because of the obstacles already described there have been significant failures in others. These must now be addressed. However, these are merely the core functions of a radiology department. Once achieved, they are no more than might be expected from a department with the highest capital costs of any within the organization. Rapid advances in imaging technology should allow significant developments across a whole range of patient pathways.

The aim should be to develop and utilize the best and most modern techniques available and to use these to improve the patient pathway, reduce length of stays, improve patient safety and ultimately drive down costs. This last statement may sit uncomfortably with some clinicians and radiologists as the NHS is always perceived as a *service* and cost savings have always been something for managers to worry about. However, the current Government initiatives are driving change and a more commercial approach is now required from all. In addition to the imaging modalities currently available, the following will or should become available in the New Hospital:

- 3T MRI scanning;
- cardiac MRI;
- MRI open magnet for small parts scanning;
- pediatric MRI utilizing the open magnet;
- MRI diffusion scanning;
- whole body MRI scanning for staging tumors and identifying bone metastases;
- PET/CT scanning;
- cardiac CT scanning;

- CT angiography (cerebral, pulmonary, body, peripheral);
- improved image guided biopsy (CT, U.S.);
- expansion of multislice CT scanning (64 slice) with 3D image manipulation;
- digital mammography;
- ultrasound 3D/4D scanning;
- ultrasound contrast techniques; and
- interventional neuroradiology (coiling etc.).

The effects of these technologies on patient care and throughput is still to be fully evaluated. However, UHCW will be one of the best equipped departments in the U.K. and it is therefore essential that the technology is exploited to its fullest.

Service Re-configuration

Flexible Working

Certain aspects of the work of the department are relatively inflexible because they involve other clinical groups (e.g. breast clinics, multidisciplinary meetings, interventional lists requiring patient admission and preparation). However, the majority of a radiologist's time may be used flexibly once it is accepted that the radiologist is not tied to a particular "list" as in the old ways of working. This should allow the individual radiologist far greater control of the working day, and should help to improve work–life balance. In order to facilitate this, we make certain recommendations regarding Consultant workload:

Recommendation 1. It must be accepted that it is very difficult to assess consultant productivity by using crude workload figures. This is due to differences in case mix, contracts (full- and part-time working, other hospitals), work not counted by the current RIS, differences in speed of working, management and teaching commitments, work not included in figures such as multidisciplinary team meetings (MDTs). Consequently there must be true capacity planning based on a detailed review of the individual job plan (a contractual requirement) for each consultant radiologist. Radiologists will be expected to meet the objectives of the job plan, subject to annual review. This is a requirement for pay progression in the NHS consultant contract.

Recommendation 2. In addition to specialist work, all radiologists must expect to contribute to the core work of the department, generally plain image reporting, which in the vast majority of cases is the first-line investigation. This is also essential to support the work of the General Practitioners in Primary Care who do not have access to the images and are consequently completely dependent on the radiology report. Also, on a regular basis they must be available for consultation with other clinicians to discuss specific images and cases.

Recommendation 3. The NHS currently has a number of national targets with regard to access to healthcare. These are rigorously imposed and a Trust's performance is monitored against these. It is accepted that diagnostic imaging is key to delivering on these targets and pressure to meet these with the associated rise in the number and complexity of MDT meetings also adds to the workload of radiologists. This has also resulted in a steady increase in the number of specialist examinations performed, specifically CT, MRI and non-vascular interventions. Consequently, detailed assessment of demand against true capacity is crucial. This should be combined with a careful review of systems and processes to ensure that the highest possible efficiencies are gained from the service. This will highlight specific areas where demand exceeds capacity. This will become important as new techniques are introduced and demand rises. Under Payment by Results (PbR, the NHS tariff system for funding each episode of healthcare), it is the only way that the department will be be able to demonstrate the need for funding additional consultants and supporting staff.

Measurement

In order to demonstrate the benefits realization of the new department, it is essential that certain key performance indicators be measured on a regular ongoing basis. These should be reviewed on a daily/weekly/monthly basis and the results should be available for all staff. The aim should be to develop "ownership" of service improvement process by all staff, and help challenge the traditional mindset of the NHS that "nothing can be improved without lots more money." These should include the following:

- Report turnaround time—measured from the time the examination is requested by the referring clinician to the time the report is verified on the RIS by the reporting radiologist. This will become practical with the introduction of electronic requesting.
- Machine utilization (this should be conducted on a daily basis).
- Individual consultant output and productivity (see earlier caveats).
- Waiting time monitoring.

All of this information should be easily obtainable through the RIS and will provide much more robust data allowing *data driven management* to monitor workflow and volumes.

The Role of Knowledge Management in Radiology

The clinical decision-making process for radiology (and associated imaging procedures) has long been an academic area of interest. Wu *et al.* (1993) discuss the use of artificial neural nets for decision-making in mammography while Redmond *et al.* (1989) tell us how MRIs can be used in the clinical decision-making process. Johnston and Goldstein's (2001) work on Noninvasive Vascular Imaging (NVI) results details how this impacts on decision-making while Walter and Covinsky (2001) describe decision processes for cancer screening for the elderly. Further examples include Schellinger *et al.* (2003) and their work on thrombolytic therapy and Johnson *et al.*'s (1991) rationale for clinical decision-making for CT cerebral blood flow imaging. A comprehensive review for decision-making in radiology by Taylor (1995) examines a variety of different ways in which computers can be used to assist in the interpretation of radiological images and in radiological decision-making. The four proposed criteria for evaluating the design of computerized decision aids are: need, practicality, veracity and relevance.

Having established that the concept of decision-making in radiology is well researched, we now explain how this notion has been transformed into KM and why this is so important in the clinical environment. Gorry and Scott Morton's (1971) concept of Decision Support Systems (DSS) was seminal and showed how computers and humans would solve problems. They proposed that computers would deal with structured issues while humans dealt with unstructured issues. From this alone we can postulate that, as (healthcare) organizations continue to become more complex, the implications for increased human judgment become more critical.

The fact that modern day organizations are facing a deluge of data and information while simultaneously lacking knowledge is very well documented (Liebowitz and Beckman, 1998; Sieloff, 1999). Technological innovations relating to workflow and such technologies as groupware systems have brought about a radical transformation in the way organizations can interact both internally and externally. These new ways of collaboration have resulted in organizations being inundated with information to an unprecedented degree resulting in data/information overload (Sieloff, 1999; Cothrel and Williams, 1999; Drucker, 1998). The widespread use of internet applications using client server architecture and web browsers has further exponentially increased our ability to draw on information in ways not previously possible.

It is now possible to allow every computer access to the entire organizational knowledge base. Technologies such as data integration, document and content management (support applications enabling users to have personalized access to the organizational knowledge base) continue to grow at an exponential rate (Bali et al., 2005; Dwivedi et al., 2007). This has implications for decision makers across all sectors including healthcare, as they have to deal with large amounts of data (Bali, 2005).

One of the major challenges that faces managers is how to make effective decisions based on the data at hand. It is acknowledged that the selection of a particular direction is both constrained and influenced by the availability of data, the ability to transform data into information and then to make recognition of it by deriving knowledge from information. Practitioners then have to decide on how best to effectively transfer this knowledge on an organization-wide basis (Bali and Dwivedi, 2007). KM tools and techniques are defined by their social and community role in the organization in:

- the facilitation of knowledge sharing and socialization of knowledge (production of organizational knowledge);
- the conversion of information into knowledge through easy access, opportunities of internalization and learning (supported by the right work environment and culture); and
- the conversion of tacit knowledge into "explicit knowledge" or information, for purposes of efficient and systematic storage, retrieval, wider sharing and application.

There are various tools that can be used to capture and codify knowledge (Wickramasinghe, 2006). These include databases, various types of artificial intelligence systems including expert systems, neural networks, fuzzy logic, genetic algorithms and intelligent or software agents.

DISCUSSION AND CONCLUSION

The traditional European culture, which is often based on protectionism, is giving rise to more openness in healthcare. Services based on new imaging infrastructures are being introduced. The European

Commission and the European Association of Radiology (EAR)-sponsored *Eurorad project* (www.eurorad.org) offers an array of radiological databases covering all aspects of radiology. Eurorad acts as a promising base for future computer-aided diagnosis and KM systems (Lemke, 2003).

Current technology allows stakeholders to separate data from client applications (where users view it, and where data processing would take place). The various modalities of clinical images can be stored on hospital-based servers (networked and perhaps located throughout the world), which are able to deliver data to the client "on demand" via these image servers. This provides the potential to integrate with current hospital image repositories such as PACS (Dupplaw *et al.*, 2004), thus facilitating superior operations in radiology departments.

As this case has outlined, a number of significant changes to the working practices of radiologists and the implementation of extensive new technology within the UHCW Trust in the U.K. is occurring. The tools and techniques of KM have been introduced as an approach that should be embraced in conjunction with these changes in order to support effective operations in any radiology setting.

Case Exercise References

Aas, I.H.M. (2005) Organizational Cooperation in Teleradiology, *Journal of Telemedicine and Telecare,* 11(1), January 6: 45–50.

Bali, R.K. (Ed.) (2005) *Clinical Knowledge Management: Opportunities and Challenges.* Hershey, PA: Idea Group.

Bali, R.K. and Dwivedi, A. (2007) *Healthcare Knowledge Management: Issues, Advances and Successes.* New York: Springer.

Bali, R.K., Feng, D.D., Burstein, F., and Dwivedi, A. (2005) Advances in Clinical and Health-Care Knowledge Management', *IEEE Transactions on Information Technology in Biomedicine,* 9(2): June: 157–161.

Cothrel, J. and Williams, R. (1999) On-Line Communities: Helping Them Form and Grow, *Journal of Knowledge Management,* 3(1): 54–60.

Cross, M. (2006) Will Connecting for Health Deliver its Promises?, *British Medical Journal,* 332, March 11: 599–601.

Drucker, P. (1998) The Coming of the New Organization, *Harvard Business Review on Knowledge Management,* Boston: Harvard Business School Press, pp. 1–19.

Dupplaw, D., Dasmahapatra, S., Hu, B., Lewis, P., and Shadbolt, N. (2004) Multimedia Distributed Knowledge Management in MIAKT (Speech), in S. Handshuh and T. Declerck (Eds), *Proceedings of Knowledge Markup and Semantic Annotation,* 3rd International Semantic Web Conference, Hiroshima, Japan, pp. 81–90.

Dwivedi, A., Wickramasinghe, N., Bali, R.K., and Naguib, R.N.G. (2008) Designing Intelligent Healthcare Organizations with KM and ICT, *International Journal of Knowledge Management Studies,* 2(2): 198–213.

Gorry, G.A. and Scott Morton, M.S. (1971) A Framework for Management Information Systems, *Sloan Management Review,* 13(1): 55–70.

Hendy, J., Reeves, B.C., Fulop, N., Hutchings, A., and Masseria, C. (2005) Challenges to Implementing the National Programme for Information Technology (NPfIT): A Qualitative Study, *British Medical Journal,* 331, August 6: 331–336.

Johnson, D.W., Stringer, W.A., Marks, M.P., Yonas, H., Good, W.F., and Gur, D. (1991) Stable Xenon CT Cerebral Blood Flow Imaging: Rationale for and Role in Clinical Decision Making, *American Journal of Neuroradiology,* 12(2): 201–213.

Johnston, D.C.C. and Goldstein, L.B. (2001) Clinical Carotid Endarterectomy Decision Making, *Neurology,* 56: 1009–1015.

Lemke, H.U. (2003) PACS Developments in Europe, *Computerized Medical Imaging and Graphics,* 27(2–3), March–June: 111–120.

Liebowitz, J. and Beckman, T. (1998) *Knowledge Organizations: What Every Manager Should Know.* Boca Raton, FL: St. Lucie Press.

Redmond, O.M., Stack, J.P., Dervan, P.A., Hurson, B.J., Carney, D.N., and Ennis, J.T. (1989) Osteosarcoma: Use of MR Imaging and MR Spectroscopy in Clinical Decision Making, *Radiology,* 172: 811–815.

Reed, D.H., Herzog, D.G. and Reed, G. (1996a) A Systems Approach to PACS: The Key to Realizing Strategic Benefits, *Radiology Management,* 18(3): 8–9.

Reed, D.H., Herzog, D.G. and Reed, G. (1996b) A Visual Guide to PACS, *Radiology Management,* 18(3): 20–22.

Schellinger, P.D., Fiebach, J.B., and Hacke, W. (2003) Imaging-Based Decision Making in Thrombolytic Therapy for Ischemic Stroke: Present Status, *Stroke,* 34(2): 575–583.

Sieloff, C. (1999) If Only HP Knew What HP Knows: The Roots of Knowledge Management at Hewlett-Packard, *Journal of Knowledge Management,* 3(1): 47–53.

Smith, E.M., Ruffel, J.D., and Fisher, M. (1999) A Generic Digital Imaging and Communications in Medicine Solution for a Bidirectional Interface Between the Modality and the Radiology Information System, *Digital Imaging,* 12(2): 93–95.

Taylor, P. (1995) Computer Aids for Decision-Making in Diagnostic Radiology—A Literature Review, *The British Journal of Radiology,* 68(813): 945–957.

Walter, L.C. and Covinsky, K.E. (2001) Cancer Screening in Elderly Patients: A Framework for Individualized Decision Making, *Journal of the American Medical Association,* 285(21): 2750–2756.

Wickramasinghe, N. (2006) Knowledge Creation: A Meta-Framework, *International Journal of Innovation and Learning,* 3(5): 558–673.

Wu, Y., Giger, M.L., Doi, K., Vyborny, C.J., Schmidt, R.A., and Metz, C.E. (1993) Artificial Neural Networks in Mammography: Application to Decision Making in the Diagnosis of Breast Cancer, *Radiology,* 187: 81–87.

Case Exercise Questions

1   Clearly outline why KM, its tools techniques, technologies and tactics are so critical in moving from data to decisions in a radiology settings.

2   What are the major barriers and facilitators in effecting such transformations? Be sure to identify these in terms of people, process and technology issues.

FURTHER READING

Davenport, T. and Prusak, L. (1998) *Working Knowledge.* Boston: Harvard Business School Press.

Lehaney, B., Clarke, S., Coakes, E. and Jack, G. (2004) *Beyond Knowledge Management.* Hershey, PA: Idea Group Publishing.

Liebowitz, J. (2008) *Making Cents out of Knowledge Management.* Lanham, MD: The Scarecrow Press Inc.

Wickramasinghe, N. and von Lubitz, D. (2007) *Knowledge-based Enterprise Theories and Fundamentals.* IGI: Hershey.

Wigg, K. (1993) *Knowledge Management Foundations.* Arlington, VA: Schema Press.

REFERENCES

Alavi, M. (2000) Managing Organizational Knowledge, in R.W. Zmund (Ed.), *Framing the Domains of IT Management*. Cincinnati, OH: Pinnaflex Educational Resources.

Becerra-Fernandez, I. and Sabherwal, R. (2001) Organizational Knowledge Management: A Contingency Perspective, *Journal of Management Information Systems:* 18(1), Summer: 23–55. Also available online at http://jmis.bentley.edu/toppage/index.html"\t"_top.

Berinato, S. (2002) CIOs at the Heart of Health-Care Change, *CIO Magazine*, June 15: 89–94.

Boland, R. and Tenkasi, R. (1995) Perspective Making Perspective Taking, *Organization Science*, 6: 350–372.

Davenport, T. and Prusak, L. (1998) *Working Knowledge: How Organizations Manage What they Know*. Boston, MA: Harvard Business School Press.

Drucker, P. (1993) *Post-Capitalist Society*. New York: HarperCollins.

Drucker, P. (1999) Beyond the Information Revolution, *The Atlantic Monthly*, October: 47–57.

Fayyad, U., Piatetsky-Shapiro, G., and Smyth, P. (1996) From Data Mining to Knowledge Discovery: An Overview, in U. Fayyad, G. Piatetsky-Shapiro, and P. Smyth (Eds), *Advances in Knowledge Discovery and Data Mining*. Menlo Park, CA: AAAI Press/MIT Press.

Grant, R. (1991) The Resource-Based Theory of Competitive Advantage: Implications for Strategy Formulation, *California Management Review*, 33(3) Spring: 114–135.

Hedlund, G. (1990) A Model of Knowledge Management and the N-Form Corporation, *Strategic Management Journal*, 15: 73–90.

Holmes, J.P., Abbott, P., Cullen, R.N., Moody, L., Philips, K., and Zupan, B. (2002) Clinical Data Mining: Who Does It, and What Do They Do?, AMIA 2002 Symposium, November: pp. 9–13.

Hope, J. and Hope, T. (1997) *Competing in the Third Wave*. Boston, MA: Harvard Business School Press.

Huber, G. (1990) A Theory of the Effects of Advanced Information Technologies on Organizational Design, Intelligence, and Decision Making, *Academy of Management Review*, 15(1): 47–71.

Kanter, J. (1999) Knowledge Management Practically Speaking, *Information Systems Management*, Fall 16(4): 7–15.

Krzysztof, J. Cios (2001) *Medical Data Mining and Knowledge Discovery*. Heidelberg: Physica-Verlag.

Liebowitz, J. (1999) *Knowledge Management Handbook*. London: CRC Press.

McGee, M. (1997) High-Tech Healing, *Information Week*, September 22.

Malhotra, Y. (2000) Knowledge Management and New Organizational Forms, in Y. Malhotra (Ed.), *Knowledge Management and Virtual Organizations*. Hershey, PA: Idea Group Publishing, pp. 35–48

Nonaka, I. (1994) A Dynamic Theory of Organizational Knowledge Creation, *Organization Science*, 5: 14–37.

Nonaka, I. (1991, 1998) The Knowledge Creating Company, *Harvard Business Review on Knowledge Management*. Boston, MA: Harvard Business School Press, pp. 21–32.

Prahalad, C. and Hamel, G. (1990) *The Core Competence of the Corporation*. Boston, MA: Harvard Business School Press.

Polyani, M. (1958) *Personal Knowledge: Towards a Post-Critical Philosophy*. Chicago, IL: University of Chicago Press.

Polyani, M. (1966) *The Tacit Dimension*. London: Routledge & Kegan Paul.

Shapiro, C. and Verian, H. (1999) *Information Rules*. Boston, MA: Harvard Business School Press.

Snowden, D. (2005) Multi-Ontology Sense Making: A New Simplicity in Decision Making. Available online at www.cognitive-edge.com/ceresources/articles/40_Multi-ontology_sense_makingv2_May05.pdf (accessed July 19, 2008).

Swan, J., Scarbrough, H., and Preston, J. (1999) Knowledge Management—The Next Fad To Forget People? in Proceedings of the 7th European Conference in Information Systems, Copenhagen, pp. 668–678.

von Lubitz, D. and Wickramasinghe, N. (2006) Creating Germane Knowledge in Dynamic Environments, *International Journal of Innovation and Learning*, 3(3): 326–347.

Weick, Karl E. (1995) *Sensemaking in Organizations*. Thousand Oaks, CA: Sage.

Wickramasinghe, N. and von Lubitz, D. (2007) *Knowledge-Based Enterprise Theories and Fundamentals*. Hershey, PA: IGI.

Wickramasinghe, N. and Mills, G. (2001) MARS: The Electronic Medical Record System: The Core of the Kaiser Galaxy, *International Journal Healthcare Technology Management*, 3(5/6): 406–423.

Wigg, K. (1993) *Knowledge Management Foundations*. Arlington, VA: Schema Press.

Zack, M. (1999) *Knowledge and Strategy*. Boston, MA: Butterworth Heinemann.

Chapter 2

Knowledge Strategies and Knowledge Capture

INTRODUCTION

As discussed in the previous chapter, KM helps organizations attain or maintain sustainable competitive advantage. This chapter discusses KM strategies. It provides a brief background to strategy, and develops arguments as to why and how strategy can relate strongly to KM, and how one can inform the other. Strategy is about long-term planning, but it is meaningless unless objectives are clear. Organizational culture is something that is slow to change, therefore strategic thinking involves considering not just what financial and technical changes may be needed, but also the human factors that may affect outcomes.

It is important that KM is not viewed by managers as a short-term project, and it is important that it is seen as contributing to strategy. KM, however, is in itself not a strategic objective, and there is no end state. It is ongoing and should be viewed as an integral part of the organization. For it to be successful, it must be embedded in the culture, as is the case for quality. Although technological development may be positive, it may also bring disadvantages. For example, the increase in technology has increased virtual contact and reduced the opportunity for face-to-face debate and conceptualization, possibly leading to the loss of tacit knowledge. It is, therefore, the setting up of appropriate and balanced systems to develop and implement KM that is derived from and informs strategy that remains difficult.

Bali and Dwivedi (2004) explore organizational culture and the implementation of management information systems, introducing the Management Information System Culture-Organization, which combines the intangible requirements of culture change with the implementation of a new IT system. In both cases the importance of balance can be recognized. Conversely, even with the highest specification technology in place, without the appropriate management style, culture and processes to embed the concept of KM, a holistic KM strategy would be difficult to implement, hence the importance of balance as argued by Dwivedi et al. (2005). They produced a holistic KM framework for healthcare institutions, within which they recognized the importance of integrating information communication technology and knowledge sharing, stating that healthcare institutions needed to "identify key sociological and technological roles" to achieve the culture change necessary to improve efficiency.

In Western economies, organizations have seen huge changes to both domestic and world trade. KM has become more relevant as the nature of Western economies has shifted from manufacturing to services. In a service-oriented economy, knowledge, rather than physical assets, is at a premium. In recent years there have been shifts from traditional, highly structured organizations, to more fluid businesses in areas as diverse as manufacturing, healthcare, entertainment and education.

Knowledge creation, sharing and retention are the keys to gaining and retaining competitive edge in this dynamic environment. Organizations could choose to let their knowledge be treated in an ad hoc fashion, or manage the asset "knowledge" in a way that would lever the best value of it and treat it as a prime resource that needs to be managed at a strategic level. This means considering how KM may help achieve organizational goals, how it may influence such goals, how knowledge may be acquired (intelligence gathering) and how knowledge assets may be measured.

CAPTURING KNOWLEDGE

Given the accepted existence of two types of knowledge (explicit and tacit), this section deals with how one can effectively capture tacit knowledge. This is because explicit knowledge has already been captured in the form of its current state (i.e. in the form of reports, charts and other documentation). Tacit knowledge is often much harder to capture as this may reside in the form of "expertise" (some authors refer to this as knowledge that may be "trapped" in somebody's head).

To demonstrate how aspects of KM have perhaps been used *avant la lettre*, most companies operate the practice of carrying out an "exit interview" with employees who are leaving an organization. This usually takes the form of a questionnaire and interview where the company tries to find out the reasons for the employee's departure. Patterns can often be detected if several employees provide the same or similar reasons. It may, however, be argued that even this is a case of too little, too late. The employee has, after all, still left (along with his or her knowledge).

Other common, effective and obvious ways of capturing knowledge include the use of qualitative and quantitative research methods, such as questionnaires, interviews and observation. The use of interviews is to be encouraged since questionnaires often only allow for a limited or "fixed" range of opinions (for example, yes/no answers or ranking-based questions which do not allow for variation, however slight —and yet important—this may be). A yes/no option does not allow for the answer "well, sometimes," which could be crucial.

KM-based innovations, such as social networks and wikis, also enable organizations to efficiently gather facts and opinions. It could be argued that the "social" nature of such knowledge capture enables the organization to garner opinions and knowledge that may otherwise remain inaccessible.

Finally, simple "brainstorming" techniques can be very effective ways of gathering tacit knowledge. In a group environment such techniques can help participants to focus their ideas and trigger new thoughts, while working with the thrust of a team. The resulting thoughts and opinions can then be used as a basis for refinement. Other terms that are used for "brainstorming" include mind shower, mind map, word storm, brain dump, word dump, thought dump or round robin.

ORGANIZING KNOWLEDGE: A STRATEGIC VIEW

Skyrme and Amidon (1997) suggest six different types of knowledge, building on the five questions: how, who, when, where, why, but also including a final category, "that."

1 *Know-how* is the knowledge of how to get things done, and some of this knowledge is made explicit in organizational procedures, but in practice much of it is tacit and in people's heads.
2 *Know-who* is about knowing who can help, and this relies on the ability to appreciate other people's skills and strengths (and weaknesses). Knowing whom not to ask is also very important.
3 *Know-when* is about sense of timing. For example, skilled stock market operators seem to have the knack of buying when everybody else is selling.
4 *Know-where* is about knowing where things are best carried out. This arises in localities where people with certain skills congregate—places like silicone valley for high technology or the City of London or New York for international finance.
5 *Know-why* is about the wider context and vision. This knowledge allows individuals to do what is right for a customer rather than slavishly following a procedure.
6 *Know-that* is the basic sense of knowing. It represents accepted facts but also experience and access to learning. A skilled mechanic may know that the cause of a problem is likely to be found in a particular component.

Sveiby (2006) splits KM initiatives into three areas: External Structure Initiatives (ESIs), Internal Structure Initiatives (ISIs) and Competence Initiatives (CIs). ESIs involve gaining knowledge from customers or suppliers and offering knowledge to customers or suppliers. For example, from 1982 General Electric (GE) (U.S.) has collected all customer complaints in a database that supports telephone operators in answering customer calls, and GE has programmed 1.5 million potential problems and their solutions into its system. The National Bicycle Industrial Company (Japan) produces bicycles that are tailored to each customer's height, weight and color choice, and this is done in a single day, by means of their customer database being integrated with computer aided design and computer integrated manufacturing. Agro Corp (U.S.) sells seed and fertilizers, and assists farmer's choices by analyzing data on their soils together with weather forecasts and information on crops.

Sveiby's (2006) Internal Structure Initiatives include things such as building a knowledge sharing culture and creating new revenues from existing resources. Examples include Outokumppu (Finland) which uses knowledge on how to build smelting plants to educate staff of customers throughout the world, with the result that this is now bigger business than the original smelting activity. Skandia (Switzerland) has a back office system that is now sold to Swiss insurance companies.

Sveiby's (2006) Competence Initiatives include creating careers based on KM and creating microenvironments for the transfer of tacit knowledge. Examples are Buckman Labs (U.S.)

where employees gain financial rewards and higher positions for knowledge sharing, and Affärsvärlden (Sweden), where team writing and piggy-backing are used to help new journalists develop more quickly.

Probst *et al.* (2000) view KM as a process that encompasses knowledge identification, knowledge acquisition, knowledge sharing and knowledge utilization. Knowledge may be considered as tacit or explicit, and this categorization is often attributed to Nonaka and Takeuchi (1995) but Polanyi (1962) is considered by many to be the original source. Explicit or codified knowledge is transmittable in formal systematic language. Tacit knowledge is personal, context specific and therefore hard to formalize and communicate. Other views of organizational knowledge include the traditional hierarchical approach of data, information, knowledge and wisdom. Yet another view is of organizational knowledge as being at the cusp of people, processes and technology.

The foregoing outline provides high-level views of knowledge and how it may be organized. The following sections discuss intelligence gathering and measuring the value of knowledge.

INTELLIGENCE GATHERING

Knowledge-based systems need to acquire various forms of knowledge, which includes knowledge of what exists and what does not (declarative knowledge—"know that") and processes (procedures—"know what," "know where," "know who," "know how"). Declarative knowledge is about facts, concepts and inference. Procedural knowledge is about rules, methods and documented organizational norms. Facts and concepts are often general in nature, while rules and methods tend to be specific to particular tasks. For example, a design engineer at an automobile plant would need to know the processes required to take an initial idea through to production.

Intelligence gathering (knowledge capture), for a knowledge-based system, links closely to concepts from expert systems, in which attempts are made to transform the knowledge of an expert into something that will be available to others. As mentioned in the previous section, one view of knowledge is that it can be divided into tacit and explicit. Explicit knowledge is relatively easily identified and codified. The challenge that still faces those engaged in KM is that the most valuable knowledge is tacit, and such knowledge is notoriously difficult to identify and to codify. Tacit knowledge is to do with "gut feel." It may be exemplified by the years of built-in experience of a senior consultant cardiologist who makes a life or death decision about a patient.

Experts are not always able to explain exactly why they have made decisions, and are therefore not necessarily able to provide the rules for such decisions. Their expertise is rare and valuable, and we put our trust in doctors, mechanics, technicians, engineers, lawyers and accountants. At lower levels, many people are able to grasp at least the fundamentals of these subject areas, but as issues become more complicated, deep and layered, most of us do not have the experience, knowledge or ability to be experts in all of these fields.

It is therefore challenging to attempt to gain knowledge from an expert, without the additional complication of transforming that knowledge into something that can be coded and shared with others. An expert might relate anecdotes or examples, but without supplying clear rules to establish patterns, it is not possible to transfer such intelligence to a knowledge-based system. Even further, experts may, in their attempts to explain tacit knowledge, inadvertently give misleading information. In addition, five experts may give five different views on a particular case, and this leads to a view of knowledge acquisition as something that evolves. One major challenge with this is that evolution can take considerable time.

The term "intelligence" has traditionally been used by military organizations to refer to information that has been evaluated in some way or another. It is about value (currency, relevance), as opposed to data, which is often evaluated in terms of accuracy and detail. Thus, intelligence is more than data and more than information, and intelligence may be equated with knowledge. It relates to context and meaning, and must therefore be current and relevant to the issues being considered.

Private and public sector organizations have begun to recognize the value of intelligence, though, initially, this was almost solely in the realm of what was then called industrial espionage. That is, spying on competitors in order to find out what their latest developments are and using this information to gain or retain competitive edge. Within organizations in today's world, intelligence gathering has other, less sinister meanings.

By way of example: there are many means of gathering intelligence. Standard searches of published material may be used to find out such things as the size of companies, their turnover, etc. Concomitantly, other approaches may be used to collect original data. These might include questionnaire surveys, individual interviews, group interviews, focus groups and other well-known approaches. A KM system would attempt to incorporate automated intelligence gathering and would try to share this where appropriate. Examples of this include organizational "yellow pages" and web folders for project teams.

MEASURING

One of the challenging areas within KM is concerned with measurement. Organizations use various strategies for value creation to attain high performance that creates profit, growth and competitive positions. Creativity is a key concept in KM. It is about developing things in new

Table 2.1 *Sample Intelligence Gathering Questions*

What is the age profile of customers?

How many members of staff hold degrees?

Who is the expert in the organization on X?

How much is spent on a particular form of promotion and what returns does that bring?

If the organization is to develop to meet the challenges it will face in five years time, what training programs will be needed, who will run them, what will they cost, and which members of staff should participate?

What are the likely trends within our market?

How will the economic downturn affect our competitors?

What do particular demographic changes mean to our organization?

ways, adapting existing practices and finding a competitive edge by being different from rival organizations. Creativity is an example of an intangible, and it is an example of the use of knowledge held by individuals and groups. An intangible is something that cannot be touched. Intangibles are nonetheless valuable, and in today's world, possibly more valuable than tangible assets.

A part of intangible assets is intellectual capital, and some authors refer to intellectual bandwidth; that is, the ability of an organization to create value with its intellectual capital. Intellectual capital may be thought of as the non-physical and non-monetary assets that are held by an organization. Traditionally, intangibles were considered as either not measurable or too difficult to measure. With the recognition that knowledge is a prime asset, or possibly the only asset, this has had to change. The challenge is to find ways to measure such things and to achieve agreed standards. Currently, that debate is still being held, and the following discussions outline a number of factors related to these issues.

The MERITUM Project (2002) was funded by the European Union to prepare guidelines for measuring intangible assets. This suggests that management organizes both critical and non-critical intangibles through knowledgeable activities to meet organizational objectives. In doing this, the organization will concomitantly engage in the value creation process.

Mehta (2007) suggests three knowledge types: core knowledge (minimum for the firm to be in the business); advanced knowledge (for competitive viability) and innovative knowledge (to enable competitive advantage). Mehta (2007) continues by highlighting the importance of assessing value and developing direct, as well as indirect, measures of value assessment. The importance of this is more to do with the overall value of the organization than a single year's profit margin.

Mehta (2007) highlights the importance of a number of factors that help make a KM strategy effective in the value creation process. These are: articulating the KM strategy; helping the organization define the KM strategy in the light of corporate strategy; facilitating knowledge flows; helping to improve knowledge flow and build appropriate human and technical infrastructures; enabling innovation; realigning an organization's institutional structures to address strategic knowledge gaps; assessing value; and developing direct as well as indirect measures of value assessment. This is associated with a view that an organization's worth is to do with direct and indirect measures to assess economic, social, intellectual and cultural value created within and outside the organization.

KNOWLEDGE REPRESENTATION

Knowledge representation is a large and complex subject that brings together facets from cognitive science, artificial intelligence and knowledge modeling. Central to knowledge representation are the key issues of how people store and process information as well as the way to store knowledge so that programs can process it and use it. Key areas in knowledge representation include:

1 language and notation;
2 ontology languages;
3 links and structures;

4 notation; and

5 storage and manipulation.

Given the problems with representing knowledge in human language such as multiple meanings and the difficulty of capturing gestures, various artificial languages and notations coupled with intricate logical structures have been developed, derived from mathematics, for representing knowledge. The important goal is to accurately and unequivocally capture and store the knowledge in computers and then be able to access it later without any confusion as to what it is representing. Developments in KM generally and knowledge representation more specifically have lead to the development and ongoing development of the semantic web.

KNOWLEDGE ENGINEERING AND THE SEMANTIC WEB

Relatively recently, a meaningful revolution in the computer science field began. The main focal points of this revolution relate to:

1 Centrality of Data

Every computer application is composed of both data and program, that according to the type of application have more or less dominance: for instance, within dynamic systems simulations the application is mostly centered on the program while in database technology, the application is almost completely centered on data. In the last few years, the interest of computer science has gradually moved from program/process centered systems to data centered ones; even the web can be described as nothing more and nothing less than a colossal amount of data distributed among a very large number of computers and daily queried by million of users.

2 Interoperability of Applications and Use of Web Technologies Different Typologies of Networks

For many years, companies have developed and used "closed" applications, operating mainly on proprietary formats of data. Nowadays it is possible to reach a reasonable level of interoperability by using technologies that, based on XML, allow the development of corporate intranets which, by integrating data and web services, "look inside" the company. However, when the application needs to overcome the boundaries of the intranet, the XML-based technologies have often proved themselves insufficient, mainly because they codify and standardize the syntax (structure) of the data but not their semantics (meaning). Interoperability in an open environment requires that the applications can access a repertoire of common knowledge and are able to exploit such knowledge in an autonomous way (without human intervention). This brings back to the fore both the XML-based technologies and the models and techniques developed in the last three decades in the knowledge engineering field.

Knowledge engineering methods enable various types of applications that have huge industrial interest to be developed. Starting from the end of the seventies up to the beginning of the nineties, a plethora of applications known as expert systems were built to support typical tasks such as: analysis of large volumes of data, diagnosis of faults in industrial implants, medical diagnosis, configuration of complex computer systems, planning of the production, etc. Nowadays, however, due to their high development costs and extreme specialization, even if expert systems will remain of interest in some niche, they will hardly result in products of large diffusion.

At the beginning of the nineties, a growing interest started to come out in another knowledge engineering field, known as the semantic web. In fact, in the original conception from Tim Berners-Lee, the web as we know it today (syntactic web) is only a single step that subsequently drives to the semantic web. In May 2001 (Berners-Lee *et al.*, 2001), it was asserted that the: "Semantic Web is an extension of the current web in which information is given well-defined meaning, enabling computers and people to work in co-operation." The concept is very simple: in order to be elaborated in a completely automated way, it is not enough that the data on the web have a clearly defined structure (syntax), as it is possible to give through XML, but it is also necessary that they share the same meaning (semantic) in the community that uses them. To support the development of the web in this direction, a set of standardized technologies (RDF, RDFS, OWL, etc.) have been proposed and are still under development.

CASE EXERCISE: NHS DIRECT[3]

NHS Direct is the combination of a telephone advisory service; with the latest computer based Clinical Assessment Software (CAS), which is staffed by trained nurses (Cunningham *et al.*, 2002), health advisers and health information advisers. The service was introduced as a 24-hour nurse-led advice telephone line, and was established to *"provide easier and faster information for people about health, illness and the NHS so that they are better able to care for themselves and their families"* (Department of Health, 1997).

NHS Direct not only offers services through multiple channels but also plays a key role within the NHS, by responding to major health scares (for example the avian flu) and other incidents of national importance (Office of Public Sector Information, 2007). The service also provides a language line for people who require information or advice in another language other than English. A text phone system is also provided so that the deaf can efficiently utilize the service (Commission for Health Improvement).

NHS Direct was first launched in 1998 with three pilot sites in Milton Keynes, Newcastle and Preston. Like many organizations taking advantage of the "internet age," NHS Direct saw the potential and developed an authoritative health website in December 1999, which is known as NHS Direct Online. Following a positive reception of the three pilot sites, NHS Direct was launched in England in November 2000 and in Wales six months later. A similar service called NHS24 was launched in Scotland in 2004, a year which also saw another aspect of NHS Direct emerge—the NHS Direct digital TV service—one of the largest interactive services in the U.K. (NHS Direct, no date). NHS Direct Interactive was rolled out onto Freeview (a free digital TV service) in December 2006 (NHS Direct, no date).

The service was managed by a central team at the Department of Health when it was initially launched. In April 2004, a Special Health Authority was recognized under the NHS

Direct (Establishment and Constitution) Order 2004 to manage NHS Direct (Office of Public Sector Information, 2007). The organization underwent a major organizational change which consolidated twenty-two organizations together to form a single national provider that provided services commissioned by local Primary Care Trusts (PCTs) (Commission for Health Improvement).

NHS Direct has grown over the years and has established its own unique identity within the healthcare industry. In April 2007, NHS Direct became an NHS Trust, a national service with national policies (NHS Direct, 2006). More recently, the organization has implemented a Knowledge Management Systems (KMS), which:

- allows all staff to deliver the NHS Direct service through systems that provide access to accurate information;
- is more specific to patients' needs; and
- allows appropriate referrals and advice locally.

This is in the context of a changing environment for unscheduled care and an increase in variation of different local services across the country. In addition, the KMS simplifies access to patient information resources and is said to improve quality and efficiency.

Knowledge Sharing Within NHS Direct

Knowledge within NHS Direct is mainly embedded in the system in the form of *structured knowledge*. This structured knowledge provides protocols/algorithms and guidance for nurses and health advisers and is in the form of a decision support system. The service is broadly based and, while it does require explicit knowledge, this is generally determined by first applying tacit knowledge.

The main objective for NHS Direct was to *"provide easier and faster information for people about health, illness and the NHS so that they are better able to care for themselves and their families"* (Department of Health, 1997). This has been achieved through nurses and health advisers (both designated call handlers) guided by a decision support system consisting of codified knowledge. The role of both of these call handlers is to use their tacit knowledge to guide the selection of the correct pathway through the codified knowledge.

Nurses sometimes also use tacit knowledge to determine the conclusions from the codified knowledge. The health advisers may use tacit knowledge to determine what the most critical symptom is at present (for example, if the patient is not being clear enough). If any of these call handlers are unsure about the outcome, they ask for help from supervisors, team leaders or other call handlers and this is where knowledge sharing occurs. Another aspect of knowledge sharing is the KMS. When patients call to ask for a specific clinic in their area, their postcode (zip code) is taken and entered into the system along with the specific requirements they require (for example, a clinic that provides advice on family planning). Once these details are input, the system executes a search and returns results of clinics near the patients' postcode.

All NHS Direct policies are available on the intranet and can be accessed while at work. Emails from management and clinicians within the service are sent regarding issues such as health alerts, job vacancies, etc. Training sessions are held to keep all staff updated with policies (for example, child protection training). Within these sessions, individuals are able to voice and share their concerns with others. When new call handlers are recruited, they undergo "buddy" training; the current call handler takes calls from patients while the new call handler listens in. A discussion and exchange of knowledge is displayed.

Conclusion

Patrick and Dotsika (2007) tell us that:

> If future competitive advantage lies in providing value-added to products and services, then knowledge creation becomes essential to providing this value-added. At the core of knowledge creation lies knowledge sharing and therein the need for collaboration.
>
> (p. 403)

While technology may help to facilitate communication between people, it is up to people to choose whether or not to communicate their knowledge. NHS Direct is very dependant on its technology for communication throughout the organization. Through the use of this technology, staffing levels, waiting times and so forth can be forecast. However, this can only be achieved if the supervisors at each site communicate both effectively and efficiently.

Based on Nonaka's model, NHS Direct is in the combination process, as knowledge is shared from explicit to explicit and again is best supported by technology. The tacit knowledge that each call handler holds is never documented; however, it is always passed on between call handlers. The only type of sharing that is carried out is the formal sharing, within offices, meetings, emails and so on. NHS Direct does not have a knowledge sharing culture between staff members, but one could argue that it possesses a "knowledge sharing culture" within the public (as knowledge about services and health information is transferred to patients). The only tacit knowledge the organization is losing is the critical thinking and the knowledge gained from that. The knowledge that nurses hold (or that which call handlers bring with them to the organization), in most cases, cannot be applied to the job.

The main barriers to sharing knowledge are those attitudes based on mutual trust, and possibly the constant changes being implemented. These changes lead to staff members leaving as knowledge about changes and conditions was not always effectively communicated and shared. People can use their abilities to create value by creating and transferring knowledge externally and internally to the organization. NHS Direct needs to focus on its employees and their abilities; by sharing and, in return, helping them to share their knowledge.

Case Exercise References

Commission for Health Improvement (n.d.) What CHI Has Found In: NHS Direct Services. Available online at www.healthcarecommission.org.uk-_db-_documents-04000053.pdf> [accessed: May 5, 2008].

Cunningham, P., Green, L., Miles, I. and Rigby, J. (n.d.) NHS Direct, An Innovation in Social Trust. Available online at www.step.no/publin/reports/d12–3ukum.pdf [accessed: May 5, 2008].

Department of Health (1997) Making it Happen. Available online at www.archive.official-documents. co.uk/document/doh/newnhs/wpaper10.htm [accessed: May 5, 2008].

NHS Direct (n.d.) Launch on Freeview. Available online at w ww.nhsdirect.nhs.uk/MediaObject.aspx? MediaObjectID=622 [accessed: May 1, 2008].

NHS Direct (2006) Connecting Health and Home, Annual Report 2006/07. Available online at www.official-documents.gov.uk-document-hc0607-hc06–0649–0649.pdf [accessed: May 5, 2008].

Office of Public Sector Information (2007) NHS Direct Special Health Authority Abolition Order 2007. Available online at www.opsi.gov.uk/si/si2007/uksi_20070504_en_2 [accessed: May 5, 2008].

Patrick, K. and Dotsika, F. (2007) Knowledge Sharing: Developing from Within, *The Learning Organization,* 14(5) 395–406.

Malhotra (2003) addresses the complexity of measuring intangibles and defines intellectual capital as wealth creating knowledge, information, intellectual property and experience. Lehaney *et al.* (2004) argue that intellectual capital, including creativity knowledge sharing, affects the organization's market value overall, but not necessarily the tangibles of profit margins. This is a key point, and it should be noted that if share values were directly related to profits per annum, they would be easy to predict. In fact, the share market is what is known as a "random walk," and predicting share values is notoriously difficult. There is some relationship with profit margins, but the long-term value of shares is more closely linked with the perception of an organization's value.

A knowledge-based organization typically has intellectual capital as its major asset but typically this value is usually not declared in annual reports and does not appear in conventional analysis models. The Danish Government has attempted to address this issue over a number of years, and has produced guidelines for intellectual capital evaluation (Danish Agency for Trade and Industry, 2000). This report indicates that:

The intellectual capital statement supports the company's KM, i.e. the part of management work that obtains, shares, develops and anchors knowledge resources. The intellectual capital statement provides a status of the company's efforts to develop its knowledge resources through KM in text, figures and illustrations.

The intellectual capital statement is both a strategic tool for adding value to the company and a communication tool for inducing employees, customers and others to engage in this process. The intellectual capital statement thus points to the future and is not primarily intended to account for the current portfolio of knowledge resources at any particular time.

The objective of an intellectual capital statement is not to calculate the value of the company's knowledge in financial terms. Also, this is probably not feasible. Thus, an intellectual capital statement cannot be used to explain the difference between a company's book value and its market value, although this is sometimes the stated purpose of intellectual capital statements. Such use of the statement is for several reasons meaningless. Firstly, the difference would depend on accounting standards and on market developments generally. Secondly, it would require that the market already knew the true value of the company, thus eliminating the need for calculating this.

(p. 3)

33

The intellectual capital statement consists of three elements: a knowledge narrative, KM challenges and KM reporting. The knowledge narrative outlines how a company meets customer's requirements, and specifies how the company has organized its resources to achieve this. KM challenges are defined from the knowledge narrative. They should be translated into actions for implementing the objectives that derive from the knowledge narrative. The report is informed by the knowledge narrative and the KM challenges.

Text, figures and illustrations are used for the external intellectual capital statement, which is the document reporting on the company strategy for KM. Text relates to the knowledge narrative, the management challenges and the specific actions. Figures document the initiatives launched to address management challenges, with actions tied to indicators. Illustrations may be photographs, charts or any graphical depictions that help to communicate the knowledge narrative and the KM challenges, and that aid the reader to gain an impression of the organization's style, character and identity (Danish Agency for Trade and Industry, 2000).

The *Skandia Navigator* model is one of the first approaches to be used in this area, and its initial internal intellectual capital report was based upon the basis proposed by Edvinsson and Malone (1997). This model divides the intellectual capital of an organization into three forms: human capital, structural capital and customer capital. Human capital includes staff competence, capabilities, skills, experiences, creativity and innovation. The infrastructure is provided by structural capital and it includes organizational processes, procedures, technologies, information sources and intellectual property rights. It may be argued that the organizational physical environment is a major factor within this. Customer capital may relate to good will, and is related to an organization's relationships with its customers, suppliers, trade and professional associations and any external links.

The *Balanced Scorecard* (Kaplan and Norton, 1996) has four general perspectives, and these are financial, customer, internal process, and learning and growth. The financial perspective considers an organization's strategy and how that contributes to profits. It incorporates the tangible outcomes of the strategy in traditional financial terms. The customer addresses the value proposition that the organization chooses to apply in order to satisfy customers and generate additional sales to the most desired customers. The internal process perspective considers processes that create and deliver the customer value proposition. It focuses on activities that are needed for an organization to provide, effectively and efficiently, value expected by customers. The learning and growth perspective links strongly to KM and is the basis of developing and increasing the intangible assets of an organization, with its focus on internal skills and capabilities that are required to support value-creating processes.

Accounting and financial measurement techniques not only tend to take a historical perspective but also focus on physical or tangible assets. Given that most of KM is concerned with intangible assets this poses a significant problem. More recently, various attempts to measure the benefits of intangible assets have been developed, including trying to value brands, trademarks and patents.

Skyrme (2005) identified approximately thirty different methods used by companies to try to measure the value of KM. These methods tend to focus on one of the following four areas:

1 valuing knowledge as an asset, potentially tradable;
2 focusing on the benefits of a KM program;

3 assessing KM effectiveness as a basis for year-on-year comparison; and

4 focusing on performance measurement.

There are other approaches to valuing and reporting intangible assets. In many ways these are variations on those discussed previously. They include the Intangible Assets Monitor (Sveiby, 1997), the IC-Index Model (Roos *et al.*, 1997), the Holistic Value Approach (Roos *et al.*, 2005), and the Technology Broker Model (Brooking, 1996). Other measurement models include Tobin's Q, Economic Value Added, Market-to-Book Value, Intellectual Asset Valuation, Total Value Creation, Knowledge Capital Earnings and Citation Weighted Patents.

While all offer various, often similar, ways to evaluate intangibles, there is no commonly agreed approach as yet. Given the myriad of systems currently developed or being developed, it is clear that there is no one unified and agreed upon method to measure knowledge at this time and this is indeed an area that requires further development.

CONCLUSIONS AND SUMMARY

This chapter discussed strategies related to organizing, gathering and measuring knowledge. Strategy is a long-term concept and involves not just traditional financial concepts, but also human dimensions, including organizational culture. KM needs to address strategic aims and to contribute to them, but as KM is not in itself a strategic objective (such as increasing market share), it has to be treated as integral to working practices and embedded in organizational culture, as is the case for quality.

A holistic approach is needed if KM is to be addressed seriously and implemented successfully. Technology may be useful in this, but it must be accompanied by an appropriate management style. Culture and processes are major aspects of KM initiatives.

The decline of manufacturing and the increase of services have been major influences in considering knowledge as a prime asset. To get the best of that asset it has to be managed and evaluated. Knowledge organization, gathering and measurement are important in gaining and retaining competitive edge. It is accepted that, in general, intellectual capital comprises non-monetary and non-physical assets that add value to an organization. There is still no generally agreed approach to evaluating such assets.

REVIEW QUESTIONS

1 Why is knowledge now considered a prime asset in Western economies?

2 What are the main models of organizing knowledge discussed in this chapter?

3 What is the difference between declarative knowledge and procedural knowledge?

4 What challenges arise in trying to capture tacit knowledge?

5 What is the Balanced Scorecard?

6 What is the Skandia Navigator?

DISCUSSION QUESTIONS

1 What is the difference between the value of an organization and the profits it makes?

2 Consider a public sector provision, such as health services in the U.K., and a private sector commercial organization. Would both be interested in evaluating organizational knowledge? Why? How would they differ?

3 If knowledge is valuable, what issues are there in trying to create a knowledge sharing culture?

4 Think of an example of a work situation, past, present or that could arise, in which organizing, gathering and evaluating knowledge would be relevant.

CASE EXERCISE: OPERATING ROOM OPTIMIZATION[4]

Introduction

As the population ages, an increasing number of people will experience debilitating, degenerative arthritis of the knee and hip joint. In degenerative arthritis, the articular, gliding surface of the joint becomes worn and exposes the underlying bone of the joint. This is a painful condition for which patients seek medical care to decrease their pain and increase their functional status. In fact, the number of persons age sixty-five or older is expected to double between the year 2000 and the year 2040 (U.S. Census Bureau, Decennial Census Data and Population Projections). One of the most successful procedures in the treatment of knee and hip arthritis is to replace the worn surfaces with the metal and plastic components of a hip or knee joint replacement. This procedure is currently completed in a hospital's operating room; the patient stays in hospital to start their recovery and is then discharged to go home or to a rehabilitation facility for further rehabilitation. For the next twenty years, U.S. domestic demand for knee replacements is expected to increase by over 10 percent per year.

Challenges

Once the patient's arthritis is end-stage and the articular cartilage is worn away, patients with painful degenerative arthritis will seek the expertise of an orthopedic surgeon. Replacement of the hip and knee joint has become one of healthcare's most successful procedures in terms of providing the patient with pain relief and improved function. These operations are performed by the surgeon in a hospital where the surgeon has been credentialed and has privileges to admit their patients and perform operations in which the surgeon has expertise. As the population requiring medical care increases, hospitals worldwide are being challenged to provide sufficient resources, including operating rooms, for these patients. These is also more pressure on the hospitals to decrease their cost structure and this is complicated by the introduction of newer medical technology, including new, and presumably more advanced, implants.

Patient preparation for a hip or knee replacement is dependant on their surgeon's evaluation and treatment plan as well as the preoperative evaluation by anesthesia providers and in many cases a medical evaluation to ensure that the operative procedure is done in the safest manner possible. Ensuring that patients are optimally prepared for the day of surgery is critical to keeping the surgeon's schedule and an operating room schedule accurate and not affected by the cancellations that lead to lost opportunity costs. Additionally, the healthcare system must provided sufficient hospital resources so that patients can efficiently move from the operating room to the recovery room to their nursing floor bed and then to either a rehabilitation hospital bed or home with the provision of home care services such as physical therapy.

The entire process can initially be represented by three distinct phases: preoperative, intraoperative and postoperative. While each of these phases is dependant on a previous state or event, the capture of the data from that previous state is important to the optimization of the next phase. Many surgeons perform only hip and knee replacements and will attest that their methods and procedures don't change from operation to operation. While this statement may be disputed to some extent by the operating room personnel, every knee replacement follows a very similar pattern of events. In fact, a surgeon's performance of a knee replacement is fairly similar across hundreds of procedures but the most significant difference between each of the operations is that the substrates change, i.e. each patient is different. Operating room success for each of these procedures is dependent on the preoperative, intraoperative and postoperative processes that comprise the spectrum of orthopedic care.

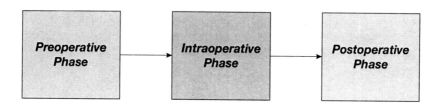

Stakeholders and Objectives

The process stream begins with a patient experiencing pain and decreased function sufficient to present their complaints to an orthopedic surgeon. Once the decision is made to proceed with the procedure, the patient is scheduled for a preoperative evaluation and the surgery is scheduled at the hospital. The surgeon will also indicate their preference for a specific implant system and the hospital will ensure that those implants and the instruments used for their insertion are present for the surgery. In further preparation for the day of surgery, the sterilization and supply teams at the hospital are charged with assembling all of the necessary materials, the operating room nursing team set up the sterile instruments and equipment and the operating room and the anesthesia is tasked with providing the patient with a pain-free operative experience. The surgeon and their assistants then can complete the operative procedure as scheduled. The postoperative recovery room nursing team provides the next step in the process by helping the patient recover from the operative episode. Then the patient will go to the most appropriate nursing floor to start their recuperation with the assistance of the nursing team, the physical and occupational therapists, the surgical team and when necessary, various medical consultants. Once specific surgeon and institutional milestones have been reached, the patient is discharged to a rehabilitation nursing facility or to go home, where further physical therapy is provided. In all, over 250 people and over 435 individual processes are involved with a single patient's operative procedure. Each entity, hospital and surgeon's office has specific fixed and variable expenses that are greatly influenced by every process in the patient's care.

Technology

Hip and knee implants are undergoing a constant state of innovation and improved technology. While the benefits of these purported improvements are not always proven in a stringent or conclusive examination, the implant companies are under pressure to improve their market share and their profitability. In the last 10 years, additional developments in the implant insertion instruments have included computerized navigation systems and newer imaging-based custom instrument development which have been marketed to surgeons and their patients. The value of the newer technologies has not been conclusively demonstrated. In some cases, the hospital bears the increased costs of the new technology while the profits of the implant companies increase.

Many hospitals are also involved in the implementation of electronic medical systems to consolidate and automate the ordering of specific medications or procedures and to electronically document nursing and physician notes regarding a patient's care. Hospital supply chain management and human resource teams have also been implementing electronic systems to improve the scheduling of personnel and the stocking, ordering and billing reconciliation of supplies and implants. These incremental costs that have been borne by hospitals and doctor's offices have occurred while the payers' ''reimbursement'' for services rendered have been decreasing consistently.

Knowledge

To improve the efficiency and efficacy of patient care, especially for those patients requiring hip or knee replacement, every process should be optimized—the inputs, transformation and outputs should be measured against specification for process time, scheduling, expenses, personnel, etc. Each individual in the long chain of processes has tacit knowledge that increases with each day of experience while the explicit knowledge in the institutional or surgeon's policies and procedures manual are infrequently updated. The opportunity to improve the knowledge spiral and use the Intelligence Continuum to capitalize on realizing the full value of the system is unparalleled. The inherent limitations of organizational structure must be overcome to make these improvements.

The first steps in a process improvement project include the identification of each knowledge point, i.e. the process mapping for joint replacement procedures with the goal of improving performance and predictability while minimizing variances, decreasing ''waste'' and increasing value while minimizing costs. The generation, representation, storage, transfer and transformation of knowledge are key steps in making the desired improvements in clinical and management practices and incorporating continuous innovation. The current state is that the daily volume data that is generated and accumulated is often lost, further increasing the gaps between data collection, comprehension and analysis. Boyd's OODA loop model of observation, orientation, decision and action can organize the inputs and provide a structure for improvement.

Conclusions and Recommendations

More patients with degenerative knee and hip arthritis will need joint replacement. Surgeons and hospitals need to use process engineering tools to identify critical path processes and the stakeholders to optimize process efficiency, efficacy, productivity and satisfaction.

Case Exercise Questions

1 What processes are involved in the care of the joint replacement patient?

2 How can the tacit, implicit and explicit knowledge be organized?

3 What are key metrics and measurements of success?

4 How can current resources be maximized and optimized?

5 What are the impediments to getting the work done?

6 How can capacity be increased?

7 What technologies would improve processes?

FURTHER READING

Helbig, H. (2006) *Knowledge Representation and the Semantics of Natural Language.* Berlin: Springer.

Sveiby, K. (1997) *The New Organizational Wealth: Managing and Measuring Intangible Assets.* San Francisco, CA: Berret-Koehler Publishers.

Wickramasinghe, N. and von Lubitz, D. (2007) *Knowledge-Based Enterprise Theories and Fundamentals.* Hershey, PA: IGI.

www.fek.su.se/home/bic/meritum/download/index.html#papers.

www.gurteen.com.

www.sveiby.com.

REFERENCES

Bali, R.K. and Dwivedi, A.N. (2004) Organizational Culture and the Implementation of Management Information Systems, *OR Insight*, 17(1): 10–18.

Berners-Lee, T., Hendler, J., and Lassila, O. (2001) The Semantic Web, *Scientific American*, May: 35–43.

Danish Agency for Trade and Industry (2000) *A Guideline for Intellectual Capital Statements—A Key to Knowledge Management.* Available online at www.ebst.dk/publikationer/rapporter/guidelineICS/ren.htm (accessed July 25, 2008).

Dwivedi, A.N., Bali, R.K., Naguib, R.N.G., and Lehaney, B. (2005) Knowledge Management for the Healthcare Sector: Lessons from a Case Study, *OR Insight*, 18(2): 3–13.

Edvinsson, L. and Malone, M. (1997) *Intellectual Capital: Realizing Your Company's True Value by Finding Its Hidden Roots,* New York: Harper Business.

Guarino, N. (1998) Formal Ontology in Information Systems, *Proceedings of FOIS '98.* Trento, Italy: IOS Press, pp. 3–15.

Kaplan, R. and Norton, D. (1996) *The Balanced Scorecard: Translating Strategy into Action,* Boston, MA: Harvard Business School Press.

Lehaney, B., Malindzak, D., and Khan, Z. (2008) Simulation Modeling for Problem Understanding: A Case Study in the East Slovakia Coal Industry. Accepted for publication in the *Journal of the Operational Research Society.*

Malhotra, Y. (2003) *Measuring Knowledge Assets of a Nation: Knowledge Systems for Development,* Research paper presented to UN. Available online at http://unpan1.un.org/intradoc/groups/public/documents/un/unpan 011601.pdf (accessed July 6, 2002).

Mehta, N. (2007) The Value Creation Cycle: Moving Towards a Framework for Knowledge Management Implementation, *Knowledge Management Research and Practice,* 5(2): 126–135.

MERITUM Project (2002) *Guidelines for Managing and Reporting on Intangibles* (Intellectual Capital Report). Available online at www.fek.su.se/home/bic/meritum/download/index.html#papers (accessed July 17, 2008).

Nonaka, I. and Takeuchi, H. (1995) *The Knowledge Creating Company: How Japanese Companies Create the Dynamics of Innovation.* New York: OUP.

Polanyi, M. (1962) *Personal Knowledge: Towards a Post-Critical Philosophy.* New York: Harper Torchbooks.

Probst, G., Raub, S., and Romhardt, K. (2000) *Managing Knowledge: Building Blocks for Success.* Chichester: John Wiley & Sons.

Roos, G., Pike, S., and Ferntröm, L. (2005) *Managing Intellectual Capital in Practice.* Amsterdam: Elsevier.

Roos, J., Roos, G., Edvinsson, L., and Dragonetti, N. (1997) *Intellectual Capital: Navigating in the New Business Landscape.* New York: Macmillan.

Skyrme, D. and Amidon, D. (1997) *Creating the Knowledge-Based Business.* London: Business Intelligence.

Skyrme, D. (2005) Measuring the Value of Knowledge. Available online at www.skyrme.com/insights/24kmeas.htm (accessed September 1, 2008).

Sveiby, K. (1997) The Intangible Assets Monitor, *Journal of Human Resource Costing and Accounting,* 2(1): 73–97.

Sveiby, K. (2006) *Knowledge Management Initiatives Round the Globe.* Available online at www.sveiby.com/ KnowledgeManagementInitiativesRoundtheGlobe/tabid/123/Default.aspx (accessed July 28, 2008).

Chapter 3

Knowledge Tools and Techniques

INTRODUCTION

There are several different tools and techniques heavily used within KM. Some actively use technology, some less so or not at all. This chapter will introduce some of the major methods in contemporary use and will provide some examples to illustrate their effectiveness.

TAXONOMIES AND ONTOLOGIES

Ontologies and taxonomies are means of classifying things. This notion is not new, and the concept is often attributed to Aristotle (384BC–322BC), who attempted to classify living things (in ways that are still familiar today, such as live-birth animals (mammals) and egg-birth creatures (birds and fish)). The term taxonomy thus began to be used within biology and was used to classify living organisms (this is now known as alpha taxonomy). It is now used in a more general sense, and may refer to the ways in which classifications are decided, not just the classification structure itself. Interestingly, systems thinking also has biological roots and this is discussed in Chapter 4.

Ontologies are often considered as broader than taxonomies, but the terms may be used in a variety of ways. Various relationships can be classified and grandparent–parent–child relationships are often depicted. The term can, however, be used to cover multi-parent relationships and networks. For example, a document may be classified with the parent Bloggs (the author). It might also have the parent June 2008 (date) or the parent Tax Office (correspondent). It could be classified by subject.

A very well-known classification scheme is that used by libraries, known as the *Dewey Decimal Classification* (DDC) or the *Dewey Decimal System*, originally created by Melvil Dewey in 1876. Within DDC, knowledge is organized into ten main classes, ten divisions per class (100 divisions) and ten sections per division (1,000 sections)—hence decimal. Non-fiction publications are classified by subject as follows.

From the above, 600 represents technology, and within this, the second digit indicates the division: 600 is used for general works on technology, 610 for medicine and health, 620 for

41

Table 3.1 *Example of the Dewey Decimal System*

000	Computer science, information, and general works
100	Philosophy and psychology
200	Religion
300	Social sciences
400	Language
500	Science
600	Technology
700	Arts and recreation
800	Literature
900	History, geography, and biography

engineering, 630 for agriculture, and so on. The third digit indicates the section with 610 used for general works on medicine and health, 611 for human anatomy, 612 for human physiology, and 613 for personal health and safety. After the first three digits a decimal point is used, followed by finer gradations, each being a factor of ten.

Just as an example, if you wanted to find out about black widow spiders of California, you would look for 595.44. Each book in a library will have its Dewey number on the spine. A major advantage of this system is that when books are left on desks or misplaced on shelves, it is extremely easy to put them back in the correct place, without having to start considering from the beginning where they should go.

The Dewey System is an example of a taxonomy that is used worldwide. It can make life easier, because as human beings we like to try and make sense of things by putting some order on them that we can understand. A problem with this is that one person's order and understanding is not the same as another's. The book *Who Moved My Cheese?* is a humorous view on change in personal and work life and nothing to do with culinary issues. Someone classifying the work might think otherwise—and so there are lots of rules about how to classify with Dewey so that the same book title would be classified in every library in exactly the same way.

A major problem with this is of course the cost of setting up all the rules, the training involved, the supervision, the checking, etc. The Dewey System has evolved over a long period of time, so this has not been the major challenge that it would be for a large organization suddenly deciding it wished to classify its knowledge. The technology aspects of KM are largely derived from computer science, within which ontology represents a domain, the concepts within it, and the relationships between those concepts. In this sense an ontology would typically comprise a structure of individuals (e.g. a specific child), classes (e.g. all children with red hair), relationships between classes and individuals, attributes (e.g. age), constraints and rules, events (how things change—e.g. hair changes from red to grey), and various other factors, such as axioms and functions. Together these all comprise the domain.

KM may use taxonomy to depict an organization, and this may be done in different ways, such as by product, by customer type, by cost center, by services bought, and so on. The driver is knowledge transfer to achieve competitive advantage, but the costs and effort of setting up such a system may be prohibitive. Attempting to organize knowledge methodically is typically a major task that is outside normal productive work. There is no immediate contribution to income, and there will be costs. Information and new ideas would have to be recognized and collated from the broadest to the most detailed level.

For the immediate future the key areas of taxonomies in KM are likely to be in helping users to navigate web-pages and PDF files on a KM intranet, and in the construction of logs of experts in an organization. Taking eBay as an example, someone searching for a DVD player would find a taxonomy of this kind:

Home > Buy > Consumer Electronics > DVD & Home Cinema > DVD Players

This can be divided further by price band, manufacturer, region code, etc.

DATA MINING TOOLS AND TECHNIQUES

Due to the immense size of the data sets, computerized techniques are essential to help decision makers understand relationships and associations between data elements. Data mining is closely associated with databases and shares some common ground with statistics since both strive toward discovering structure in data. However, while statistical analysis starts with some kind of hypothesis about the data, data mining does not. Furthermore, data mining is much more suited to dealing with heterogeneous databases, data sets and data fields.

From a micro perspective, data mining is a vital step in the broader context of the knowledge discovery in databases (KDD) that transforms data into knowledge by identifying valid, novel, potentially useful, and ultimately understandable patterns in data (Adriaans and Zantinge, 1996; Fayyad et al.,1996; Cabena et al.,1998; Bendoly, 2003) KDD plays an important role in data-driven decision support systems that include query tools, report generators, statistical analysis tools, data warehousing and online analytic processing (OLAP). Data mining algorithms are used on data sets for model building, or for finding patterns and relationships in data. How to manage such newly discovered knowledge, as well as other organizational knowledge assets, is the realm of KM.

STEPS IN DATA MINING

The following steps are typically undertaken in data mining (Fayyad et al.,1996; Becerra-Fernandez and Sabherwal, 2001; Holsapple and Joshi, 2002; Choi and Lee, 2003). These steps are iterative, with the process moving backward whenever it is required to do so.

1 Develop an understanding of the application, of the relevant prior knowledge, and of the end user's goals.
2 Create a target data set to be used for discovery.
3 Clean and pre-process the data (including handling missing data fields, noise in the data, accounting for time series, and known changes).
4 Reduce the number of variables and find invariant representations of the data if possible.

5 Choose the data-mining task (classification, regression, clustering, etc.).
6 Choose the data-mining algorithm.
7 Search for patterns of interest (this is the actual data mining).
8 Interpret the patterns mined. If necessary, iterate through any of steps 1–7.
9 Consolidate the knowledge discovered, prepare reports and then use/re-use the newly created knowledge.

A data mining project usually starts with data collection or data selection, covering almost all steps (described above) in the KDD process. In this respect, the first three steps of the KDD process (i.e. selection, pre-processing and transformation) are considered exploratory data mining, whereas the last two steps (i.e. data mining and interpretation/evaluation) in the KDD process are considered predictive data mining. The primary objectives of data mining in practice tend to be description (performed by exploratory data mining) and prediction (performed by predictive data mining). Description focuses on finding human-interpretable patterns describing the data while prediction involves using some observations and attributes to predict unknown or future values of other attributes of interest. The relative importance of description and prediction for particular data mining applications can vary considerably. The descriptive and predictive tasks are carried out by applying different machine learning, artificial intelligence and statistical algorithms.

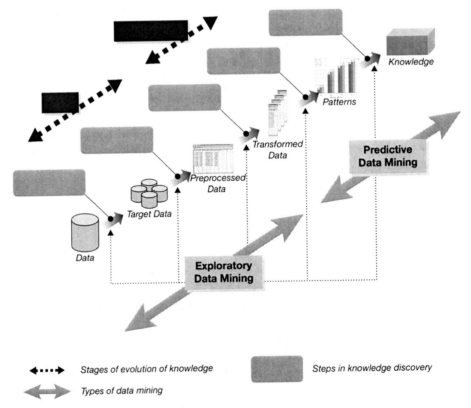

Figure 3.1 *Essential Aspects of Data Mining.*
Source: adapted from Fayyad *et al.* (1996)

Major goals of exploratory data mining are data cleaning, unification and understanding. Some of the data operations undertaken during exploratory data mining include: sampling, partitioning, charting, graphing, associating, clustering, transforming, filtering and imputing. Predictive data mining deals with future values of variables and utilizes many algorithms; including regression, decision trees and neural networks. Predictive data mining also involves an assessment step, which compares the effectiveness of different models according to many performance metrics. Figure 3.1 shows an integrated view of the knowledge discovery process, the evolution of knowledge from data to information to knowledge, and the types of data mining (exploratory and predictive) and their interrelationships. In this one figure, all the major aspects connected with data mining are captured, emphasizing its integral role in knowledge creation. This is not normally explicitly articulated in the existing literature although the connection between data, information and knowledge is often discussed; for example (Chung and Gray, 1996; Becerra-Fernandez and Sabherwal, 2001; Holsapple and Joshi, 2002; Choi and Lee, 2003).

Data mining then, is the non-trivial process of identifying valid, novel, potentially useful, and ultimately understandable patterns from data (Fayyad *et al.*,1996). It is essential to emphasize here the importance of the interaction with experts who always play a crucial and indispensable role in any knowledge discovery process in facilitating prediction of key patterns and also identification of new patterns and trends.

CASE EXERCISE: KM AND PERSONAL HEALTH RECORDS— A MALAYSIAN PERSPECTIVE[5]

Background

In trying to propel Malaysia into a "developed nation" status, the Government of Malaysia has formulated vision and mission statements such as the Malaysian Vision 2020 as well as the Malaysian Healthcare Vision. In trying to actualize both these visions into reality, the government and the Ministry of Health of Malaysia (MOHM) have started preparing through the *Integrated Telehealth Initiative* where the Lifetime Health Record (LHR) is used as the basis for continuous care.

The LHR is the central key delivery of Malaysia's integrated telehealth application. The LHR correlates each episode of care for an individual into a continuous health record. It is the summarized health record of every individual compiled from their electronic medical records. These records refer to a patient's electronic medical records that are cumulatively derived from the clinical support system (such as clinical information system, laboratory information system, pharmacy information system and patient management system) and it can be collected and gathered from the various spectrums of health information systems and healthcare levels. The most important consideration, however, is that the LHR should contain not only longitudinal health summary information but also incorporate online retrieval of patient health histories whenever required. In order to achieve this, standard data sets for LHR should be established for supporting the implementation of the integrated telehealth initiatives for collecting and generating the national LHR repository. This research aims to produce the optimal amount of patient health data for developing and proposing standard data sets of LHR that would be used to support the implementation of Malaysia's integrated telehealth system and creating the national LHR repository.

Methods

The research was carried out through a case exercise approach conducted at the outpatient department of MOHM. The data obtained from the case exercise (by way of structured interviews and accessing archived records) would be used to develop standard data sets of LHR. The interviews were carried out by ten assistant researchers who were appointed to conduct the interviews with thirty doctors in thirty outpatient clinics. The assistant researchers were selected from medical graduates who had extensive knowledge in the medical domain. By doing this, the discussion between interviewer and respondent was conducted smoothly.

Background of Malaysia Healthcare System

Current Healthcare Delivery System and Physical Set-up

The Malaysian public healthcare system is structured in a hierarchical pyramid-based concept. At the base of the pyramid is a broad array of primary healthcare services (such as health centers, polyclinics, mobile clinics and maternal and child clinics) spread throughout the country. The next level consists of district hospitals in every one of 120 districts, feeding into state general hospitals in each state capital. At the top of the pyramid lies the Hospital Kuala Lumpur, which is the national tertiary reference centre that provides specialist and super specialist services for the nation. In terms of the physical healthcare facility setup, the healthcare premises are normally developed within the area where the most population is living. Since 1998, 95 percent of the population were living within a 5-kilometre radius of the nearest healthcare facility. This setup enables patients from anywhere in the country to be referred to the appropriate hospital, to access and visit several healthcare facilities through a nationwide network of clinics, hospitals and other health programs in a convenient manner.

Background of Outpatient Clinics

The outpatient clinics department administratively reports to the Family Health Division of Public Health Services of MOHM. Healthcare services are provided through various health centers and community polyclinics strategically located in the most populated areas in the district. The health centers and community polyclinics comprise the first level of service made available to the community. The services provided are comprehensive at this level, essentially comprising maternal health, child health, acute care of diseases, chronic care of diseases, mental health, geriatric care, community-based rehabilitation, well person services and health promotion.

These services are provided as outpatient treatments. In order to support such services, there are laboratory services and also radiological services. The pharmaceutical services are also provided in-house. With these comprehensive services and workflows, it was a significant reason that the outpatient clinic department was selected as a case exercise organization for advancing knowledge on the case under study. The selected organization will cover most of the processes of consultation and medical diagnosis workflow in the outpatient clinic. The healthcare setting provides relevant evidences and extensive information about patient demographic and clinical data that would contribute in developing the LHR components and structure.

Results

A. Findings from the Analysis of Patient Demographic and Clinical Data

The findings and evidences obtained from the primary data collection shows that seamless and continuous access to patient demographic and clinical data was critical and crucial. This fact was supported from the findings during the primary data collection, which include: approximately 52 percent and 35 percent of the doctors strongly agreed that they faced difficulties if they could not access a patient's medical history. Additional findings were that approximately 74 percent of the doctors strongly agreed that by sharing the health records with the patient, the quality of healthcare services will be improved.

The demographic data elements include Patient Name, Date of Birth, Gender, Race and Occupation. The clinical data elements include Patient's Problem/Diagnosis, Allergies, Chief Complaint, Symptoms, Test Conducted/Result, Medication Ordered and Onset Date of Diseases. These are the minimal clinical data elements required, from which a prompt and accurate treatment could be provided. Other data elements include Home Address, Telephone Number, Test Date, Type of Test and Test Result/Report. It was noted from the findings that doctors in outpatient clinics have limited time to consult patient problems from which the average consultation duration was normally finished in twenty minutes. This shows that the patient health records required by the doctors (for helping them to diagnose the patient problem) could be simplified (number of attributes and size in bytes) for facilitating the consultation process to be finished efficiently and effectively. It also facilitates the doctor to maintain the LHR continuously within the limited time allocated for each patient in the consultation room. Based upon evidence obtained from the primary data collection, the LHR could be simplified and it could be categorized into several components.

B. The Proposed LHR Data Sets

Based on inputs and evidences obtained from the case exercise, the LHR was divided into three components: (1) Patient Master Information, (2) Health Condition Summary and (3) Episode Summary.

Patient Master Information (PMI)

Patient Master Information comprises of administrative records and the required information to identify and distinguish the patient across healthcare facilities and levels. It is often used to locate patient identifier, including patient demographic and the related health administration information. The patient master information comprises the following set of information including demographic record, next of kin record, birth record, family health record, medical insurance record, employment record and organ donor record. It was noted from the findings of the primary data collection (the analysis of patient demographic information to be viewed by doctors during consultation) that the patient demographic information is highly required during consultation and medical diagnosis workflow. The demographic information is indicated as compulsory due to the fact that the demographic information is a key identifier for the patient. The administrative records (examples are next of kin record, birth record, family health record, medical insurance record, employment record and organ donor record) could be included in the patient information as optional records.

Health Condition Summary

The Health Condition Summary comprises of records that summarize the illness and wellness condition of the patient. Each condition has a status indicator to indicate whether the condition is active or inactive. This summary of a patient's condition will enhance the continuity of care by providing a method for communicating the most relevant information about a patient and providing support for the generation of LHR. It was noted from the primary data collection that the first step of patient care or treatment was that the doctor will gather information about the patient's current health status. Here, many types of information were collected about the patient and placed in the patient's health record. By giving the latest health condition summary of the patient at the beginning of a first doctor–patient encounter, the accuracy, quality, safety and continuity of care would be given. The health condition summary component could be added and enhanced in future and the set of information given below are the initial information revealed from the primary data collection and system analysis. The health condition summary comprises such information as chronic disease record, allergy record, immunization/ vaccination record, social history record, surgical medical procedure record, disability record and obstetric record.

Episode Summary

The Episode Summary is comprised of data for a particular episode or visit. If required, it provides the necessary data for reference to the source of the information where details of the episodes are stored. It comprises the following information: episode record, encounter record, symptoms record, diagnosis record, lab test record, radiology record, medication record, vital sign record and health plan record. The LHR components defined above provide the conceptual structure of LHR information and it is envisaged that the many LHRs could be collected and generated continuously from telehealth applications and various health information systems.

Knowledge Management Implications and Practice

Platform for Research and Development

The integrated telehealth system, via its role as the premier database repository for patient's LHR in the country, will function as the health knowledge platform from which a variety of research and development activities within the healthcare domain can be launched. These research and development initiatives will spearhead the development and establishment of initiatives that will produce innovative healthcare products and services of national and international significance.

Health Group Data Services

The standard data sets of the LHR would ensure that everyone's lifetime health record could be mined from various applications transcending geographical and service level constraints. The LHR repository would be a premier health database repository in the country and it will be an important source for health knowledge data mining purposes.

Health Knowledge Communication Protocol

The benefits of standard LHR data sets are numerous. The interaction various applications within healthcare facility and between healthcare facilities will be facilitated through a standard LHR document as a means for communication protocol. The LHR data sets ensure the many applications could be integrated and increase the interoperability of the telehealth system for integrating with other health information systems.

Personalized Lifetime Health Plan

The LHR data sets enable the many LHRs of individuals to be mined continuously. The LHR repository contains the medical records of a person for his/her lifetime chronologically. Through proper KM applications with standardized practices, personalized health plans could be created or suggested that are tailored to the specific needs of the individual and formulated based on the person's complete and integrated LHR. The health plans and health records created by the patients and healthcare professionals would generate personalized lifetime health plan for individuals and become critical health knowledge for quality healthcare.

Future Work

The next step of the research would be to finalize the LHR structure and LHR messages in detail and actualize it in Malaysia's telehealth framework into a working prototype system and pilot the system in certain healthcare centers.

BUSINESS INTELLIGENCE AND ANALYTICS

Business intelligence (BI) has now become synonymous with an umbrella description for a wide range of decision-support tools, some of which target specific user audiences (Wickramasinghe, 2006; Wickramasinghe and Schaffer, 2006). At the bottom of the BI hierarchy are extraction and formatting tools, which are also known as data-extraction tools. These tools collect data from existing databases for inclusion in data warehouses and data marts. Thus the next level of the BI hierarchy is known as warehouses and marts.

Because the data come from so many different, often incompatible systems in various file formats, the next step in the BI hierarchy is formatting tools; these tools and techniques are used to "cleanse" the data and convert it into formats that can easily be understood in the data warehouse or data mart. Next, tools are needed to support the reporting and analytical techniques. These are known as enterprise reporting and analytical tools. OLAP (on-line analytic process) engines and analytical application-development tools are for professionals who analyze data, for example by forecasting, modeling and trend analysis. Human intelligence tools form the next level in the hierarchy and involve human expertise, opinions and observations to be recorded to create a knowledge repository.

These tools are at the very top of the BI hierarchy and serve to amalgamate analytical and BI capabilities along with human expertise. Business analytics (BA) is a newer term that tends to be viewed as a sub-set of the broader business intelligence umbrella and concentrates on the analytic aspects within BI by focusing on the simultaneous analysis of patterns and trends in a given context (Wickramasinghe and Schaffer, 2006).

COMMUNITIES OF PRACTICE

The term "Communities of Practice" (CoP) is largely attributed to the work of Wenger (1998). The term refers to a network of people, working on the same or similar areas, coming together (either physically or virtually) to share and develop their collective knowledge. The intention is that this would benefit them as individuals as well as the organization.

By way of example, a CoP might be working in the area of healthcare modeling, and, more specifically, might be attempting to provide decision support tools in order to make better use of resources. Aspects of CoPs include communal support, social learning and shared culture. As with all organizational culture, it can be learnt by new entrants. In relatively recent times, CoPs have been considered in the context of KM, and they relate to developing social capital and sharing tacit knowledge. While a lot of KM initiatives are intra-organizational, CoPs may be intra-organizational, inter-organizational, or a mix of both. They may even be trans-national.

The notion of CoPs incorporates learning as a major focal issue, and this relates strongly to organizational learning and learning organizations (discussed later in this book). Learning is generally a social activity and therefore participation and its nature within social communities is of importance in CoPs. Engagement in CoPs may be viewed as a way in which the individual helps establish his or her own identity and this identity relates to processes of change. Change management, therefore, is an interesting link, but change management is normally considered as a concept that is used within an organization. Without an organizational structure and without effective line management, lots of complex questions arise, such as who decides what changes should be made, how should they be made, what are their benefits and cost, how are these measured, who decides and negotiates meaning, and who manages all of this?

CoPs may be within a subject discipline, or they may be within an application area that involves people from a variety of subject disciplines. The latter may enable more holistic approaches to be taken to viewing areas of interest, and it also adds to the richness of perspective, while offering theoretical triangulation. This is about looking at something from different theoretical perspectives. If there is convergence of views, it provides stronger credibility than would be gained from a single theoretical view, as the latter might have a particular bias. The learning aspect of CoPs is inherent within the concept of organizational learning. It is about how flexible an organization may be and how easily it can adapt to new situations that reflect changes in the internal and external environments.

Within the business world, CoPs are now considered to be much more than merely sharing day-to-day practices within the community. Wenger explains practice as *meaning*—an experience that is of interest located in a process referred to as the *negotiation of meaning*. This negotiation requires active *participation*, defined as:

> . . . the social experience of living in the world in terms of membership in social communities and active involvement in social enterprises . . . it can involve all kinds of relations, conflictual as well as harmonious, intimate as well as political, competitive as well as co-operative.

(Wenger, 1998: 55–56)

Figure 3.2 KARMAH "Starwheel".

Source: www.coventry.ac.uk/karmah/—reproduced with permission

Table 3.2 *The KARMAH Research Group's Spread of Competencies*

OB	Organizational Behavior including change management, strategy, ICTs, clinical governance, etc.	
CI	Clinical Informatics and Engineering including AI, cybernetics, expert systems, etc.	
ET	Education and Training including HRM, work study, industry-academic interfaces, etc.	
PS	Privacy and Security including technical, legal, ethical and organizational aspects, etc.	
DM	Data Mining including algorithms, knowledge discovery, genomic mining, etc.	

A schematic may help to explain the concepts. Figure 3.2 depicts the "KARMAH Starwheel", a representation of a CoP created and facilitated by the Knowledge Management for Healthcare (KARMAH) research group at Coventry University, U.K. Essentially, as the group's interests match those of KM within the healthcare environ, the span of knowledge is widespread, depicted by five distinct avenues (expanded in Table 3.2).

At the time of writing, participation in KARMAH's CoP is by invitation only. Having recognized that the nature of Healthcare KM is such that a blend of key skills is required to achieve true progress in this rapidly evolving area, the "Starwheel" depicts the group's strategy for efficient sharing and debate of current knowledge in the field. The schematic shows how participants, with expertise and competencies in the given areas (e.g. OB, CI, etc.) can bring key ideas to a central repository (the centre of the star), from which other members can draw/amend/add before returning back to the centre for final refinement. At the same time, members are free to interact by moving directly across the wheel. In this manner, it is envisaged that this will lead to an increased and rapid level of publication and/or collaborative projects for all active participants. This is a useful example of a multidisciplinary CoP.

STORYTELLING AND THE POWER OF NARRATIVE

The Girl and the Frog

A five year old girl was playing in the garden early one evening while her parents and her parents' friends chatted and sipped Martinis on the deck. After a few minutes, the girl walked to her parents, with her hands gently clasped, and showed them her new friend: a frog. "I'm going to call him Freddy—Freddy the Frog" she said.

The parents duly complimented her and Freddy. Perhaps startled by all of the attention, Freddy leapt out of the girl's hands and jumped into a hole. The girl screamed for the grown-ups to rescue Freddy. Their adult responsibility perhaps fuelled by their drinks, the grown-ups attempted to retrieve the frog. They tried to reach him with their hands and arms but Freddy was out of reach.

They then thought of placing a long stick in the hole, perhaps in the vain hope that Freddy, grateful for the support, would clutch the stick and be rescued. Sadly, the slightly drunk adults only succeeded in occasionally poking the frog with the stick. "You're hurting him!" cried the girl. "Stop it!"

After a few minutes, despite the girl's protests, the adults gave up. After attempting to comfort the crying girl, they returned to the deck and their conversation. Five minutes later, the girl joined them on the deck, her hands again gently clasped around Freddy. "How did you get him out?" the puzzled adults asked.

The girl smiled. "Oh, I just filled the hole with water".

HAVE YOU HEARD THE ONE ABOUT ... ?

The power and efficacy of narrative in the workplace has been well documented (Polkinghorne, 1988; Clandinin and Connelly, 2000). The use of effective narrative attempts to understand behavior by way of collections of anecdotal material. Narrative can be defined as a method that uses a variety of different data-based sources (for example, journals, notes, letters, transcribed conversations and discussions, interviews, photographs, etc.). The experience behind these items is of importance. It can be argued that narrative is closely related to qualitative research; they both share the trait of human knowledge.

Effective narrative should be finite and possess a longitudinal time sequence (i.e. it should have a beginning, a middle and an end). As Greenhalgh and Hurwitz (1999, p. 48) say, narrative:

. . . should also presuppose both a narrator and a listener whose different viewpoints affect how the story is told. Thirdly, the narrative is concerned with individuals; rather than simply reporting what they do or what is done to them it concerns how those individuals feel and how people feel about them.

There is much academic debate over the exact distinction between the terms "narrative" and story. It is beyond the remit of this book to become embroiled in such a complex argument. We would, however, agree with Denning's (2008) perspective (Table 3.3).

Storytelling can be a very useful and powerful communication tool, offering several advantages over more conventional mechanisms. These include Weaver (2005) who says that:

Stories communicate ideas holistically, conveying a rich yet clear message, and so they are an excellent way of communicating complicated ideas and concepts in an easy-to-understand

Table 3.3 Difference Between Story and Narrative

Story	the telling of a happening or connected series of happenings, whether true or fictitious; account; narration.
Narrative	the broadest sense is: anything told or recounted; more narrowly, something told or recounted in the form of a story; account; tale.

form. Stories therefore allow people to convey tacit knowledge that might otherwise be difficult to articulate; in addition, because stories are told with feeling, they can allow people to communicate more than they realize they know.

Storytelling provides the context in which knowledge arises as well as the knowledge itself, and hence can increase the likelihood of accurate and meaningful knowledge transfer.

Stories are an excellent vehicle for learning, as true learning requires interest, which abstract principles and impersonal procedures rarely provide.

Stories are memorable—their messages tend to "stick" and they get passed on.

Stories can provide a "living, breathing" example of how to do something and why it works rather than telling people what to do, hence people are more open to their lessons.

Stories therefore often lead to direct action—they can help to close the "knowing–doing gap" (the difference between knowing how to do something and actually doing it).

Storytelling can help to make organizational communication more "human"—not only do they use natural day-to-day language, but they also elicit an emotional response as well as thoughts and actions.

Stories can nurture a sense of community and help to build relationships.

People enjoy sharing stories—stories enliven and entertain.

The more interesting and powerful the tale, the more one is likely to remember it. Whether or not this makes it more useful in the workplace is a different matter. By way of example, the following is an example of a powerful hospital-based tale.

The Patient's Eye

A man ran into the Accident and Emergency department of his local hospital. In obvious pain, he clutched his right eye which was swollen to almost three times its normal size. Tears streaming down his eyes, he managed to convince the reception nurse of his urgent need. He told the doctor that his contact lens had somehow "fused" to his eyeball. "I was taking out my contacts and one is stuck on my eyeball! Help me, please!"

The doctor was horrified but, after careful examination of the eye, could find nothing obviously wrong (apart from the immense swelling). The patient howled in pain, all the while attempting to itch and scratch his eye. "My eye!" he cried. "For God's sake, fix my eye!"

The doctor called two of his senior colleagues who rushed the now hysterical patient to a lab. After administering a pain-killing injection (which helped somewhat to calm the patient down), all manner of additional lighting and laser-based medical equipment was wheeled in to analyze the patient's eye. After several minutes, the doctors had drawn a blank. They scratched their heads and looked at each other.

One doctor suddenly had a thought. "Actually . . . are you absolutely sure you hadn't already removed the lens?"

The full impact of this option dawned on everyone in the lab. What the patient had in fact tried to do was to "peel" away part of his cornea.

We fully acknowledge that this story is particularly graphic. However, once we look past this, what—if anything—have we actually learnt? To be careful? To be sure? What organizational implications are there? If we adapt the story though so that the doctor who, at the end of the story, had the idea now appears as a junior doctor, or perhaps an attending nurse or auxiliary, the story suddenly has implications for practice within the hospital. The ability to examine all options, no matter where they come from, becomes very important. The experienced doctors examined the patient using all manner of expensive medical equipment and were unable to come to a diagnosis. The answer came from an unexpected source. There are potential lessons here, including the ability to consider all possible options. The simplest may be correct.

Operating Theatre

A group of business analysts were asked to evaluate the routines of an operating theatre unit in a Northern European hospital. The gathered data was input into a simulation software package, the objective of which was to identify any possible process bottlenecks. In this way, the analysts would discover whether any of the clinical and healthcare processes could be made more efficient. After running the simulation, the following was discovered:

- The average time spent per operation was twenty-two minutes in this specific operating unit.
- The average amount of operations conducted per unit between 0700 hrs and 1500 hrs was 1.6 operations.
- Out of thirty operating rooms, ten were vacant all the time (yet the staff demanded additional operating rooms).
- The average time between anesthesia and the beginning of the operation was approximately seventeen minutes; in some rare cases, this increased to 100 minutes (without any statistical explanation).
- Most operations took place between 0900 hrs and 1430 hrs.
- Most units did not commence a new operation after 1430 hrs because the nursing staff were scheduled to finish their shifts at 1500 hrs.

Additionally the analysts found that, on Tuesdays, all activities tended to start one hour later. Upon interview, staff revealed that weekly meetings took place on Tuesday mornings. The analysts suggested that this weekly meeting be moved to Monday afternoons (since hardly any operations took place then). This was strongly rejected—based on the fact that the routines of this department has always been the same. "We can't move the meeting— everyone's used to Tuesdays now," said one Doctor.

The power of storytelling (and a good narrative) boils down to accessibility. No technical knowledge per se is required. Any organizational member can understand a good tale. As understanding of the "meaning behind the tale" is grasped, this may lead to members sharing their own anecdotes and experiences. In this way, members can learn from each other.

SOCIAL NETWORKS (AND SOCIAL NETWORKING SITES)

In its simplest form, a social network is a structure comprised of several nodes (entities that could be companies, institutions or people), which are interconnected according to varying dependencies and interdependencies (Figure 3.3). These could include common interest, value, linkages and so forth. Given the myriad of different possibilities, the resulting visualization can be very complex (see Figure 3.3). Social Network Analysis (SNA) examines these relationships as linkages (ties) between nodes (the actors within the network). The social networks (and contacts) combine to form *social capital*, considered to be of vital importance for communities and individuals (Putnam *et al.*, 2000).

The fact that relationships matter is a key concept within social capital theory (Field, 2003). As interactions allow people to create communities and a sense of belonging, the rich experience of a trustworthy social network can produce great advantages to the individuals within the social network. The "trustworthiness" of the network is essential as trust between individuals (known persons within the network) has broader implications for people outside the network (strangers) with whom interactions (face-to-face) would eventually take place (Beem, 1999). Without this essential interaction, trust breaks down causing major social problems.

SOCIAL NETWORKING (INTERNET-BASED)

The proliferation of web-based social networking includes recent phenomena such as wikis, blogging, chat, instant messaging, file sharing, file exchange, video and contact management. The "social" aspect (the ability for individual users within the trustworthy environment to "tag" important documents and items—thus saving valuable time for other interested users) has key advantages for contemporary organizations. When this is combined with opinion and fact-finding from individuals, these comment-based contributions can combine to provide the basis for a useful CoP.

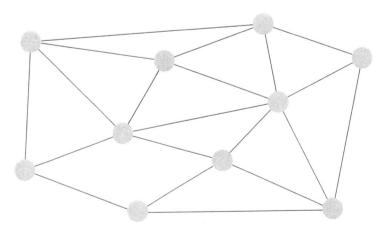

Figure 3.3 *Simple Social Network.*

INTELLECTUAL CAPITAL

Intellectual capital is essentially knowledge that can be exploited for financial purposes. It combines knowledge present in the minds of individuals with the more traditional (and economic) aspect of capital. The knowledge can be both tacit and explicit. Due to the inherent nature and importance of *trust*, explained earlier in this chapter, it is implicit that intellectual capital also contains social capital.

KNOWLEDGE ASSETS

Knowledge assets refer to knowledge of products, services, processes, technologies, competitors and so forth that organizations require to gain and to maintain competitive edge and adapt to changing circumstances. The inherent issue remains the fact that such knowledge is always nearly "intangible," thus making it difficult to codify. Knowledge resides in the minds of individuals and the teams in which they function and therefore both teams and individuals have value for an organization that may be measured.

KNOWLEDGE NUGGETS

A knowledge nugget is a small item or piece of useful knowledge in categories of interest to the user. Sometimes the nugget can consist of relevant files, hyperlinks or dialogue boxes. In the contemporary web-enabled environment, nuggets can include external links to wikis, podcasts and videocasts.

CONCLUSIONS

There are key tools and techniques closely related to contemporary KM (in addition to those which evolve), several of which have been outlined in this chapter. Some of these techniques utilize IT but all rely on an effective human component to both enliven and enable them.

SUMMARY

Key KM-related tools and techniques have been outlined. These include taxonomies and ontologies (the Dewey Decimal System being a prime example), data mining, business intelligence and analytics, CoPs, the usefulness of storytelling and the power of narrative, social networks (with the growth of social networking sites being of contemporary relevance), intellectual capital, knowledge assets and knowledge nuggets.

REVIEW QUESTIONS

1   What are contemporary KM-related tools and techniques?

2   What is data mining?

3   What is storytelling?

4   What is social networking?

DISCUSSION QUESTIONS

1   How may data mining be used to create useful knowledge?

2   Why can CoPs be so useful?

3   Can data mining be carried out without human involvement?

4   How may storytelling and narrative be used to collect and analyze *tacit* knowledge?

CASE EXERCISE: INCREASING BREAST CANCER SCREENING ATTENDANCE IN THE U.K.[6]

Introduction

Breast cancer is the most common cancer in women with over 40,000 women being diagnosed with the disease each year in the U.K. (Cancer Research U.K., 2005). Any information related to the breast can largely affect a women's consciousness and a threat of breast cancer will have varying impacts on female psychology. Typically breast cancerous cells originate in the mammary glands (lobules) or in the ducts connected to these glands or in other tissues around these glands (American Cancer Society, 2005). When in close proximity to the lymphatic system, these cells can result in being carried to other organs of the body. This subsequently results in cancerous growth in that organ and is described as metastatic breast cancer (American Cancer Society, 2005). Although many causes had been identified for breast cancer, the knowledge of finding a cure is still not within the reach of modern medicine.

Breast Cancer

Breast cancer should ideally be diagnosed at the earlier stages of its development. Possible treatments include removing or destroying the cancer cells to avoid the spread of the affected cells. Breast self-examination (BSE) is an effective and non-intrusive type of self-diagnosis exercise for checking any abnormalities/lumps in the breast tissue. Unfortunately this greatly depends on the size of the lump, technique and experience in carrying out a self-examination by the woman. An ultrasound test using sound waves can be used to detect lumps but this is usually suited for women aged below thirty-five owing to the higher density of breast tissue (American Cancer Society, 2005).

Having a tissue biopsy via a fine needle aspiration or an excision is often used to test the cells for cancer. These tests are mostly employed in treatments or post-treatment examination and as second rung diagnostic confirmation methods. Performing a Computed Tomography (CT) or a Magnetic Resonance Imaging (MRI) scan would result in a thorough examination of the breast tissue but this technique is not favored due to reasons including that it may not be economical, needs preparation, noisy, time consuming and images may not be clear (Marcela, 2004).

Breast Screening Programme

Mammography is a technique for detecting breast tissue lumps using a low dosage of X-ray. This technique can even detect a three millimeter sized lump. The X-ray image of the breast tissue is captured and the image is thoroughly read by experienced radiologists and specialist mammogram readers. Preliminary research suggests that women aged fifty-five and above are more susceptible to breast cancer; mammography is more suited to the women aged fifty-five and above (due to the lower density of breast tissue) (Blanks et al., 2000).

Even though mammography has its critics—mainly due to its high rate of false positives and false negatives (Burton, 1997)—it has still become the standard procedure for screening women by the NHS National Breast Screening Programme U.K. (Forrest, 1986). Mammography is the best and most viable tool for mass screening to detect cancer in the breast at an early stage (Medicine net, 2002); however, the effectiveness of diagnosis through screening is directly dependent on the percentage of women attending the screening program.

The NHS Breast Screening Programme, catering to the entire eligible female population is funded by the Department of Health in the U.K. and is the first of its kind in the world. It covers nearly 4 million women and detected more than 13,000 cancers in the screened population for the year 2005 (NHS Review, 2006). Currently the screening programme routinely screens women between

Table A Extrapolation of Cancer Not Detected Due to Non-attendance

Screening Year	Number of Women Invited	Acceptance Rate	Number of Cancers Detected	Probable Number of Cancers Not Detected
1996–97	1,558,995	75.1	7,141	1,776
1997–98	1,668,476	75.5	7,932	2,635
1998–99	1,669,727	75.5	8,771	2,580
1999–00	1,811,541	75.4	9,525	3,110
2000–01	1,815,610	75	9,866	3,286
2001–02	1,752,526	75.5	10,003	3,237
2002–03	1,873,470	74.7	10,467	3,539
2003–04	1,998,989	75.2	13,064	4,284

the ages of fifty and seventy, and employs two views of the breast, medio-lateral and cranio-caudal. Breast cancer is still one of the major cancer killers in women.

The lack of breakthroughs in finding a definitive cure means that preventive medicine is the only viable alternative to reduce deaths due to breast cancer. The U.K. NHS National Breast Screening Programme (NBSP) is unique as it provides free breast screening for the female population aged between fifty and seventy at a national level (Forrest 1986; Cancer Research U.K. 2004). The recent increase of the upper age limit from sixty-three to seventy for screening and making a two-view mammogram mandatory has greatly increased the efficiency of benign or malignant tumor detection.

The NBSP currently runs a massive screening programme catering to almost 2 million eligible women across the U.K. (Cancer Research U.K., 2004). This programme runs on a call/recall cycle that screens all eligible women in a three-year interval. The information published by the U.K. Government Statistical Service (NHS Health and Social Care Information Centre) in its Community Health Statistics report for the year 2006 agrees that, for the past ten years since 1995, the uptake has remained constant at around 75 percent.

Knowledge Management

The healthcare domain not only provides challenging opportunities for managing knowledge but it is also one of the areas where it is often most poorly understood and deployed. This predicament is slowly being addressed as more and more KM-focused projects are initiated and professionals with better understanding of KM are being involved. This work has strong orientation towards KM tools and technologies. The knowledge created by prediction and screening outcome is the focus of this research. This research leverages the knowledge created and shares it with the healthcare deliverers to alleviate the predicament faced by the limited uptake rate. This project also sheds more light on the efficacy of tools and technologies that can be utilized in knowledge creation and its management through AI and EDI messaging respectively.

Research Objective

The question is whether the screening programme is working efficiently. The efficiency can be mapped to the screening attendance. The number of non-attendees has been significantly increasing and has reached half a million. Simple projection of this data, through translation (Table A), submits that nearly 4,000 cancer incidences would not have been diagnosed. Even if a small percentage of these non-attendees could be made to attend, it would result in the saving of significant lives. Indirectly we can also infer that, despite focused efforts on these non-attendees for the past ten years, there was no real effect on their attendance. Moreover, early stage cancer detection would have a huge impact in reducing cancer related deaths. From these facts and data, we see that the primary concern is to reduce non-attendance (Bankhead et al., 2001).

Solution Proposed

The challenges already discussed can only be addressed by a resource-saving strategy that has better healthcare at its core. The first component in the proposed strategy is related to knowledge via Artificial Intelligence (AI), employing Neural Network (NN) algorithms. This strategy also includes a Service Oriented Architecture (SOA) to deliver the envisaged knowledge as the second component. This research proposes to unify the existing National Breast Screening Computer System (NBSS) software onto a single platform and create prototype software component based on Open Source technologies. The proposed prototype software would be automated to produce the pre-processed data and eventually normalize the data for AI (neural network) assimilation. These activities would be performed sequentially without human involvement for repeatability, reliability and accuracy. The Java Based Attendance prediction by Artificial Intelligence for Breast Screening (JAABS) model itself would be simulated on the Open Source technology platform. This model incorporates all additional transformations occurring within the screening process (including the change in the screening upper age limit).

The prototype framework proposed will incorporate the AI model for creating a list of predicted non-attending women. The prototype combines the demographic data pertaining to the non-attending women and information related to her General Practitioner (GP) as a messaging package. This package triggers the generation of an electronic message based on the Health Level 7 (HL7) version 3 standards and utilizes Service Oriented Architecture (SOA) as the message delivering technology.

Questionnaire Based Survey

The recent advances in IT prompted us to collect additional data to determine the best possible use of the knowledge, in particular data about the preferred mode of information delivery to GPs, their opinion on the interventions and their perceived need for additional resources/assistance. The survey was conducted in the summer of 2006 through a mailed four page questionnaire that enquired about GPs belief on the screening prediction, mode of knowledge delivery, intentions with the proposed sharing and any additional resources required to intervene. The survey design and analysis was approved by the NHS Local Research Ethics Committee (LREC).

The response to the questionnaire has suggested the following. If such kind of interventions (based on prediction or post-screening results) are to be made effective, some form of compensation to cover economical overheads in surgeries is essential, otherwise these initiatives are destined to fail. The responses did not provide a clear picture on the preference of opportunistic intervention over the traditional telephone- or letter-based interventions. More focused studies in this area can shed light on these aspects. Earlier studies on computer generated reminders for GP interventions had suggested an increase in screening uptake. Hence an electronic version of knowledge and subsequent flag reminders is highly favored by the GPs. All the above inferences are very encouraging and provide the required evidence that GP interventions are effective and can improve screening attendance; further, it reveals that computer initiated interventions would be economical and effective.

Project Outcomes

- An evaluation report on the suitability of the HL7 Version 3.0-based XML standards was completed to highlight its appropriateness to the proposed BSP Messaging (BSPM) protocol.
- The report included a comparison of the proposed HL7 Version 3.0 with EDIFACT based protocol for highlighting salient features.
- A framework was designed for implementing the JAABS algorithm.

■ A prototype was implemented to predict non-attendance by the JAABS algorithm.

■ The prototype was evaluated and tested with real-time dataset.

■ An architecture for the proposed prototype for knowledge exchange was proposed.

■ A questionnaire-based evaluation of the GPs' role in reducing the BSP non-attendance was designed, conducted, analyzed and reported.

■ Technical reports.

Conclusion

The objective of this work was to identify the challenges that are being faced by the U.K. NHS' national breast screening programme and find approaches to alleviate these impediments and eventually reduce mortality due to breast cancer. Based on JAABS algorithm's negative prediction value (for the first to sixth episode) the number of non-attendees correctly predicted *a priori* to screening date would be at least forty-two women for every 100 screening non–attendees. When such knowledge is shared with the GPs (with whom the women are registered), they can initiate interventions. Such interventions can educate the non-attending women and clarify their attitudes and beliefs. The expected outcome is that the woman commits to a positive informed decision, which would culminate in attending the screening appointment.

This work not only confirms that breast screening attendance can be predicted through an automated software solution, but also can be leveraged to increase screening attendance by employing emerging KM tools and techniques. This research work draws its strength from such KM tools and techniques. This work is also one such initiative addressing the NHS' breast screening attendance through efficient KM methodologies. A 25 percent success in GP interventions will result in saving more than 350 women's lives per year. Even if one woman's life can be saved by our approach, this approach can be deemed as a success. The new bespoke software prototype, incorporating JAABS algorithm, can be easily converted and integrated into the NBSS software.

The current work has already designed HL7 v3.0 messages for delivering the knowledge package as part of the new protocol (BSAMP). This message design has been developed on the same modus operandi followed by NHS CFH for easy integration. The National Care Records Services (NCRS) are already being field tested at cluster level and once the national network is established would form the backbone of all NHS' future clinical messaging across the country, including the proposed protocol (BSAMP).

Case Exercise References

American Cancer Society Inc. (2005) Cancer Reference Information. Available online at www.cancer.org/docroot/CRI/content/CRI_2_4_1X_What_is_ breast _cancer_5.asp (accessed August 10, 2005).

Bankhead, C., Austoker, J., Sharp, D., Peters, T., *et al.* (2001) A Practice Based Randomized Controlled Trial of Two Simple Interventions Aimed to Increase Uptake of Breast Cancer Screening, *Journal of Medical Screening*, 8(2): 91–98.

Blanks, R.G., Moss, S.M., McGahan, C.E., Quinn, M.J., and Babb, P.J. (2000) Effect of NHS Breast Screening Programme on Mortality from Breast Cancer in England and Wales, 1990–8: Comparison of Observed with Predicted Mortality, *British Medical Journal*, 321(7262): 665–669.

Burton, G. (1997) *Alternative Medicine*. Washington, DC: Future Medicine Publishing.

Cancer Research U.K. (2004) *Breast Cancer Factsheet*. Available online at http://publications.cancerresearchuk. org/epages/crukstore.sf/en_GB/?ObjectPath=/Shops/crukstore/Categories/BrowseBySubject/BreastCancer (accessed September 18, 2004).

Cancer Research U.K. (2005) *CancerStats Incidence-U.K.* Available online at www.cancerresearchuk.org/about cancer/statistics/statsmisc/pdfs/cancerstats_incidence_apr05.pdf (accessed August 10, 2005).

Forrest, P. (1986) *Breast Cancer Screening—A Report to the Health Ministers of England, Scotland, Wales and Northern Ireland*. London: HMSO.

Medicine net (2002) *Breast Cancer*. Available online at www.medicinenet.com/breast_cancer/page3.htm (accessed August 10, 2005).

NHS Information Standards Board (2006) *Information Standards Board for Health and Social Care*. Available online at www.isb.nhs.uk (accessed May 16, 2007).

NHS Review (2006) *The Breast Screening Programme Annual Review 2005*. Available online at www.cancer screening.nhs.uk/breastscreen//publications/ 2005review.html (accessed July 14, 2007).

Case Exercise Questions

1 What is the role for KM in this context?

2 Outline how both tacit knowledge and explicit knowledge would increase the efficacy of the breast screening program.

3 In order to develop an appropriate KM solution, it is necessary to consider people, process and technology issues. Outline how the key considerations of people, process and technology are relevant to the current work.

4 How can the knowledge created through artificial intelligence be mapped to KM and its core components? Justify your explanation with appropriate examples.

5 What strategies would you recommend to foster a KM culture in healthcare (similar to the breast screening case exercise)?

FURTHER READING

Wenger, E. (1998) *Communities of Practice: Learning, Meaning, and Identity*. Cambridge: Cambridge University Press.

Wickramasinghe, N. (2006) Knowledge Creation: A Meta-Framework, *International Journal of Innovation and Learning*, 3(5): 558–573.

REFERENCES

Adriaans, P. and Zantinge, D. (1996) *Data Mining*. Reading, MA: Addison-Wesley.

Becerra-Fernandez, I. and Sabherwal, R. (2001) Organizational Knowledge Management: A Contingency Perspective, *Journal of Management Information Systems*, 18(1) Summer: 23–55.

Beem, C. (1999) *The Necessity of Politics. Reclaiming American Public Life.* Chicago, IL: University of Chicago Press.

Bendoly, E. (2003) Theory and Support for Process Frameworks of Knowledge Discovery and Data Mining from ERP Systems, *Information & Management,* 40: 639–647.

Cabena, P., Hadjinian, P., Stadler, R., Verhees, J., and Zanasi, A. (1998), *Discovering Data Mining from Concept to Implementation.* Upper Saddle River, NJ: Prentice-Hall.

Choi, B. and Lee, H. (2003) An Empirical Investigation of KM Styles and Their Effect on Corporate Performance, *Information & Management,* 40: 403–417.

Chung, M. and Gray, P. (1996) Special Section: Data Mining, *Journal of Management Information Systems,* 16(1), Summer 1999: 11–16.

Clandinin, D.J. and Connelly, F.M. (2000) *Narrative Inquiry: Experience and Story in Qualitative Research,* San Francisco, CA: Jossey-Bass Publishers.

Fayyad, U., Piatetsky-Shapiro, G., and Smyth, P. (1996) From Data Mining to Knowledge Discovery: An Overview, in U. Fayyad, G. Piatetsky-Shapiro, and P. Smyth (Eds), *Advances in Knowledge Discovery and Data Mining,* Menlo Park, CA: AAAI Press/MIT Press, pp. 1–36.

Greenhalgh, T. and Hurwitz, B. (1999) Narrative Based Medicine: Why Study Narrative?, *British Medical Journal,* 318: 48–50.

Holsapple, C. and Joshi, K. (2002) Knowledge Manipulation Activities: Results of a Delphi Study, *Information & Management,* 39: 477–519.

Polkinghorne, D. (1988) *Narrative Knowing and the Human Sciences.* Albany, NY: SUNY Press.

Putnam, R.D., Feldstein, L.M., and Cohen, D. (2000) *Bowling Alone: The Collapse and Revival of American Community.* New York: Simon & Schuster.

Weaver, C. (2005), *Storytelling.* Knowledge Management Specialist Library. Available online at www.library.nhs.uk/knowledgemanagement/ViewResource.aspx?resID=93580 (accessed May 29, 2008).

Wenger, E. (1998) *Communities of Practice: Learning, Meaning, and Identity.* Cambridge: Cambridge University Press.

Wickramasinghe, N. (2006) Knowledge Creation: A Meta-Framework, *International Journal of Innovation and Learning,* 3(5): 558–573.

Wickramasinghe, N. and Schaffer, J. (2006) Creating Knowledge Driven Healthcare Processes with the Intelligence Continuum, *International Journal of Electronic Healthcare,* 2(2): 164–74.

Chapter 4

Knowledge Management: A Systems View

INTRODUCTION

This chapter provides a background to systems thinking and develops arguments as to why and how systems thinking can relate strongly to KM. Successful KM requires the tools of operational research (OR) that assist managers to forecast, manage, monitor and plan; yet managers have often ignored the methodologies provided (Lehaney *et al.*, 1994). The reasons for this are manifold, and there has been a great deal of argument as to why, in practice, greater use is not made of modeling methodologies.

One view is that relatively "hard," prescriptive, goal seeking or optimizing methods have been perceived to fail. Problem structuring methodologies were developed within the concept of soft systems thinking, partly as an attempt to address this perceived failure by focusing on process issues. Later, critical systems thinking was developed as an approach that attempted to widen the issues and consider choice critically. These developments are related to systems thinking in general and they will be discussed in more detail later in this chapter.

Essential features of systems thinking include the legitimacy of holism as opposed to reductionism. Reductionism may be considered as the process of simplifying the complex to define a specific experiment and provide a minimum explanation and analysis of a problem, component by component. Within the concept of reductionism the whole is nothing more than the sum of its parts. Within the concept of systems thinking the whole is greater than the sum of its parts (emergent properties).

A simple example of this is a bicycle. This is made up of a number of different systems: the gear system, the braking system, the transmission system, etc. Each of these systems has an emergent property associated with its purpose. Depressing the brake lever will cause the brake blocks to close on the wheel rim and stop the wheel turning. None of these systems has the emergent property of the bicycle (the whole system), which is a machine that enables a human being to travel from A to B. The following discussion helps to place this introduction in the context of the debates that have arisen in the management science and systems arenas from World War Two until the present day.

GENERAL SYSTEMS AND HARD SYSTEMS THINKING

Bertalanffy (1968) is considered as the founding father of General Systems Theory, having started to write and publish in the 1940s and 1950s. The early systems works developed largely from biological roots, and though they attempted to discover cross-discipline concepts that would relate to systems of all types, writing of the time tended to be couched in terms of biological analogies. Many different writers have explored more directly management related systems concepts in many different ways.

General systems thinking is interdisciplinary and is intended to provide an approach to enable understanding and analysis of complex systems, whether in nature, society, science or technology. In the context of this discussion, the term "system" refers to emergent purposeful activity, the boundaries of that activity, associated entities, and all of the relationships that exist between them in undertaking the sub-system activities needed for that system to exist. The system as a whole cannot be understood simply by studying its constituent parts. Systems thinking may be thought of as being about the organization of parts and their dynamic relationships, that comprise a whole, rather than the study of static organizational parts. This is counter to the traditional approach of Taylorism, which is based on classical assumptions (Taylor, 1911).

Within systems thinking phenomena may be considered as relationship networks within a boundary. The boundary encompasses the system, but the system has external connections, to other systems, and thus is considered open rather than closed. Common patterns, properties and behaviors are key aspects of systems thinking. It is about looking at the whole rather than trying to solve each individual problem in isolation. Other key characteristics include emergence and hierarchy. Emergence has been mentioned previously and is the notion that a system will display at least one emergent property that none of its constituent parts can display individually. Hierarchy is the concept of systems within systems.

The Earth is a system within the Solar System, within the Milky Way, within the Universe. Within the Earth, the human being is a system. Within a human being are the respiratory, circulatory and other systems. Within these systems are the systems of molecules, and within these, systems of atoms. Hierarchy in a systems sense does not imply the ranking that is found in the political sense. It is simply an order of connectivity between systems. Bertalanffy (1968) was attempting to find a theory of general systems that would be able to address all systems in all scientific disciplines. He wished to use his observations from biology to describe attributes of systems in general. In particular, he argued that there are concepts and principles that may be applied generally to systems, regardless of their nature. He considered that there should be universal laws for general systems and not just theories that refer to specific types of systems. Bertalanffy (1968) identifies three major areas of systems thinking: philosophy, science and technology. Banathy (1966) considered four areas of enquiry that could be integrated. These are philosophy, theory, methodology and application, all integrating in a recursive relationship to make systems enquiry become knowledgeable action. Knowledgeable action is within the realm of KM.

From the concept of general systems came hard systems approaches. These assume that:

- well-defined problems exist that can be solved with a single optimal solution;
- a rigid scientific approach is the way to solve problems;

- everyone shares the same view of problems; and
- problems are technical in their nature.

Checkland (1981) suggests that systems thinking has the two complementary processes of systems analysis and systems synthesis. He argues that there are two paradigms related to these processes. The first views the world as systemic and it requires systematic study. The second views the world as problematic and it requires systemic study. In this case, problematic means "open to many different interpretations" (pluralistic). The first paradigm reflects hard systems thinking and the second reflects soft systems thinking.

Hard systems thinking works on the view that a problem can be solved by structuring a system to achieve the desired outcome. Typically such problems are quantifiable or technical. Systems analysis and systems engineering are forms of hard systems thinking. Structured Systems Analysis and Design Method (SSADM) is a particular hard systems approach that has been used for the design of information systems. This is a form of the more general Waterfall Model that views any development as flowing downwards through stages: requirements analysis, design, implementation, testing, integration and maintenance. Hard systems thinking requires rational analysis, and as a scientific mode of investigation has limitations when transferred to social environments such as organizations. Key aspects of the hard systems approach are:

- reductionism, which is the process of simplifying the complex to define a specific experiment and provide a minimum explanation and analysis of a problem, component by component;
- experimentation in a controlled environment; and
- repeatability.

A major problem with the hard systems approach is its inability to cope with the complexity of social or organizational problems. For example, a reductionist approach requires simplification of problems by separating them into manageable parts resulting in experimentation and analysis being conducted in isolation from variables and external forces that could result in a different outcome. Such an approach does not consider changeable circumstances, and further, speculation cannot be accepted until experimentation and repeatability is achieved. As such, quantitative measures can be recorded and repeated more easily than qualitative findings. Hard systems thinking is goal directed and requires clearly defined problems to achieve solutions, with a philosophy based on ontology.

Considering hard systems in relation to KM, it is apparent that the ideas of a controlled environment and isolationist approach are inappropriate in what is essentially a social process. The concept of reductionism could be beneficial in the initial exploration of a complex area that involves people, processes, technology and environment. It is of little use if such areas are explored in total isolation from each other as each impacts significantly upon the other. Equally, experimentation and repeatability are not achievable in organizational contexts, as there will be different outcomes according to various internal and external influences. Other things cannot be "held equal" (remain the same) in an organization while one thing is changed to find out its effect.

SOFT SYSTEMS THINKING

Soft systems thinking aims at understanding problem situations and agreeing what problems exist, with a view to resolving the problem situation. Resolution, as opposed to solution, is the nature of soft systems thinking, and its philosophy is based on epistemology. Soft systems thinking is a holistic approach that recognizes organizations as complex social systems, and this view counters the conventional reductionist models that focus on departments and individuals as being separate from the whole. It is interdependence between individuals and groups, and the processes in which they engage, that help create a system.

Jackson (1993) provides an excellent background to the issues that led to the development of soft systems thinking:

> It was in the second world war that approaches such as operational research came into their own. These were used to help the allied war effort and quite successful they were . . . They assumed that people would share values . . . there are difficulties when you seek to extend the range of application of these approaches . . . Often the situation will be pluralistic, there will be different value positions, or it will be conflictual.

The successes of operational research during World War Two were expected to be mirrored in both private and public sector post-war organizations:

> In its heyday of the 1960s and early 1970s this approach was widely seen as the rational way to take decisions.
>
> (Rosenhead, 1989)

> It is, then, proposed that the development of man-machine digital systems be conducted as an applied scientific enterprise, regulated in accordance with an evolving set of hypotheses that relate systems design to systems performance, and are experimentally tested in anticipation of, and in response to, changing conditions.
>
> (Sackman, 1967)

The hopes for operational research were dented as a result of the more flexible and open social structures that existed in Western countries after World War Two. While technical problems suited a technique-oriented approach, many post-war organizational difficulties had much more to do with social science than physics:

> Unfortunately "management science" has not been able to resolve these problems. Hence there is an incentive to examine alternative paradigms to those of natural science, while continuing to build on the scientific bedrock: rationality applied to the findings of experience.
>
> (Checkland, 1981)

> . . . the basic philosophy and methodology of the "hard" systems approaches makes them unsuitable to applications in social situations, for there exists much corroborating evidence of failure in such situations
>
> (Lewis, 1994: 27)

A much-quoted example of such hard systems failure is the RAND Corporation's experiences with the New York public health sector, using methods that had proved successful with the New York fire service (Greenberger *et al.*, 1976). A more recent example involved the failure of the London Ambulance Service Computer Aided Despatch system. The important thing to note from the findings is that it was not essentially a technical failure, but a failure with many causes, with a series of mistaken judgments. In particular, the report notes that senior managers lacked understanding as to how to manage this type of project, and there was failure to approach the development of the system in a totally open way (Prince User Group, 1993). In other words, a hard systems approach was mistakenly used to address a complex system involving human interaction.

Critics of OR in practice argue that failures have arisen because of OR's concentration on problems which have clearly defined, agreed objectives (e.g. Churchman, 1967; Ackoff, 1979). Partly, this perceived failure may arise through the difficulties associated with attempting to introduce change that is not in line with the organizational culture (Johnson *et al.*, 2007). Partly it may be linked to a lack of recognition of human factors, particularly in an IT environment (Boddy and Buchanan, 1992).

As a response to the issues that arose, a range of so-called "soft" methods have been developed over the last thirty years or so. Soft Systems Methodology (SSM) is regarded by some as a problem structuring exemplar (e.g. Rosenhead, 1989), and it is also one of the most widely-used and widely-known of the problem structuring methodologies (Mingers and Taylor, 1992). SSM was developed by Checkland (1981) and Wilson (1984), and was not based on any particular theory at that time. Checkland (1981) describes the complexity of social situations as compared to a scientific basis through three main features:

- Generalizations that might be made will be inaccurate in comparison to physical, quantitatively based controlled experiments.
- The researcher or investigator will always be an active participant in the situation being investigated resulting in personal perspectives, meanings and values. For example scientists' observations may include interpretations *for* others, the social scientist requires a sympathetic appreciation of the situation from the viewpoint of others.
- Making predictions about social situations is problematic, because although there might be particular outcomes intended, when these are observed and shared, through learning and increased knowledge with others the outcomes may change. In contrast, physical systems cannot react to predictions made about them.

From these observations and through action research, SSM developed as a learning process and is underpinned by four key principles, identified by Lehaney *et al.* (1999):

- holistic systems thinking based on the concepts of emergence and hierarchy, and communication and control;
- a learning rather than an optimizing approach to problem situations;
- relationship handling as opposed to goal achieving; and
- an action research paradigm.

Emergence, hierarchy, communication and control are core to systems thinking. Emergence relates to properties at a particular level, which cannot be reduced to lower levels for explanation, unlike the reductionist approach. Emergence *and* hierarchy together relate to emergent properties at particular layers in the structure of a system, which interact to make up the whole system. Communication and control relate to the overall direction and development of the system. All of this relates to the complete organization of a system, which is complex yet organized.

Checkland (1993: 280–281) uses Burrell and Morgan's (1979) framework (Figure 4.1), to draw out the social theory implicit in SSM stating that it would lie in the left-hand quadrants with hermeneutics and phenomenology toward regulation. The left-hand quadrants relate to the subjective, where social reality is perceived as having an existence that is a product of individual or shared consciousness. The subjective domain endeavors to seek knowledge by attempting to understand the views of others in creating social reality. At the extreme, people possess free will and the preferred method of gathering knowledge is by getting as close as possible to the subject under investigation.

Regulation is about understanding the status quo, with the perspective that society is basically consensual and change is generally incremental. Hermeneutics and phenomenology provide the philosophical base for interpretative studies. Interpretive sociology assumes that access to reality is only through social constructions such as language, consciousness and shared meanings. Interpretative studies generally attempt to understand phenomena through the meanings that people assign to them. Jackson (2000) points out that the combination of people and free will means that it is not normally possible to construct a model of such a system and

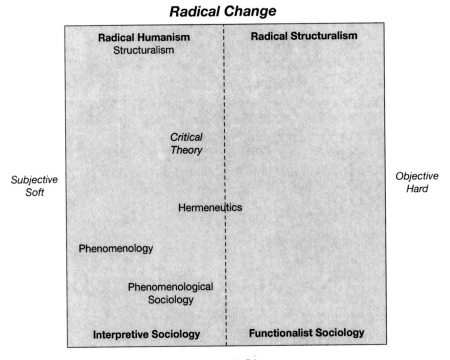

Figure 4.1 *A Grid of Social Theory.*

Source: Burrell and Morgan (1979) in Checkland (1993: 280)

the purpose is to understand the status quo better so that predictions and control can be better facilitated.

Hermeneutics is defined as knowledge gained by interpretation and became the established definition through Wilhelm Dilthey (1822–1911) who described it as historical, cultural and social facts that require interpretation and understanding. Considering this with KM, the knowledge cycle of gathering and interpreting information is influenced by the cultural and social present and past of an organization. It is contextualized by individuals or groups and enhances understanding and knowledge. Phenomenology has its origins in the work of Edmund Husserl (1859–1938) and is the attempt to describe experiences directly and independently of causal explanations. In this case, the relationship with the concept of KM may fall into the area of creativity and the notion of "thinking outside the box."

There have been many versions of SSM. Within the original version (Checkland, 1981) the unstructured problem situation is expressed, often by what is known as a "rich picture." This is used to search for relevant notional systems that are encapsulated as root definitions and conceptual models (4). Each conceptual model is compared with the "real world" in stage 5. The stage 5 comparison may undergo many iterations. Stage 4 originally included sub-sections 4a and 4b, which were formal and informal systems thinking inputs, but Checkland and Scholes (1990: 41–42) argue that with the development of CATWOE, 4a and 4b are not needed. (CATWOE—customer, actor, transformation, weltanschauung, owner, environment). Stage 6 is the assessment of changes that are both desirable and culturally feasible. Stage 7 is where action is taken to improve the situation (implementation). The cycle continues.

As an example of a root definition, consider the following definition of KM. Within this, the customer is not stated. The actors are the private or public concerns. The transformation (purpose) is to influence and achieve strategic aims. The weltanschauung (world view) is that using KM will do this better than not using KM. The owner is the public or private sector concern. The environmental constraints are financial, legal, resource, political, technical, cultural and societal:

> KM refers to the systematic organization, planning, scheduling, monitoring, and deployment of people, processes, technology, and environment, with appropriate targets and feedback mechanisms, under the control of a public or private sector concern, and undertaken by such a concern, to facilitate explicitly and specifically the creation, retention, sharing, identification, acquisition, utilization, and measurement of information and new ideas, in order more effectively to influence and achieve strategic aims, such as improved competitiveness or improved performance, subject to financial, legal, resource, political, technical, cultural, and societal constraints.
>
> (Lehaney et al., 2004)

The foregoing discussion considers SSM as a logical process. This logical process has a parallel cultural analysis: intervention or role analysis, social system analysis and political system analysis (Checkland and Scholes, 1990). Intervention (role) analysis considers the roles of client, would-be problem solver and problem owner. Social system analysis examines the problem situation as a culture, and the significance of social roles, norms and values, within that culture. Political system analysis considers how power is obtained and disposed, and how that power is utilized in relationships between different interest groups.

CASE EXERCISE: LOUISIANA MASS IMMUNIZATION EXERCISE (2007)[7]

Introduction

Currently there are a total of thirty-three vaccines that target human disease, which are produced by nine manufacturers (CDC, 2008). The majority of the vaccines are made by three companies: Sanofi-Pateur (Aventius), Merck and GlaxoSmithKline, with Sanofi-Pateur being the largest supplier. Sanofi-Pasteur's recent announcement of a new high-tech facility to produce vaccines against twenty diseases and the capability to switch to a sole pandemic influenza vaccine production environment indicates their commitment to continue to be the leading provider of vaccines on a global scale. In 2007, Sanofi-Pasteur shipped over 1.6 billion doses of vaccine worldwide, including 130 million doses of influenza vaccine (de Reuil, 2008), which illustrates their global commitment to produce vaccine to meet the global demand if a pandemic were to occur.

With the limited number of vaccine manufacturers in the U.S., coupled with the fact that the major supplier of pandemic vaccine is not based in the U.S., vaccine production should be considered a critical resource challenge for U.S. preparedness. The probability of a major health-related event causing a disruption in the vaccine supply chain should be of concern to health officials. The U.S. Centers for Disease Prevention and Control (CDC) has recognized the critical nature of vaccines to support preparedness and has established specific influenza vaccine goals (Vanderwagen, 2007):

Vaccine Goal #1

To establish and maintain a dynamic pre-pandemic influenza vaccine stockpile available for 2 million persons: H5N1 stockpiles (40 million doses).

Vaccine Goal #2

To provide pandemic vaccine to all U.S. citizens within six months of a pandemic declaration: pandemic vaccine (600 million doses).

Antivirals Goal #1

To provide influenza antiviral drug stockpiles for treatment of pandemic illness for 25 percent of the U.S. population who we estimate will become clinically ill during a pandemic (75 million treatment courses).

Antivirals Goal #2

To provide influenza antiviral drug stockpiled for strategic limited containment at the onset of a pandemic (6 million treatment courses).

Diagnostics Goal #1

To develop new high throughput laboratory and Point of Care influenza diagnostics for pandemic virus detection.

Given the emphasis placed upon this resource as a component of the health infrastructure, the organizational level that will most likely be ultimately responsible for managing this resource will be state health departments. For state preparedness directors, emergency co-ordinators and public health officials, the key questions specific to vaccine will be:

- Where is the State's current influenza vaccine inventory located?
- Is it distributed appropriately to respond to the demand?
- How do I monitor the utilization rates to redistribute or reorder?

To address this issue, health departments are examining their information infrastructure that would support the administration and utilization of vaccines in their communities. One of the most important information environments within health departments is a statewide immunization registry. Currently forty-nine of the fifty U.S. states have implemented a state registry (AIRA). These registries, which were originally developed with an emphasis on children of school age, now have evolved to include doses administered to all age groups. With this information resource it is now possible to identify at-risk populations to an event based on current vaccine converge rates. In turn, this provides public health professionals decision data on which to distribute and allocate vaccines to regional locations.

In 2007, the State of Louisiana conducted a statewide Influenza Mass Vaccination Event drill for emergency Preparedness, simulating a Mass Immunization event. One objective of this drill was to determine the value of using the state's immunization registry to provide real-time information to decision makers in emergency command centers to support vaccine utilization and regional needs. The goal was to determine the value of real-time data and in particular to determine how the statewide registry could support these efforts.

The Louisiana Immunization Network for Kids Statewide, (LINKS), developed by Scientific Technologies Corporation, has been in operation for over seven years. LINKS was utilized extensively after Hurricane Katrina in 2005 and validated the importance of utilizing electronic immunization records to support mass displacement events (Urquhart et al., 2007). Given this rich resource and a proven history of utilization by the provider and emergency operations centers, a project was designed to exercise health providers at specific state-designated vaccine Points of Distribution (POD) to capture vaccine utilization data with real-time reporting to command centers to determine demand and availability of vaccine supplies.

Background

Public health mass immunization or dispensing responses to outbreaks of communicable disease has been greatly aided with the advent of secure network or internet accessible population-based databases. States are successfully tracking childhood and adult immunizations through access by both private and public providers to the statewide database. These immunization management systems have also proven to reduce the "over-immunization" of patients due to lost or incomplete hand-carried vaccination records. A second important result of this has been to reduce the total doses used of publicly or privately supplied vaccine inventories, thus reducing costs, and equally important, increasing the availability of this crucial resource in a critical event.

Statewide registries such as the LINKS have evolved to a robust suite of applications catering to the needs of the patients, parents, the private and public providers, and the CDC. The registries are feature-rich with the ability to capture hundreds of data elements related to patient demographics, vaccines, inventory, and information about the participating medical organizations and the users. They are designed to provide standard and customized reports, reminder/recall processes, automated and manual patient record matching, and algorithms to forecast vaccinations for which a patient may be due or past due. In the case of a major health-related event in which mass immunization of individuals would be required, the use of electronic information systems to support management of critical resources is not the norm.

Data collection, for example, has historically been accomplished through handwritten forms followed by electronic data entry accomplished after the event. Manual counts by staff of on-site inventory levels, volumes of patients being served and staffing levels at the PODs are common. Reporting to decision makers at emergency operation centers (EOC) through mobile communications is the mode for information flow. Vaccine allocation, movement of supplies, and reordering from vaccine distributors is delayed and inefficient. In an environment of demand being greater than vaccine supply, the ability to determine exact needs would reduce the current tendency to overestimate the orders, thus potentially consuming resources that are best utilized in other locations.

With a paper-based data collection process, not only is the tracking of the general population patient not shared in a real-time manner with the EOC, but data about those considered to be first responders, including essential healthcare support staff, critical infrastructure workers, public health emergency response workers and high risk patients, are not efficiently categorized with aggregated data made available to the EOC decision makers at the time of the encounters. Furthermore, after dispensing medicine or giving an immunization there is no opportunity to easily monitor an adverse reaction or to contact an individual at a later date for a follow-up.

The Louisiana Experience

As a result of the post-Katrina response in 2005, the electronic data capture of patient services specific to immunizations was established within the refugee shelter environments. Since then, the Louisiana State Office of Public Health (OPH) has proactively sought to increase the capability of the statewide immunization registry to further support real-time data capture and real-time information for EOC management decision support. Various statewide preparedness drills, including its Plague Drill in 2005, its Statewide Mass Immunization in 2006, and this most recent Mass Vaccination Event drill and flu season preparation in 2007, have continued to increase lessons learned and demonstrate the value of real-time data collection and information.

Both the 2005 and 2006 drills showed increasing levels of preparedness for public health responses to emergencies (Welch, 2006). The efficiency and value of the use of electronic data collection is evident in the rapid setup of data collection at community-based PODs and the distribution of critical resources such as vaccines and other pharmaceutical product inventories among the PODs. Past experience has also pointed to needs for continual improvement in electronic system capabilities. Improvements are needed at two levels: the complete elimination of paper forms as backup processes to online information systems at each POD and the need for a consolidated view of the resources and event activity across all PODs at the EOC level.

2007 Louisiana Drill Results

In previous preparedness exercises the immunization registry was accessed in real time at each POD and a specific user interface allowed for rapid web-based data entry to capture the minimal data set. Since there was no guarantee that online access could be provided or sustained, the backup system used was the paper form. The forms replicated the data elements collected in the Mass Immunizations Module, the rapid data entry tool. This data would then be electronically entered once connectivity had been restored and as the POD workflow allowed.

In the 2007 drill, one of the nine statewide PODs lost connectivity for a period of several hours and the data entry personnel reverted to paper forms. This constituted approximately 6 percent of the total data from the six-hour drill and all data was in the central LINKS system within twenty-four hours. Experience has shown that in nearly every Louisiana mass vaccination event, especially where PODs are quickly established in community centers, network or internet connectivity is lost for at least some period of time, typically for an hour or less. In such cases, data collection using paper forms has been the only recourse. Paper increases the workload, real-time information to support decisions is not readily accessible, and the quality of data entered after the healthcare service is less accurate. As a result, it was determined that a paperless system would be a preferable means of backup.

As the drill progressed, the value of the online data entry at time of service became more apparent to the health professionals in the EOC. Real-time, accurate information is critical to EOC personnel charged with monitoring the activities of the PODs during mass events. Within a few hours of operation, the EOC staff was able to determine from the patient flow and vaccine inventory information that all of the PODs would deplete their inventories of flu vaccine at their then current rate of use. To alleviate the projected shortfall of vaccine, the immunization registry was used to determine locations of additional vaccines near each POD. EOC staff were able to co-ordinate the transfer of flu vaccine to the PODs, thereby preventing any of the PODs from running out of vaccine and having to turn away patients during the six-hour drill.

This was a critical metric to manage this valuable resource. Specific lessons focused on the fact that the EOC decision makers need access to information from all of the PODs in real time as the event progresses. Decision makers required the ability to answer the following questions without the need for numerous voice communications or extensive manipulation of data gathered from running various reports:

- Facilities (PODs)—Are the facilities located properly? Do others need to be opened?
- POD staff levels—Are the intake, vaccination and data entry personnel able to keep up with the patient flow?
- Patients—Is the targeted population being served? Are there geographically (or other) defined groups not being served?
- Pharmaceutical inventory—What is the current inventory? What is the rate of use? What/where are the sources of resupply?
- First responders and other essential personnel—How many and what categories of essential personnel have been vaccinated and are prepared to render services?

During the 2007 drill, the EOC staff found that they had sufficient information to determine vaccine levels and patient flow for each POD.

The Solution

To ensure the greatest patient coverage rate and the protection of public health in a public health emergency and to employ the most efficient utilization of resources, such as responders and vaccine inventories, two problems need to be solved:

1 Point of service data collection at the POD level must be done in real-time, or in the case of connectivity loss, the quality of the data must be maintained—that is, all the information should be entered electronically, not collected on paper forms.
2 The systems in use by the EOCs need to be enhanced to eliminate or reduce the need for manual manipulation to the lowest possible level.

For the 2007 drill, the solution to the point of service back-up challenge was the migration of the current web-based Mass Immunization Module to a standalone tool for local and non-connected data entry. The tool was implemented in a USB to allow for connectivity to any computer such that the entire application and database resided on this device. Thus no software was required on the host computer and no special connection or hardware was necessary. This application replaces the need for paper forms with all point of service data entry activity continued electronically and data uploaded to the state registry when network or internet access is restored. This ensures the shortest possible lapse of real-time information for the EOC, but most importantly, maintains the accuracy of the patient demographic and vaccination information.

A solution to the second problem has not yet been implemented, as in effect the recommendation was to establish an EOC immunization dashboard to create a consolidated view of the real-time data flowing from each POD. The proposed solution would eliminate the need for additional data consolidation at the EOC, which utilizes spreadsheets that require labor intensive maintenance. As a result of the most recent drill, an EOC immunization dashboard has been designed and is intended to derive and display information such as projected inventory depletion times as the data flows in from the event PODs.

Outcome

The 2007 drill validates the usefulness of the state's immunization registry as an EOC management tool for the management of vaccines during a mass immunization event. This real-time information allowed an assessment of vaccine utilization rates, assessed local stockpiles of vaccines and prevented PODs from running out of vaccine prior to the end of the drill. Prior to the drill, it was estimated that each POD would experience a workload of approximately 200 patients per hour, resulting in 11,000 vaccinations statewide for the six hours. Surprisingly, the actual workload was more than double this number and the 27,000 vaccinations were administered with over 90 percent of the data recorded in a paperless process. This drill further demonstrated the likelihood that in an event, the demand will outweigh the expected workload and available vaccine resources. Resources will be challenged and only through rapid and real-time data collection can decision support staff maximize the use of resources while minimizing the burden on their time to process and analyze data.

This case exercise focused on the single critical resource of vaccines. Information and decision support tools to manage inventory and distributions served to maximize the ability of the state public health officials to protect individuals from vaccine preventable diseases. Vaccine resources are a critical U.S. element to the overall infrastructure supporting preparedness. There is no guarantee that there will be sufficient vaccine to support all potential events but as was demonstrated in this Louisiana Case Exercise there are tools and data workflows to support and manage the use of a limited resource.

Case Exercise References

AIRA (n.d) Registry Profiles, Association of Immunization Registries. Available online from http://immregistries.org/public.php/ImmRegs/regMain.php [accessed August 21, 2008].

CDC (2008) U.S. Vaccines, CDC website. Available online from www.cdc.gov/vaccines/pubs/pinkbook/downloads/appendices/B/us-vaccines.pdf [accessed August 20, 2008].

de Reuil, V. (2008) France Press Release, June 25, 2008.

Urquhart, G., Williams, W., Tobias, J., and Welch, F. (2007), Immunization Information Systems Use in a Public Health Emergency in the United States, *American Journal of Public Health*, 13(5): 481–485.

Vanderwagen, W.C. (2007) Statement by RADM W. Craig Vanderwagen, MD, Assistant Secretary for Preparedness and Response U.S. Department of Health and Human Services on Pandemic Influenza: HHS Progress in National Preparedness Efforts before Committee on Homeland Security and Governmental Affairs Senate Subcommittee on State, Local and Private Sector Preparedness and Integration United States Senate, October 3, U.S. Dept of Health and Human Services. Available online from www.hhs.gov/asl/testify/2007/10/t20071003a.html [accessed August 21, 2008].

Welch, F. (2006) The Louisiana Immunization Registry (LINKS) after Hurricane Katrina: Unexpected Success, 2006 National Immunization Conference website. Available online from www.cdc.confex.com/cdc/nic2006/techprogram/P11707.HTM [accessed August 21, 2008].

Checkland (1993, p. 281) notes that SSM "covers the area in which Burrell and Morgan locate the critical theory of the Frankfurt School," for example the theory of Knowledge Constituitive Interests (Habermas, 1972). Here Habermas distinguishes between three primary cognitive experiences through which people create knowledge, termed technical, practical and emancipatory interests. These areas define cognitive experiences or learning domains and are grounded in different aspects of social existence—work, interaction and power.

The technical interest is linked to work, and involves people achieving goals and material well-being. The technical interest is especially concerned with prediction, control and manipulation of the physical world. The generation of knowledge in this case is based on instrumental action using empirical analytical methods within the positivistic sciences, e.g. physics chemistry and biology. The practical domain identifies human social interaction or communicative action, involving mutual expectations, understanding of participants and debate. The criterion of clarification of conditions for communication and understanding of meaning is used to determine what action is appropriate. The practical domain falls within the historical hermeneutic methods; for example, social sciences, history, legal, etc.

The emancipatory interest relates to coercion and power, which can hinder (or help) the progression of work and interaction. This domain identifies self-reflection and involves ones own history, social conditioning, values and norms. The emancipation refers to the ability to free oneself from environmental constraints, power of others over self and the awareness necessary to release oneself from such constraints. The importance of the emancipatory interest can be seen in debate, which occurs in the practical interest. A debate that does not deal with the concept of emancipation will develop under constraint and stunt a beings potential for development. Knowledge in the emancipatory domain is generated through self-reflection leading to a change in consciousness and perspective.

Applying Habermas' Knowledge Constituitive Interests to SSM, SSM falls primarily within the practical domain because it is aimed at consensual debate, which explores alternative Weltanschauungen and has criteria of success established through action research. Comparing

Table 4.1 *Knowledge Constituitive Interests, SSM and Knowledge Management*

Knowledge Constituitive Interests	SSM	Knowledge Management
Technical—prediction, control, manipulation of physical world	Primary task root definitions.	Technical control of objectified processes—use of IT and clearly defined system to share information. (KM Process)
Practical debate, participation	Issue based root definitions. Learning cycle, CATWOE	Maintaining, creating, communicating, and improving knowledge. (KM Activities)
Emancipatory—power and politics	Political analysis	Critical reflection, understanding and freedom to create and share knowledge. (KM Development)

SSM, KM and Habermas' Knowledge Constituitive Interests, the components may be linked as per Table 4.1. The following critique led to a development known as critical systems thinking. This will be discussed on p. 81.

CASE EXERCISE: INTERVENTION IN AN OUTPATIENT'S DEPARTMENT

This case is drawn from Lehaney et al. (1999)

In the U.K., publicly funded hospitals (National Health Service or NHS) run outpatient clinics. These enable patients who have been referred by their general practitioner (family doctor) or from elsewhere in the hospital, to receive diagnosis, treatment and prognosis within a scheduled appointment. The nominal appointment duration is ten minutes, but in practice the appointment might take from five to thirty minutes. The work attempted to address gaps between customers' and providers' expectations and the intervention used a soft systems approach, coupled with simulation modeling. Simulation modeling is a means by which the activities and entities in a system, and their relationships, can be captured, usually on a computer, and usually with graphics that represent what is going on in the system.

The hospital faced some issues that it had to address. In particular, patients were queuing (waiting in line) for longer than was desired. There were also concerns about the number of patients who did not turn up for appointments (did-not-attends, or DNAs). The intervention was initiated as a result of U.K. Government pressure on the NHS to improve its service. This was as a result of a number of factors, including increasing pressures on health service expenditure driven by advances in medical treatment, social pressures such as the elderly living longer, and the inefficiencies of such a large public sector organization. An NHS Performance Guide is published annually (from 1993–1994), and this indicates how local health services are performing. For each hospital, outpatient statistics show the percentage of patients seen within thirty minutes of appointment time, and this is a key statistic.

Long outpatient queues in the NHS were not new, but the pressure to reduce them was. The task was to reduce such queues, but without using additional resources. It is not a straightforward challenge, as having queues of patients avoids the possibility of doctors having to wait for the next patient to arrive. Given that doctors are an extremely expensive resource, this is an unacceptable scenario. Through existing networks, we met with the Associate Director of Information Services (Associate Director) of a local NHS Trust. He felt that "pressure to perform" had increased in recent years, and was searching for ways to make noticeable improvements. He was not clear as to what, where and how. We felt that such case material would be useful for us in many ways, and we agreed that mutual benefit might be gained by collaboration on a research project. At this stage, the Associate Director appeared to be in the roles of client, would-be problem solver and problem owner, while we were would-be problem solvers and would-be problem owners.

The Consultant Dermatologist was a major participant and if improvements to performance could be made at this outpatients' clinic, it might be possible that similar issues could be addressed elsewhere. A second meeting with the Associate Director, the Consultant Dermatologist (Consultant), the Outpatients Department Manager (Manager) and the Senior Ward Sister (Sister) was held, and it became very clear that if any one of these individuals withdrew co-operation the intervention could not continue. Hence they are termed "key stakeholders." The intervention was undertaken in four linked stages. Cultural analysis was done in Stage 1. In this, the roles of the participants and the social and political systems were considered. This enabled soft objectives to be set and the nature of the project and likely timescales to be agreed. The areas were considered against desirability, feasibility, and participants' expectations and observations.

In Stage 2 the group favored the use of simple flowcharts, which were compared with participants' expectations and observations, and adjusted as work progressed. These flowcharts were extremely useful in many ways, not least because they helped the participants gain a greater understanding of their own organization. Eventually, most of the charts were dropped in favor of a flowchart of the patients' experiences from entering the clinic to leaving. The reasoning was that this was the one area that the group could influence with any hope of success. The key stakeholders were keen to see a computer simulation model, and a series of iterations took place involving the flowcharts and computer models. Eventually flowcharts were dropped and development took place solely on computer models. Flowcharts provided only a static representation of the systems, whereas computer simulation models would enable dynamic depictions.

In Stage 3, simulation modeling began and models were compared with expectations and observations, and adjusted accordingly. The desirable and feasible outcomes of Stage 3 were that operational (process) actions were taken to reduce both queuing times and the incidence of patients not attending. Patient waiting time and doctor utilization were reaffirmed as the major issues for consideration, and simulation models were built to mimic patient arrival to patient departure. A prototyping approach was used in building the models until a satisfactory outcome was achieved.

Stage Four moved the project on from operational to strategic level. Instead of the simulation helping solve a single problem, a system of intervention was developed and agreed to help address ongoing complex situations. The intervention resulted in a procedure to reduce unexpected non-attendance of patients and a system to schedule patient bookings according to simple rules was developed, with an associated reduction in clinic waiting times. In order to achieve these things it was important to address the overall situation as more than a technical problem. The technical issues were important but equally important were the perceptions of those involved in running the clinic. Based on this, key stakeholders helped develop and accepted the simulation models, and a model of the intervention process itself, which they hoped to use for continuing investigations. In addition, participants increased their knowledge of their own systems.

CRITICAL SYSTEMS THINKING

SSM has been criticized for not fully addressing the issue of political domination and emancipation. For example, Mingers (1984) argues that two forms of subjectivism, strong and weak, should be considered. He suggests that pure, strong subjectivism that does not allow for the possibility of some extra individual reality, creates a weakness in the value of SSM, as any one view of the world is as valid as any other. In addition, the proposition that the world is socially constructed must also be a socially constructed view. Mingers goes on to advocate weak subjectivism in which the subject is emphasized, but extra individual structures are accepted. This subjectivist stance raises criticisms of the ability of SSM to be utilized as a tool of radical change, as social norms might work to preserve the status quo.

Recognition of this is important because if an organization wishes to engage in KM, it requires understanding about its own human activity systems. In particular, the recognition of social constraints and obstructions is important if progress is to be made to free individuals and groups from political issues that may impede the successful implementation of KM. Such issues may be considered through the theory of Knowledge Constituitive Interests (Habermas, 1972), which has provided much of the basis for critical systems thinking.

Critical theory assumes that social reality is historically constructed. Critical theory suggests that although people are constrained by various forms of social, cultural and political constraints, exposing such constraints is necessary to achieve emancipation. If KM involves innovation and creativity to think and produce beyond individual experiences, then social, cultural and political domination should be key considerations. Ulrich (1983) describes Habermas' theory of Knowledge Constituitive Interests as the process of learning, gaining experience and knowledge through different contexts and action, influenced by social and historical experience.

Critical systems thinking attempts to bring together systems thinking and participatory methods to help address boundary judgments and complexity. Just as SSM is one approach within soft systems thinking, Critical Systems Heuristics (CSH) is an approach within critical systems thinking. CSH was developed by Ulrich (1983), and it focuses on discovering whose interest a system serves by examining any assumptions and values associated with the system, and the purpose of the system. To be critical is to be "self reflective in respect to the presuppositions flowing into one's own judgments, both in the search for true knowledge and rational action" (Ulrich, 1983: 20). CSH uses questions relating to control, expertise, legitimization and motivation. The idea is that these may help expose and free the design from individual organizational, cultural, societal and political value assumptions that may be hidden and coercive. In this way CSH lays claims to being an emancipatory approach. In terms of KM the design should include consideration for individual, organizational, cultural, societal and political issues, and how these might be addressed and dealt with in an organization.

Critical Systems Heuristics studies existing or planned systems, from a point of view of discovering whose interests the system serves. It considers the assumptions and values associated with the system (or proposed system). It uses "boundary questions," such as "What is the actual purpose of the system design?" These questions are aimed at the system planners and also the people affected by the system. The power of the questions to reveal the normative content of the system design is best seen if they are put in "is" mode and "ought" mode.

Thus, the questions, "Who *is* the actual client of the systems design?" and "Who *ought* to be the client of the systems design?" would be asked. The boundary questions are designed to highlight sources of control, expertise, legitimacy and motivation (Jackson, 1992: 191). These can then be used by planners, and others involved in the situation, to show underlying value assumptions of the system design. The purpose is to expose, and hopefully free, the design from individual, organizational, cultural, societal and political value assumptions that may be hidden and coercive. By doing this, it is using an emancipatory systems approach. This revealing of "true" motives in a planning situation may itself lead to new planning proposals.

Ulrich (1987) proposes a list of twelve questions. Each question is to be asked in the "is" mode and the "ought" mode, thus making twenty-four questions in total. The questions are within the domains of four basic boundary issues, which are as follows:

- The basis of motivation: where does a sense of purposefulness and value come from?
- The basis of power: who is in control of what is going on and is needed for success?
- The basis of knowledge: what experience and expertise support the claim?
- The basis of legitimacy: where does legitimacy lie?

Questions 1–9 are about those involved with issues. Questions 10–12 are about those affected by issues. Tables 4.2–4.5 (from Ulrich, 1987) provide a checklist of boundary questions.

While CSH purports to be emancipatory, it can be argued that this methodology does not contribute enough to how any changes, by which the design is freed of hidden value assumptions, are undertaken. Willmott (1989) doubts the efficacy of the methodology, on the grounds that it neglects the structural aspects and development of social systems favored in a strucuralist analysis.

Table 4.2 *Sources of Motivation*

(1) Who is (ought to be) the client or beneficiary? That is, whose interests are (should be) served?

(2) What is (ought to be) the purpose? That is, what are (should be) the consequences?

(3) What is (ought to be) the measure of improvement or measure of success? That is, how can (should) we determine that the consequences, taken together, constitute an improvement?

(Source: Ulrich, 1987)

Table 4.3 *Sources of Power*

(4) Who is (ought to be) the decision-maker? That is, who is (should be) in a position to change the measure of improvement?

(5) What resources and other conditions of success are (ought to be) controlled by the decision-maker? That is, what conditions of success can (should) those involved control?

(6) What conditions of success are (ought to be) part of the decision environment? That is, what conditions can (should) the decision-maker not control (e.g. from the viewpoint of those not involved)?

(Source: Ulrich, 1987)

Table 4.4 *Sources of Knowledge*

(7) Who is (ought to be) considered a professional or further expert? That is, who is (should be) involved as competent providers of experience and expertise?

(8) What kind expertise is (ought to be) consulted? That is, what counts (should count) as relevant knowledge?

(9) What or who is (ought to be) assumed to be the guarantor of success? That is, where do (should) those involved seek some guarantee that improvement will be achieved—for example, consensus among experts, the involvement of stakeholders, the experience and intuition of those involved, political support?

(Source: Ulrich, 1987)

Table 4.5 *Sources of Legitimation*

(10) Who is (ought to be) witness to the interests of those affected but not involved? That is, who is (should be) treated as a legitimate stakeholder, and who argues (should argue) the case of those stakeholders who cannot speak for themselves, including future generations and non-human nature?

(11) What secures (ought to secure) the emancipation of those affected from the premises and promises of those involved? That is, where does (should) legitimacy lie?

(12) What worldview is (ought to be) determining? That is, what different visions of "improvement" are (should be) considered, and how are they (should they be) reconciled?

(Source: Ulrich, 1987)

CONCLUSIONS AND SUMMARY

This chapter discussed general systems thinking, hard systems thinking, soft systems thinking and critical systems thinking. It has provided an overview of these and developed some links with KM. System thinking has a range of methodologies or approaches for addressing interventions, and two of these, Soft Systems Methodology and Critical Systems Heuristics, have been outlined. The links between Knowledge Constituitive Interests, Soft Systems Methodology and KM have been tabulated. Hard systems thinking may be appropriate for technical or quantitative problems that can have an optimal solutions. Soft systems thinking is to do with problem situations and the resolution (rather than solution) of those. Critical systems thinking attempts to address emancipation, and the defining of roles and interests within contexts. Each of these forms of systems thinking may have something to offer to KM. Each may be criticized in various ways.

The work in this area is not fully developed as it is a fairly recent innovation, but it would appear that systems thinking and KM may be complementary, and may be stronger together than separately.

REVIEW QUESTIONS

1 In general, what is systems thinking about?

2 Why did soft systems thinking develop?

3 What is the main approach within soft systems thinking covered in this chapter?

4 What is the main approach within critical systems thinking covered within this chapter?

5 What are the two modes of enquiry in Critical Systems Heuristics?

DISCUSSION QUESTIONS

1 How can systems thinking be linked to KM?

2 Why might this potentially be useful?

3 How might systems thinking and KM be used together in a past, present or future work situation?

CASE EXERCISE: EMPOWERING PATIENTS: IMMUNIZATIONS AND KNOWLEDGE-BASED PERSONAL HEALTH RECORDS[8]

Background

Day in and day out there are press releases from healthcare providers, vendors and departments of health stressing the value of individuals assuming a greater role in managing their healthcare. The economic cost impacts of a proactive health program are well known and encouraging individuals to be a catalyst to accelerate proactively is a win for all. As such, individuals require health information and knowledge, they need to know what it means, and they need to know how to use it. They need to be able to make decisions, ask questions and stay informed.

The provider community understands the value of historical and real-time information and knowledge to support healthcare decisions for their patients. They understand the need to share information as patients receive services from a variety of healthcare professionals. Providers address this need through information and knowledge sharing. Whereas the expanding electronic medical record (EMR) environment is facilitating an infrastructure to support the provider community, the emerging personal health record (PHR) will facilitate the use of the individual's medical records to support management of their specific care. The question will become how to populate a PHR.

It is difficult for individuals to contribute to their own healthcare team if they do not have ready access to their own personal health information and knowledge. Patients empowered through information are more likely to understand the risks and benefits of certain activities (e.g. immunizations, disease screening) and are more likely to be proactive in their own healthcare. Health informatics, together with (knowledge-enabled) medical compunetics, provide the tools for information to significantly shape an individual's personal healthcare environment. Accessible information will facilitate informed decision making and contribution by ALL members of the healthcare team: physicians, other healthcare partners (e.g. pharmacists, specialists), and most importantly, the patient. Better informed healthcare teams should translate into better personal care, providing a long-term economic benefit for societies by preventing disease, mitigating direct healthcare costs, and promoting a healthy and more productive workforce.

Despite the promise of better healthcare through information-centric patient empowerment, little progress has been made. And although progress is being made to implement EMRs, significant barriers exist to enable wide-spread direct patient electronic access to this information. This paper presents an approach to achieve immediate real gains in patient empowerment by facilitating electronic access to a key component of an individual's personal health record: their immunization data.

The Need for Personal Immunization Records

Access to immunization records through health informatics and decision support through health compunetics presents an easy-win opportunity to significantly empower individuals. Whether it is a yellow fever, malaria, hepatitis, measles, or new vaccines for emerging infectious diseases or chronic illnesses, immunizations are universally available. Understanding what is required and when, and ensuring a family is fully protected is complex.

Immunizations are recommended and provided to new babies, adolescents and the elderly. From Hepatitis B given at birth, to adult boosters including those for tetanus, pertussis and influenza and new vaccines for pneumonia and shingles, the need for immunizations persists throughout an individual's entire life. As such, a complete immunization history should be a required component of a person's health record. The value of health compunetics is that this record can then be evaluated to determine what risks an individual has to vaccine-preventable diseases. Having an immunization history and tools to determine risks will empower individuals to be proactive.

An individual's immunization record needs to be complete to provide an accurate assessment of risk. Immunization records are retained by individual providers, but rarely consolidated into a single medical record across the patient's healthcare lifecycle. Each vaccine that is provided by a healthcare professional results in a paper or electronic record, retained in the custody of the primary provider. When individuals move and/or change physicians, records will exist in multiple locations.

With the advent of electronic health records, individual immunization data may eventually be consolidated under the patient's current provider but these records are not likely to be as mobile as the patient. Patients can request from past providers copies of their families' immunization records but often the effort required to do this is seen as prohibitive, and for the provider such requests add administrative costs to search, retrieve and provide this information (cost studies in 2003 have shown economic impacts of $5 per chart to retrieve medical files).

The first challenge is where or how to generate a single complete immunization record for an individual. Ultimately, there are three locations where complete records are found. The most likely is in a home paper record kept by conscientious individuals themselves. The second location is with third party organizations that ultimately pay for the services. And finally, at least in North America, records may end up in a consolidated regional immunization registry that is used by public health organizations to support vaccine-preventable disease programs. For example, in the U.S., forty-nine of the fifty state health departments have implemented statewide immunization registries (American Immunization Registry Association, www.immregistries.org/public.php/ImmRegs) and in Canada all provinces will be expected to implement immunization registries in the next few years. It is the state and provincial immunization registries where the combined patient records can be found and they will become the trusted source of this information. However, no public access is offered for this information.

Personal immunization records must be easily accessible. Individuals do not have access to their own immunizations records even if they exist in an electronic database. Without easy access it is difficult for an individual to review their own and their family's immunization status. The primary challenge standing in the way of patient empowerment is the lack of priority by immunization data custodians to open these registries to the public. Data confidentiality is the key barrier. As such, there is a source for a combined patient record but no mechanism for sharing this with the public. The challenge then becomes the second gap to overcome: how to make available this resource.

The National Committee for Quality Assurance (NCQA) is a U.S. federal agency that evaluates quality of care. All insurance companies provide reports annually on the level of their services. A key measurable criterion is immunization coverage. This is determined from the immunizations histories of patients who are members of the insurance plan. A significant effort is made by insurance companies to gather this data, often through costly on-site provider visits involving the review of a random subset of patient records. With the implementation of statewide immunization registries at the health departments, insurance companies now can receive electronic copies of all their member records if desired. The key to patient access and thus a successful patient empowerment project is through the insurance companies.

Immunization Recordkeeping and Patient Empowerment: Arizona Case Exercise

Since 1994, the State of Arizona has had in operation a statewide immunization system. Data are collected directly from providers through electronic information exchange and through direct data entry. Currently this registry has over 18,400 users, including providers, school nurses and state health professionals. The system maintains immunization records (over 31 million to date) for approximately 3.2 million individuals, most of whom are under the age of eighteen. The state total population is over 6 million and there are new initiatives underway to include adult immunizations in the system.

Immunization data is utilized by providers to determine the next appropriate vaccination, by public health officials to support immunization programs that minimize the impact of vaccine-preventable diseases on the populations at risk, and by third party insurers for their quality of care programs as well as pay for performance. Individuals do not have access to their personal immunization records in this closed system. Given that the immunization registry infrastructure is in place to collect, store and retrieve this information, the next step is to implement a patient access view into these records. This is achievable by establishing the following criteria for patient access:

- The data are secure and only available to the individual.
- No identification or location data is provided or can be viewed, but only immunization histories.

- No user access is available to the immunization record source network (i.e. providers or state health departments).
- No special software or equipment is required to access information.
- Additional immunization tools are available to support an individual's ability to use this information in the management of their own healthcare, to include forecasting next due date, identification of missing vaccines and risk assessments.

With these criteria, a secure web-based patient access health portal is recommended. A portal that leverages existing security and record access tools limits access to information to the specific individual that is authenticated through password protection and a portal that provides the most complete online record available with standardized tools to support immunization record assessment for patient decision management.

Our proposed solution leverages the health insurance/third party payer environments by providing access to records through the health portal of an individual's current insurer. When a member connects to their insurance company's health portal, an option exists to access their immunization records that would be retained as a copy from a source data repository such as a state immunization system. Family records would also be available. The insurance company becomes the repository of the record, which is also used to support their vaccine preventable programs and their quality of care programs.

Our proposed solution would include processes to access the patient historical records and advice on immunizations due and date required, recommended optional vaccinations, and additional immunization-related information as appropriate. Members would not need to access this health portal to be proactive in maintaining their family immunizations as the system would automatically, through an electronic notification feature, email or text message, send a reminder that an immunization is due. The solution as envisioned does not require a complex technical component. The most difficult element will likely be the establishment of memorandums of agreement between participating organizations.

Conclusions

Although the solution described in this paper is within the current technical environments of all parties, personal electronic immunization health records have yet to be implemented in North America. It is simply a matter of time until individuals will have electronic access to their immunization records. This will be driven not through government or provider initiatives, but from consumers demanding access to their own personal health data or through the economics of healthcare.

Although there are ongoing debates relating to the potential costs and benefits associated with providing consumers access to their entire medical records, access to personal knowledge-based immunization records is a universally accepted concept. Enabling access to these knowledge-based records provides a low-cost, low-risk, first step towards more broad-based access to personal health information. The economic and health benefits to individuals and communities associated with patient empowerment through information access will be profound.

Case Exercise Questions

1 What systems-oriented issues may need to be overcome before successful implementation of the proposed system?

2 The technical issues appear to have been overcome. What people and process issues remain?

FURTHER READING

Bali, R.K. (Ed.) (2005) *Clinical Knowledge Management: Opportunities and Challenges*. Hershey, PA: Idea Group.

Jackson., M. (2000) *Systems Approaches to Management*. New York: Kluwer Academic/Plenum Publishers.

Lehaney, B., Clarke, S., Coakes, E., and Jack, G. (2004) *Beyond Knowledge Management*. Hershey, PA: Idea Group Publishing.

REFERENCES

Ackoff, R.L. (1979) The Future of Operational Research is Past, *Journal of the Operational Research Society*, 30(3): 189–199.

Banathy, B. (1996) *Designing Social Systems in a Changing World*. New York: Plenum.

Boddy, D. and Buchanan, D. (1992) *The Expertise of the Change Agent*. London: Prentice-Hall.

Burrell, G. and Morgan, G. (1979) *Sociological Paradigms and Organizational Analysis*. London: Heinemann.

Checkland, P.B. (1981) *Systems Thinking, Systems Practice*. Chichester: Wiley.

Checkland, P.B. (1993) *Systems Thinking, Systems Practice*. 2nd edn. Chichester: Wiley.

Checkland, P.B. and Scholes, J. (1990) *Soft Systems Methodology in Action*. Chichester: Wiley.

Churchman, C. (1967) Wicked Problems, *Management Science*, 14: 141–142.

Greenberger, M., Crenson, M., and Crissey, B. (1976) *Models in the Policy Process*. New York: Russell Sage.

Habermas, J. (1972) *Knowledge and Human Interests*. Boston, MA: Beacon Press.

Jackson, M. (1992) *Systems Methodology for the Management Sciences*. London: Plenum.

Jackson, M. (1993) Beyond the Fads: Systems Thinking for Managers, *Centre for Systems Studies Working Paper Number 3*, University of Hull.

Jackson, M. (2000) *Systems Approaches to Management*. New York: Kluwer Academic/Plenum Publishers.

Johnson, G., Langley, A., Melin, L., and Whittington, R. (2007) *Strategy as Practice: Research Directions and Resources*. Cambridge: Cambridge University Press.

Lehaney, B., Warwick, S., and Wisniewski, M. (1994) The Use of Quantitative Modeling Methods in the U.K.: Some National and Regional Comparisons, *Journal of European Business Education*, 3(2): 57–71.

Lehaney, B., Clarke, S., and Paul, R.J. (1999) A Case of an Intervention in an Outpatients Department, *Journal of the Operational Research Society*, 50(9): 877–891.

Lehaney, B., Clarke, S., Coakes, E., and Jack, G. (2004) *Beyond Knowledge Management*. Hershey, PA: Idea Group Publishing.

Lewis, P. (1994) *Information-Systems Development*. London: Pitman.

Mingers, J. (1984) Subjectivism and Soft Systems Methodology — A Critique, *Journal of Applied Systems Analysis*, 11: 85–103.

Mingers, J. and Taylor, S. (1992) The Use of Soft Systems Methodology in Practice, *Journal of the Operational Research Society*, 43(4): 321–332.

Prince User Group (1993) *Report of the Inquiry into the London Ambulance Service*. London: Prince User Group, Binder Hamlyn.

Rosenhead, J. (Ed.) (1989) *Rational Analysis for a Problematic World*. Chichester: Wiley.

Sackman, H. (1967) *Computers, Systems Science and Evolving Society: The Challenge of Man-Machine Digital Systems*. New York: Wiley.

Taylor, F. (1911) *The Principles of Scientific Management*. New York: Harper Bros.

Ulrich, W. (1983) *Critical Heuristics of Social Planning: A New Approach to Practical Philosophy*. Berne: Haupt.

Ulrich, W. (1987) Critical Heuristics of Social Systems Design, *European Journal of Operational Research*, 31(3): 276–283.

Wilson, B. (1984) *Systems: Concepts, Methodologies, and Applications*. Chichester: Wiley.

Chapter 5

Knowledge: The Organization, Culture and Learning

INTRODUCTION

This chapter will introduce key organizational concepts (e.g. organizational structures, the learning organization, organizational culture and organizational change) and discuss how these essential components relate to effective KM implementation. This will be followed by a discussion of the benefits offered to companies introducing KM into their organizations as well as the socio-technical perspectives on KM. The application to, and impact on, contemporary businesses will be described (and illustrated by way of case exercises).

THE LEARNING ORGANIZATION

The concept of the learning organization (LO) is said to have been coined by Chris Argyris (a Harvard-based academic) but seems to have been popularized by the seminal work of Peter Senge (and his book *The Fifth Discipline*, first published in 1990). We should emphasize that, although closely linked, the terms "learning organization" and "organizational learning" are not the same. The overlap occurs because organizational learning is a prerequisite for a learning organization.

Senge (1992) describes learning organizations as places "where people continually expand their capacity to create the results they truly desire, where new and expansive patterns of thinking are nurtured, where collective aspiration is set free, and where people are continually learning to see the whole (reality) together". Pedler *et al.* (1991) agree with this viewpoint by stating that "...a Learning Company is an organization that facilitates the learning of all its members and continually transforms itself."

A learning organization is essentially one where the objectives and the company are one and the same. The organization encourages learning and sharing and dissemination of information and knowledge (and an appropriate infrastructure is in place to ensure this). New ideas, and change associated with them, are achieved by way of shared vision. The organization's culture is central to any change process and this is discussed in detail later in this chapter. The LO is in a position to continuously transform itself (perhaps because of external pressures or even internal efficiency and effectiveness) and has the freedom to let go of the past and attempt novel, innovative ways forward to achieve this. The LO is a unique organization inasmuch that both successes and failures are examined for their potential for learning; there is very much an "anti blame" culture in place as mistakes are permitted (in the very best LOs, mistakes may even be encouraged for their learning potential and value). It could be argued in fact that without trying new ideas, and an element of trial and error, true innovation is not possible. The following table summarizes the four levels of learning.

Senge describes five disciplines as being essential and conducive to learning and engagement, allowing organizational actors to become active participants in the learning (and associated change) process. The five components are:

Personal Mastery

This component refers to the ability and discipline of an individual to clarify and deepen his/her personal vision. By doing so, energy can be focused, hopefully allowing the individual to view things in an objective manner. Clarity is of paramount importance here, as is the constant technique of checking/re-checking where one currently is towards attaining the vision. By way of a simple analogy, is an individual embarks on a personal and professional development (career) plan, goals should be set which are both ambitious and realistic. Milestones should also be incorporated that allow the individual to check on progress and, if necessary, to reappraise or even add or amend additional goals and milestones.

Team Learning

This component aims to align and developing the capacity of a team to create the results they desire. It is a truism that people (actors) within an organization require the ability to work well with one another in order to, collectively, achieve organizational goals. This process may start with actions as simple as brainstorming (or mindstorming), suspending personal assumptions and working together "as one."

Table 5.1 *Levels of Learning According to David Skyrme Associates (2008)*

Level 1	*Learning facts, knowledge, processes and procedures* Applies to known situations where changes are minor
Level 2	*Learning new job skills that are transferable to other situations* Applies to new situations where existing responses need to be changed. Bringing in outside expertise is a useful tool here
Level 3	*Learning to adapt* Applies to more dynamic situations where the solutions need developing. Experimentation, and deriving lessons from success and failure is the mode of learning here
Level 4	*Learning to learn* Is about innovation and creativity; designing the future rather than merely adapting to it. This is where assumptions are challenged and knowledge is reframed

Shared Vision

This component focuses on the ability of a group to perceive and rely upon a common viewpoint of a desired future. This aspect provides the focus and energy of learning that reflects both individual (personal) and organizational goals and visions. If carried out correctly, this component tries to align both personal and organizational goals; individuals strive to learn and the positive culture within the organization is highly conducive to enable this.

Mental Models

Senge describes mental models as assumptions that influence how individuals perceive and influence the world and, as a consequence, how we choose to take action. The value of mental images comes when individuals compare new ideas with their (internal) perception of how the world works; if these new ideas are significantly at odds with the mental images (perception), this can prevent them from being turned into reality.

Systems Thinking

Very much at the heart of Senge's thinking comes Systems Thinking. Having acknowledged that organizations are inherently complex entities with various and varied key components, the approach attempts to understand how these components interact with each other and how these interactions affect the organization. In order to function correctly, the approach requires managers to think from a systems perspective and thus also have a long-term perspective. More detail on systems thinking and its importance to KM can be found later in the book.

THE IMPORTANCE OF ORGANIZATIONAL CULTURE

The term *culture* can be used in a variety of contexts. For example, we can describe a person as cultured when (s)he comes to appreciate fine art or literature; on a biological level, cells can be grown in cultures or we describe a country's culture (those national characteristics indigenous to that country). Definitions of culture are notoriously widespread. The difficulty in refining to a single definition is exacerbated when it is considered that, according to the anthropologists Kroeber and Kluckhohn (1952), over 150 different definitions of the term "culture" have been formed. Little wonder then, that confusion over the accepted definition of culture exists.

Smircich (1983) suggests that the plethora of definitions can be readily explained by the fact that the entire concept of culture has been extrapolated from the area of anthropology where there is "no consensus of meaning" (Smircich, 1983: 339–358). Brown (1995) cites Edward B. Tylor's (1871) definition of culture as "the complex whole which includes knowledge, beliefs, art, morals, law, custom . . . acquired by man" (Tylor, 1871: 3).

Pheysey (1993) suggests that culture is "a way of seeing that is common to many people" (p. 3). Perhaps the most cited definition of culture is that of Geert Hoftstede (1994), a leading academic and consultant in organizational anthropology and international management. Based in the Netherlands, and the founding director of the Institute for Research on Intercultural Cooperation (IRIC), Hofstede's professional career has spanned foreman, plant manager and chief psychologist on the international staff of IBM. In his book *Cultures and Organizations*, Hofstede analogizes organizational culture as the "software of the mind" and suggests that culture can be thought of as the ". . . collective programming of the human mind that distinguishes the members of one human group from those of another" (Hofstede, 1994: 5).

In simple terms, describe organizational culture as "an attitude which governs the way things are done in an organization," closely aping the viewpoint of Bower (1966) who describes culture as "the way things are done around here." Hofstede (1994: 4) further states that each person carries patterns of thinking and feeling that stay with them throughout their life. Acquired and learnt during childhood, when the person is most open to learning, assimilation and dissemination of information, these patterns gradually become entrenched within the persona.

Figure 5.1 (Hofstede, 1994: 6) depicts the distinction between human nature on one side and an individual's personality on the other side. When learning something else, the established patterns must be *unlearnt,* which Hofstede (1994) says is inherently more difficult (perhaps a case of old habits dying hard?). Following on from this, Hofstede puts forward the idea that all countries possess a factor called *management,* its meaning changing from one country to another. In order to understand its processes and problems, historical and cultural insights into local phenomena are taken into account.

In yet another of his works, Hofstede (1993) has suggested that universal management theories are non-existent and vary according to the country in which they are applied. It may seem that we have over-examined Hofstede's work but we would argue that this only serves to reinforce its importance. Indeed, such is its acceptance that various authors agree that his work ". . . has had a major influence on how we think about the culture of organizations in different countries" (Brown, 1995: 46).

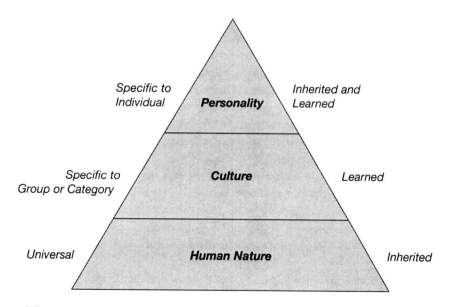

Figure 5.1 *Levels of Mental Programming.*

Table 5.2 *Kroeber and Kluckhohn's Cultural Traits*

Culture can be Shared	by individuals in families or by individuals in society
Culture is Learned	by the acquisition and transmission of teachings and experience
Culture is Transgenerational	and is passed from one generation to another
Culture is Influenced by Perception	in the shaping of mannerisms, behavior and provides the structure to how a person regards their environment
Culture is Adaptive	and is based on a person's ability to change or adapt

Various studies (Pennings, 1993; Thornhill, 1993; Vitell *et al.*, 1993) use Hofstede's various contributions to explain the effects of culture on decision making, executive award systems and training regimens respectively. But how exactly can culture be measured? According to Kroeber and Kluckhohn (1952), culture possesses the following traits.

ORGANIZATIONAL CULTURE

Much like trying to pinpoint a single definition of culture, defining and classifying *organization* is equally difficult and opinion is divided. Robbins (1991) suggests that an organization is a systematic arrangement of people who come together to achieve a common purpose, while Hutchison and Rosenberg (1994) argue that the issue is clouded as the definition changes depending on "who is asking and why they are interested" (p. 101). March and Simon (1958) concur, adding that it is substantially easier to give examples of formal organizations than to pinpoint a universally-accepted and formal definition. It would, however, still be beneficial to attempt, for the purposes of this book, an "uncontroversial" definition of organization.

We would therefore support the view that an organization is a ". . . social arrangement for the controlled performance of collective goals" (Huczynski and Buchanan, 1991: 1). According to Gibson *et al.* (1994), in order to animate the organization, *processes* (such as communications and decision-making) and *structures* (formalized patterns of how its people and jobs are grouped) are used. Extending the notion of culture into an organization leads us to the definition of *organizational culture*. Schein (1990) highlights the pattern of basic assumptions used by individuals and groups to deal with an organization's personality and *feel* which forms the basis of that organization's culture.

A biography of Richard Branson (Jackson, 1995) profiles the conception and growth of the *Virgin* brand. Great insight is provided into Branson's corporate philosophy with Branson himself attributing his personal and corporate success to the organizational culture present. Jackson (ibid.: 303) summarizes the *Virgin* culture as one where ". . . it was idle to ask whether something could be done. Virgin people would assume that it could, and confine themselves to asking how."

Some examples (the list is not exhaustive) of indexes that can combine to form the basis of an organization's culture include reports, letters, memos, emails, health and safety regulations and rulebooks (Bali, 1999). Some examples of protocols of a more-verbalized nature are given:

forms of addresses, repeated stories/myths, "in"-jokes, rumors and speculation. Factors such as dressing styles/requirements and *de rigueur* career paths are cited as additional factors that can contribute to and act as a measure of an organization's culture.

It is this same organizational culture that defines behavior and which motivates its individuals and affects the way that the organization processes information. Many researchers and authors (among them Gibson *et al.*, 1994; Gummesson, 1988) compare organizations to an iceberg. According to Gummesson (1988), an iceberg only shows 10–15 percent of its total mass above the surface water and the iceberg is thus a valid and appropriate model to show the visible and non-visible facets to an organization's culture. We would submit that this conceptualization upholds the importance of deeper research into an organization in order to gain access to the "hidden" 85–90 percent of the organization's value and belief system.

Academic studies and consultancy projects in the U.K., Europe and the U.S. have been carried out by Hampden-Turner (1990) in order to better understand the nature of organizational culture. Hampden-Turner, educated both in the U.K. and America, regularly lectures on the topic throughout the world and is in a position to comment on different cultural attitudes between countries. He suggests that the concept of organizational culture can also be compared to the notion of Rorschach inkblots (used in psychology), where a patient is asked to describe what (s)he "sees."

We would offer the suggestion that shared thoughts, ideals and procedures all contribute to forming a company's culture. The culture of some Japanese-owned car manufacturers, such as Nissan and Honda, starting their day with cross-plant exercises in the yard serves as a suitable

Table 5.3 *Robbins' Ten Characteristics*

Individual Initiative	describing the degree of freedom, flexibility and responsibility an individual has
Integration	or the extent to which units within the organization are encouraged to operate in a co-ordinated manner
Control	deals with the rules and regulations that govern an individual's working day
Risk Tolerance	describing the extent to which individuals are encouraged in terms of innovation and aggression
Direction	describing the extent to which an organization develops clear objectives for staff to follow
Reward Systems	including the degree to which factors such as salary increases are based on employee performance criteria
Communication Patterns	deal with the way an organization's communications are related to the management structure
Conflict Tolerance	details whether individuals are encouraged to air (and hopefully resolve) grievances freely
Management Support	includes the extent to which management provide clear channels of communication
Identity	takes into account the way in which individuals identify with and "fit in" to the organization, rather than their own (often narrow) sphere of experience

example. It should be remembered, however, that the Japanese, as opposed to the British or the Americans, live in quite different environments in anthropological and commercial terms. Initially in the U.K., cross-plant exercises must have seemed alien to the workers but, as suggested by Fiedler *et al.* (1988), the feeling of togetherness and bonding has combined to overcome any awkwardness to make this "norm" work in the U.K.-based plants.

The prevailing patterns of behavior that form a company culture are generally less explicit than formal rules and procedures. Nevertheless, these patterns can often be a powerful influence on the way that employees and managers approach commercial objectives, be they profit maximization or customer care. Robbins (1991) identifies organizational culture as being a mix of ten key characteristics.

Additionally, company cultures can have either a positive (helping productivity) or negative (hindering productivity) effect. Increasingly, greater importance has been attached to improving or, in some cases, creating a corporate culture. While there is nothing inherently incorrect with Robbins' "ten-point" approach, it is our contention that this approach is too formal and regimented in its outlook. We believe that a "softer" approach would be beneficial in the interests of clarity and understanding and agree with the "alternative" characteristics cited by Williams *et al.* (1993) (a group of U.K. researchers who were commissioned to write a book by the Institute of Personnel Management with the aim of shedding light on the U.K. experience of cultural change), who argue that:

- *Culture is learnt*—environmental conditions are the foundations for individual's beliefs, attitudes and values, which in turn dictate the culture of the organization. Both internal (the socio-technical facets of the organization, encompassing the internal mechanisms such as planning, control, technology, decision-making processes and training) and external (factors such as economic, legislative and technological influences) organizational environments can affect organizational culture.
- *Culture is both an input and an output*—influenced by the socio-technical systems of the organization, organizational culture is the result of actions and elements of future action, best depicted by Figure 5.2.

Figure 5.2 shows that organizational culture is influenced by the socio-technical systems of the organization, which are in turn influenced by the common beliefs, attitudes and values of its members. The procedures adopted by management create the work environment for the other members of the organization. If managers have been members of the organization for some time, they themselves can be a product of the culture. Hence their strategies and procedures have, almost inevitably, been conditioned by the culture. Given that culture is both an input and output, it is likely that this attitude is both self-perpetuating and highly resistant to change.

Culture is partly unconscious—commonly held beliefs are unconscious on two levels. Firstly, members unconsciously process information that influences the way in which they think. Secondly, the conscious beliefs, attitudes and values that underlie behavior may repeatedly lead to success to the extent that they are taken for granted.

Culture is historically based—organizations are based on the assumptions and structures of their original founders. Once a particular business direction has been decided upon, successive management generations are often tied to the inherent structures and organizational assumptions

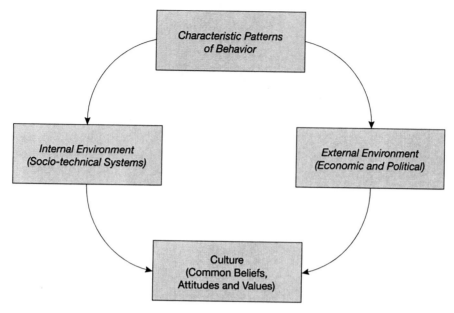

Figure 5.2 *Culture as both an input and an output.*

Source: Williams *et al.* (1993: 16)

that have been set. The original beliefs, attitudes and values (that make up the original organizational culture) may influence successive management generations as organizational decisions are made within the context of the pre-existing culture.

Culture is commonly-held—culture, on an organizational and societal level, can be shared, as different individuals would be affiliated to groups containing similarly like-minded individuals. For example, an organization spread over many sites may comprise individuals who possess common attitudes, thoughts and behavior, despite being separated geographically.

Culture is heterogeneous—in reality, beliefs, attitudes and values are common to work groups, departments, organizations and society. Hence, culture can be common between individuals in a marketing department of a large organization but this culture may not be shared with, perhaps, the IT department (who would possess their own, distinct, set of beliefs, attitudes and values). The existence of sub-cultures can be beneficial if a department's culture results in increased focus on their aims and objectives. Conversely, sub-cultures can also have a detrimental effect if common co-ordination over the organization is limited.

In order to depict the manifestation of culture at different levels in an organization, Hofstede (1994) developed the concept of the "Cultural Onion." For the purposes of this book, we have adapted the diagram (Figure 5.3) to also include organizational structures.

Referring to Figure 5.3 (and paraphrasing Hofstede's (1994) thoughts), at the heart of the cultural onion are the organization's core *values* (beliefs that hold and guide the organization's progress). Surrounding this layer is the *ritual* layer (for example, the organization's approach to employee relations or the tendency to arrange office parties). The next layer is *heroes* and describes the individuals in the organization and their respective competencies and behaviors. This layer is surrounded by *symbols* (the outward signs of the organization, for example the corporate image). The final layer, *structures*, encases the inner layers and is the control and

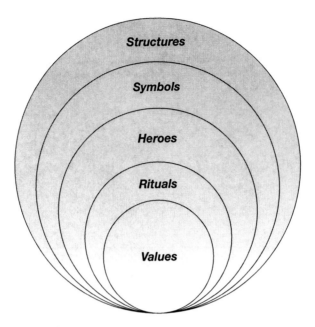

Figure 5.3 *The Cultural Onion.*

Source: adapted from Hofstede (1994)

guidance mechanism of the firm, which dictates how the organization's activities are planned and co-ordinated.

After analyzing the various layers to the diagram, it is our contention that organizational change consultants (and researchers) try to change and influence the outer layer (structure) and make little inroads into the deeper layers of the "onion." To paraphrase the thoughts of an anonymous author on the internet (Anon, 1997), we would urge caution when attempting to change organizations as *real* change has to cut right through to the core of the onion, which, like the vegetable, often leads to tears.

The manifestation of culture at different levels in an organization leads us to define *management*. Authors such as Earl (1989) and Mintzberg (1989) present management as a generic term that describes how different activities are completed efficiently with and through other people. This notion is extended by breaking down management into the four distinct functions of *planning* (the definition of goals, strategy establishment), *organizing* (which tasks are to be done by whom and reporting structures), *leading* (motivation of employees, conflict resolution) and *controlling* (monitoring activities ensuring fulfillment to prior objectives). As U.K. organizations become increasingly oriented towards a European, if not global, market, the significance of cultural understanding becomes increasingly important. Dudley (1990) puts forward the notion that an organization that fails to reflect the changing needs and requirements of a (global) market will fail in its attempt to re-focus any competitive edge it may already have. Hence, competitively, it will be outperformed.

Having given definitions for culture, organization and organizational culture, we can now apply these aspects to the structures of an organization. Harrison's (1972) framework consists of four cultural types and is used as a basis for comparison between organizational cultures. The four cultural approaches (termed orientations) are:

- *Power*—demonstrated by power-hungry and power-motivated organizations who seek to dominate their environment. These organizations treat individuals, departments and other companies as commodities, with no real regard for personal feeling.
- *Role*—generally equate to bureaucratic organizations, where strict adherence to rigid procedures is the norm. In this type of organization, status and titles are important.
- *Task*—is where structures and actions are judged by their contribution to the main organizational objectives. Executing these aims successfully is of paramount importance.
- *People*—where employees are regarded as the organization's most important asset. Action by consensus of opinion is normal. Staff welfare, personal and professional development are key facets.

After analysis of Harrison's (1972) typologies, we would simplify his orientations by typifying *power cultures* as those whose managerial stance is "do as I say," *role cultures* as those whose management attitude is "rules and regulations are King," *task cultures* as those whose managerial style is "teamwork gets the job done" and *people cultures* as those whose managerial stance is "people first."

Carnall (1995), carried out studies in the U.K. and focused on change on three levels: (1) *Psychological*, identifying the attitudes and skills needed to be an effective change leader; (2) *Managerial*, detailing how managers plan the change process to help ensure implementations without setbacks; and (3) *Strategic*, showing how change must be managed as part of a coherent strategic plan. Carnall (1995) broadly suggests that there are six model structures:

1 *Entrepreneurial structure*—a relatively simple model where everything depends on the owner of the business who makes all decisions. Other employees are taken on to carry out specific tasks but, because of little or no departmental structuring, this actually increases the organization's flexibility.
2 *Functional structure*—where an organization is split into distinct activities (such as marketing, legal, IT) and co-ordination takes place by a board of directors, overseen by a managing director.
3 *Product structure*—building on the precepts of a functional structure, the product structure makes individuals responsible for particular products and services. A group is allocated responsibility for particular products or range of products and/or services and are allocated specialists from disciplines such as marketing, legal and engineering. In this manner, these product groups are better equipped to respond to the demands of the market.
4 *Divisional structure*—as an organization increases in size, senior management become less concerned with the day-to-day operations, preferring to concentrate on medium to long-term strategies. Dividing the company into autonomous divisions means that everyday decisions are carried out by each separate division, perhaps concentrating on products or markets. Each division often has management committees which would then report to the organization's senior management. The divisional structure means that considerations regarding costs and profit are left to the committees of the autonomous divisions, leaving Senior Management to concentrate on other matters. Accountability and responsibility is "pushed down" through the organization.
5 *Matrix structure*—are often found when an organization deals with more than one project at a time, calling for various co-ordination skills. As projects may be medium to long-term,

this would require the co-ordination of projects, in terms of specialist knowledge and the timely deployment of necessary resources. Matrix structures enable the effective development of specialists who are working towards the objectives of a project while providing a base for the flexible use of these professionals.

6 *Federal structure*—building on the foundations of the divisional structure, distinct business units are introduced. Each unit has autonomous responsibility over its product market without resort to a divisional structure. Federal structures allow for clear accountability and ensure that the bulk of resources is not expended at divisional level.

There is common agreement (Harrison, 1972; Handy, 1985; Robbins, 1991; Pheysey, 1993; Carnall, 1995) that organizational model structures and cultural orientations are not mutually-exclusive and can be integrated with one another depending on the circumstance, the culture in force and the management *in situ* at an organization.

CASE EXERCISE: KM IN AMERA (THE AFRICA MIDDLE EAST REFUGEE ASSOCIATION IN CAIRO)[9]

by David Johnston

Background

AMERA is a charity that has a large team of healthcare workers and lawyers who represent persons who lack protection from their national governments to flee their countries and become refugees. AMERA, through their volunteers, provide healthcare and legal assistance in many countries throughout the world. Their volunteers sacrifice substantial fees to provide assistance in some of the poorest and most ravaged areas. The healthcare volunteers and lawyers representing these stateless individuals may be requested to assist their clients via the *UNHCR*, an agency of the United Nations, or through individuals presenting themselves at their offices.

Requirement for a Knowledge Management System

The requirement was to provide an online repository containing all the legal and healthcare bulletins issued by the UN and other agencies relating to all the countries from which the refugees originated. The online library therefore contains details sorted by country of origin. The information in the online library had to be easy to extract and insert into local case documentation for presentation in court. This requires the Knowledge Management System (KMS) to be able to merge documents downloaded from the library with local case notes, such that the original page numbers and formats are retained. The documents to be downloaded from the online Refugee library are HTML files, Microsoft Word documents and Adobe PDF files. Once a person's case has been processed, the IT solution creates a local case library of all completed cases. These are necessarily confidential but can be accessed by the local lawyers in the office that handled the original case. The Case Law Library, as the above library is known, must be searchable by the same user interface as the online library.

The Solution

The IT solution implemented contained a number of components:

The Refugee Library

This online library provides fast and easy dissemination of legal bulletins organized by country of origin. Because some of the material was proprietary, web services were required to ensure that only authorized staff could access the information. This meant providing a web browser solution to manage who could access the different sections of the Refugee Library. This was achieved using web services written in C#.Net. An advanced "keyword" search engine was written in C++ so that all of the lawyers could locate the information they needed as easily as possible. This "Search Engine" provided a similar user interface to file servers of documents as Google provides to websites. The biggest challenge was to write a "Search Engine" that recognized both Microsoft and Adobe document content (as routines provided for searching documents do not search documents from Adobe and, equally, Adobe search tools do not go near Microsoft formats). Microsoft SQL Server 2005 was utilized and combined with filters from Adobe to achieve the objective. The resulting solution is extremely fast and much praised by users.

The volunteers wanted to contribute to the library, so a vetting process was implemented and managed by local "librarians" such that they could upload additional information to the Refugee Library. So that the local librarians in the many countries could customize the user interface to their own country standards, web services were implemented so that they could easily be called using web pages built using the Macromedia Dreamweaver toolkit. This has proved extremely successful. A Refugee Library in the U.K. now has over 40,000 web pages and several million documents. The task of allowing the lawyers to download information into their current cases was not easy to implement as the offices had anti-virus software and many security devices that prevented some of the documents from downloading easily. A MS-Windows solution was implemented that could identify itself to the central web services to provide the additional security necessary to overcome the network security in place.

The Case Law Library

This is the library of completed cases. It also acts as an archive for the local offices, which can be accessed by authorized UN staff. This mostly contains legal documents, but pertinent healthcare records are also retained. Forensic and psychosocial analysis form an intrinsic part of many Refugee records. Special care has to be taken over the care of "Minors." A strict and very secure envelope had to be built to ensure that the very sensitive case data relating to a client could never be accessed by unauthorized staff. As a case is completed, the process of merging all the information together was automated using the "Bundle Maker" (described later). The Case Law Library has the same fast "keyword" searching mechanism found in the Refugee Library. Users like this easy access mechanism and use it to find their way around their case notes.

The Case Management System

A Knowledge Management System needs to integrate with all the other applications in place. Central to all the activities of the lawyers is a "Case Management System." This records all the core client details, activities and events, produces "standard letters" and supports all the services that can be offered to clients. Existing "Case Management Solutions" were extremely inflexible and provided no scope for integration with KM solutions, and they do not cater for the healthcare side of client management. A full case management system was written that could interact with both local and global online libraries and KM solutions. To cater for change, web services were utilized as the key interface mechanism between all the components. The Case Management System provides for an extensive audit trail of who accessed what information and why. The Case Management system maintains a complete Case History for each client as well as a complete audit trail of every lawyer's activities.

The Bundle Maker

The business of preparing papers for presentation in court is very time-consuming, boring and labor intensive. A "bundle maker" was written to merge and consolidate all of the electronic documents that were to be presented in court. This was in fact a great challenge, since the preferred tool of the volunteers was Microsoft Word and it is quite difficult even for an advanced Microsoft Word user to merge documents such that they maintain their exact page formats. In addition, we had to create a master index and add additional sequential page numbers to every page so that individual pages could be referred to in court. This was made more difficult by the fact that some of the documents, which needed to be merged, were PDF and HTML files. We used Adobe to merge the documents and used a combination of Microsoft tools to add the additional page numbers.

The Interpreters Booking System

An additional module had to be incorporated to cater for the booking of interpreters, the monitoring of their work, their invoicing and payment. Since interpreters are paid either by the hour, or by the number of words they translate from the KM solution, tools were provided to verify the number of words translated. Since the interpreters live some distance from the offices, the system was integrated with the client and case worker diaries maintained by the case management system and generate email reminders and confirmation notes. Requests for translations directed to the interpreters were automated via email. The integration of email with any KM solution was much appreciated.

Summary

This project was very exciting for all the participants. The technical challenges to be overcome in order to implement this "global" KM solution were not inconsiderable. Indeed, even before starting, there was some doubt expressed as to whether it was possible to integrate local and remote databases, email and online libraries into a working solution. This project has proved that KM systems can indeed be very complicated and yet they can also be easy to maintain. For example, skilled IT staff are not easy to find in Egypt but the Cairo office of AMERA found that they were able to manage all the components with their limited resources. Since the initial implementation, the KM solution has advanced to add facilities to monitor the performance of all the volunteers and to further reduce the workload of the AMERA volunteers.

Future Work

AMERA currently stores all its information in the language of most of its volunteers. With the opening of offices in countries such as Thailand, Ecuador and the Far East, the organization is now seeing a demand for such a solution in multiple languages (requiring a Unicode solution to integrate documents in many languages). With the introduction of Unicode, further issues need to be addressed. When Unicode documents are sorted, the computers use a Unicode sorting sequence to retrieve the results of "keyword" searches, but this is not necessarily the order that users expect. Would you expect to see Mandarin documents before Arabic in a list of documents? If you naturally speak Mandarin you would want this, but if you are from the Middle East, perhaps you would like to see Arabic before Mandarin?

SOCIO-TECHNICAL ISSUES

The Impact of Technology

A diagram from Williams *et al.* (1993), reproduced in Figure 5.4, shows the major determinants of culture and illustrates that culture (the common attitudes, beliefs and values) results from the external environment, the systems, structure and technology of the organization and from the behavior of the work group. The external environment impacts on the organization's cultural behavior as variations such as legislation and politics place varying demands on the organization. This has an influence on the strategy of the organization and the systems and technology that are implemented. The recruitment of persons from a wide-ranging social, cultural and educational background will result in idiosyncratic behavior when these persons are placed in the organization.

Hofstede (1994) explains how the technology of an organization can impact on culture in terms of the *boundaries* of an organization, the degree of *differentiation* and *integration* of the technology. As Wiseman (1985) tells us, the changing nature of IT over the years has resulted

103

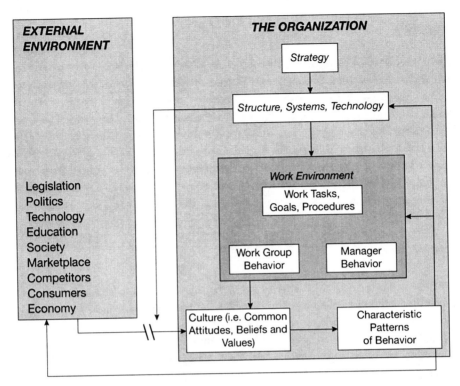

Figure 5.4 *Culture — The Organization and the External Environment.*

Source: Williams *et al.* (1993)

in three distinct conceptual models of IT (namely Data Processing, Management Information Systems and Strategic Information Systems), each model having a different effect on the organization–technology relationship.

Apart from Zmud (1984), there appears to be little evidence of research into the cultural aspects of the Business–Technology boundary of an organization. From Ward and Peppard (1995) we find a reference to an article in the *EDP Analyzer* (Organizing for the 1990s, Volume 24, No.1) that discusses the merits and demerits of various organizational structures and the varying skills required by IT managers. Little mention is made of the close relationship necessary between IT and business objectives. They go on to argue that Johnson's (1992) *Cultural Web* (reproduced in Figure 5.5) offers great insight to understanding the cultural aspects of the IT–Business relationship.

Figure 5.5, the *Cultural Web*, apes closely the reasoning behind the earlier diagram of the *Cultural Onion* and takes the view that while individuals in an organization may hold distinct attitudes, beliefs and values from their colleagues, each set of attitudes, beliefs and values is nevertheless held at the core of the organization (the Paradigm circle in the *Cultural Web*).

Ward and Peppard (1995) go on to suggest that the IT and business aspects to a business are two distinct paradigms and, furthermore, because of these respective paradigms: ". . . each creates a relatively homogeneous approach to the interpretation of the complexity that the organization faces" (p. 18). The perception of Johnson (1992) is that the paradigm (in our case,

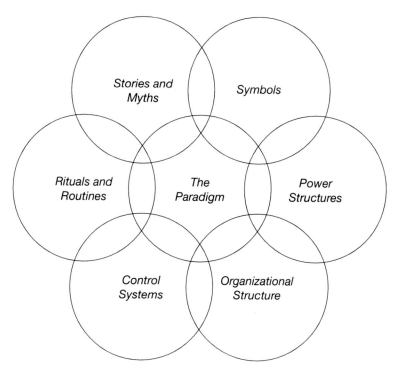

Figure 5.5 *The Cultural Web.*

Source: Johnson (1992)

either the Business or IT paradigm) is surrounded by six components through which core attitudes, beliefs and values are communicated:

1   *Stories and Myths*—almost part of an organization's folklore and includes tales that employees relate to new employees warning them of past failures/consequences and the fate of maverick recruits.
2   *Symbols*—includes such aspects as dress codes, job titles, executives' cars and *de rigueur* attitudes such as addressing directors as "Sir."
3   *Rituals and Routines*—range from director's signing requisitions to required attendance at weekly board meetings. No real business advantage may be gained by carrying out these duties, but they all encompass rituals that may have historical relevance to the organization.
4   *Control Systems*—pay and reward systems and the managerial hierarchy serve as examples of control systems that monitor performance.
5   *Organizational Structures*—hierarchical structures and product or service-based business units are examples of organizational structures. This includes the position of the IT organization relative to the position of the Business organization.
6   *Power Structures*—are often an indicator of where the major organizational influence is and is often the main target for any change programs. A common difficulty is when the main personnel targets for change are also those who hold the power.

The growth of IT, and society's increasing dependence upon it, has been both prolific and extensive. As more and more technology found, and continues to find, its way into the commercial environment, several researchers confirmed that organizational structures and cultures altered to reflect the changing circumstances and to exploit the competitive advantages from increased efficiency and effectiveness (Bessant and Cole, 1985; Johnston and Vitale, 1988; Laver, 1989; Boddy and Gunson, 1996).

The technical steps have been summarized in various sources (e.g. Bali, 1999) in order to highlight the major developments that have taken place in computing. This historical perspective is useful for providing insights into the *causes* behind technical changes and also the *effects* of the changes, in organizational and commercial terms, brought about. Additionally, the question of whether these developments were as a result of direct pressure from increasingly complex business environments, for example managers wanting more pertinent information, has been included.

New methodological and business processes have necessitated the use of new and novel ways of working. Human attitudes to the new computing technology (Human Computer Interaction—HCI) have been of prime importance. The position occupied by technology in organizations throughout the years has depended on the commercial aspirations of the organization and also the industry in which the organization operated. The review has shown that computers have been used to facilitate and disseminate innovation in organizations. A simplistic SWOT (Strengths, Weaknesses, Opportunities, Threats) analysis would reveal the benefits, together with relative weaknesses, of IT at each key chronological stage outlined.

Some of the more major evolutionary steps of IT took place in the 1950s, with the U.S. leading the global transformation from the industrial to the information age. The acceptability, however, of the ongoing changes was far from unanimous. A study conducted at that time by Garrity and Barnes (1968) indicated that only nine out of twenty-seven installations surveyed covered their initial operating costs. However, progress was being made on other aspects of the new technology and as cost, performance and potential usage of the technology improved, acceptability began to replace the initial skepticism. According to Schultheis and Sumner (1995), IT implementations in organizations occur for the following reasons (either individually or in combination):

- *To improve efficiency*—the execution of tasks *correctly*. Generally this refers to the automation of routine paper-based tasks. An example would be using IT to process hundreds of works orders per day.
- *To improve effectiveness*—executing the *right* tasks. Using a computer database to select likely prospects for a marketing campaign would be an example of using IT effectively.
- *To bring about transformation*—changing the *manner* in which the business is executed. By way of example, diversifying the business, via the strategic use of IT, to provide goods or services distinct to those originally provided.

Mintzberg (1989) set out to order the literature on organizational structuring and to extract its key messages and to synthesize these into an integrated picture of the structuring of organizations. According to him, an organization's structure consists of a highly specialized and skilled operating core, taking the form of individuals under a professional and regulatory body, confirmed by Handy (1985). Anthony (1965) substantiates by offering several schematics

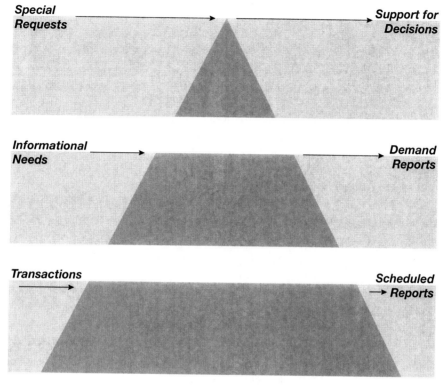

Figure 5.6 *Activities and Framework for an Organization's IS Requirements.*
Source: adapted from Anthony (1965)

depicting the three kinds of activity of an organization, together with the typical managerial layers and functions affected:

- *Operational planning* (the day-to-day activities of the organization and where first-line managers collect data, results and events).
- *Tactical planning* (where operational activities are reviewed and appraised by middle managers in order to ensure their adherence to pre-set targets and goals).
- *Strategic planning* (usually carried out by the top-layer of management, where data and information from the operational and tactical planning stages is used to set the organization's long-term agenda).

For reasons of brevity and clarity, we have adapted and combined two of his diagrams as shown in Figure 5.6. This diagram shows the need for computer-based, pertinent information systems that would be of strategic interest to managers, particularly in the form of Management Information Systems (MIS). As Schultheis and Sumner (1995) explain, the fast-moving strategies in modern organizations leading to the increasing needs of IT have clouded the area of MIS to the extent where, as Lucey (1991) says, there is ". . . no universally accepted definition of a MIS and those that exist reflect the emphasis of the particular writer" (p. 1).

Despite this, Lucey (1991) attempts to put forward a definition of a Management Information System as an ". . . integrated structure of databases and information flows over all levels and components of an organization whereby the collection, transfer and presentation of information is optimized to meet the needs of the organization" (p. 2); while Long (1989) is of the opinion that a MIS is more of a ". . . system to convert data from internal and external sources into information and to communicate that information . . . to managers at all levels in all functions to enable them to make timely and effective decisions" (p. 547).

For the purposes of this book, we have decided to put forward, as an acceptable definition of a MIS, the most contemporary description as given by Licker (1997): ". . . an integrated user+machine system that provides information to support operations, management analysis and decision-making functions in an organization" (p. 5).

The integration of IT, Management Information Systems, information flows and management is best typified by the schematic (Figure 5.7) given by Lucas (1990). Although we would agree with all of the definitions given in this section, we would suggest that, in a commercial environment (and for the layman), the purpose of IT for organizations is to provide the *right* information at the *right* time. It should be noted that this is particularly relevant for KM-based initiatives. The "value-chain," dividing an organization into *value activities* (distinct activities— such as order processing, advertising, marketing—necessary in order to carry out day-to-day business), confirms our current, and increasing, reliance on information.

However, Scott-Morton (1995) reports that Information Systems only became computer-based after the accepted advent of IT systems. Before this, information would have been paper-based, by the use of filing cabinets. Earl (1989) confirms the organization-wide impact

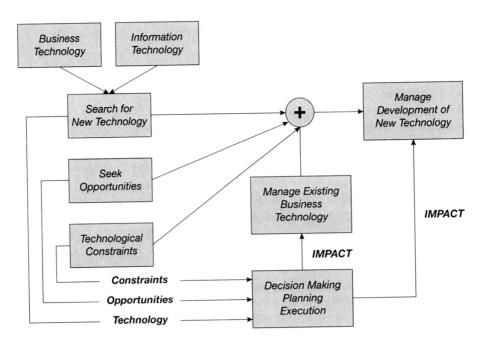

Figure 5.7 *The integration of MIS and management.*
Source: Lucas (1990)

and importance of IT given the increasing importance of the information created and used (Porter, 1985) by that organization. This ties in with the inherent structure of the organization in question.

EVOLUTION OF KNOWLEDGE MANAGEMENT SYSTEMS

The discussions on MIS given earlier are not meant to be merely tangential. Evolution within the IT industry as well as the progression of contemporary business meant that change was, and remains, inevitable. Some argue that KM is a relatively new form of MIS and decision making (Reference for Business, 2008) but this is a very simplistic as well as unrealistic perspective. Spender (1996) argues that confusion arises as we do not always have a clear idea of the significant differences between IT and KM. We prefer to argue the case of Gray and Meister (2003), who state that MIS differs from IT in its attention to the people and social systems into which computing systems are projected; it is this aspect that may make MIS and KM to appear similar. The following schematic (provided earlier in the book) may aid understanding.

The schematic attempts to portray the importance of three essential elements for the presence of knowledge (people, process and technology). The initial arguments for the adoption of MIS followed this same logic, often necessitating cultural and organizational (process) change for successful deployment (Bali, 1999). We would submit that the schematic successfully mirrors our contemporary work environment. The socio-technical nature of contemporary human-machine interaction is evident, even during an action as simple as surfing the web. Coakes' (2002) work defines the socio-technical approach as ". . . the study of the relationships and interrelationships between the social and technical parts of any system" (p. 5).

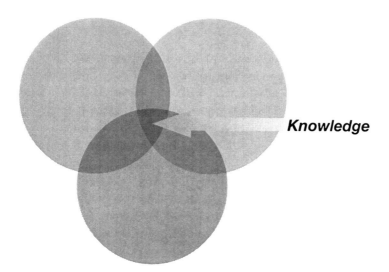

Figure 5.8 *Knowledge: Intersection of People, Process and Technology.*

Reproduced with kind permission of Doctrina Applied Research and Consulting LLC—www.consultdoctrina.com

The notion of a Knowledge Management System (KMS) often appears to fall between two stalls. Alavi and Leidner (2001) argue that KMS was "developed to support and enhance the organizational knowledge processes of knowledge creation, storage, retrieval, transfer and application" (p. 114). This perspective is detailed by Gupta and Sharma (2004) who state that "knowledge management systems are divided into several major categories, as follows: groupware, including e-mail, e-log, and wikis; decision support systems; expert systems; document management systems; semantic networks; relational and object oriented databases; simulation tools; and artificial intelligence."

While there is nothing inherently wrong with these viewpoints, one must bear in mind that knowledge-creating activities (perhaps including creativity) "take place within and between humans" (Davenport and Prusak, 1998). Combining these opinions gives us the necessary human-centric and technology-based (socio-technical) components for our schematic.

"DOUBLE LOOP" LEARNING

We described earlier the notion and importance of the learning organization to contemporary KM initiatives. The true value of any and all knowledge that resides within, lies not through mere ownership but, rather, through effective communication and dissemination methods. After all, what use is knowledge if no one can make effective use of it?

Hence, the ability to both learn and share knowledge (within the learning organization) is of paramount importance, particularly the capability and capacity of the organization to respond to internal and external demands. Senge (1992) commented on the inextricable link between individual and entity learning by stating that:

> Organizations only learn through individuals who learn. Individual learning does not guarantee organizational learning but without it no organizational learning occurs.
>
> (Senge, 1992: 139)

If we assume that learning constantly evolves within organizations—and the true value of any worthwhile knowledge lies in its contemporary application or "freshness"—then iterative knowledge is required. When an individual learns within the organization, it is imperative that this knowledge is both retained and assimilated within the organization.

Argyris and Schön (1978) developed approaches that were intended to assist organizational learning, and they distinguished single loop from double loop learning. Single loop learning involves the modification of behavior based on expectations when compared with outcomes. Double loop learning involves the questioning of values and assumptions that led to the initial behavior. Thus, double loop learning would be considered as critical in its nature, and it is about learning about single loop learning. A further development is triple loop learning (see for example Flood and Romm, 1996), in which there is learning about the learning about single loop learning.

Learning incorporates the concepts of tacit and explicit knowledge (Polanyi, 1967). These concepts were developed by Nonaka and Takeuchi (1995) as a spiral model of organizational learning that comprises four stages. Explicit knowledge may be codified, systematic, formal and easily communicated. Tacit knowledge is personal, context specific and difficult to communicate. One of the difficulties is that our world views are not always explicit to ourselves, so communicating some of these things to others poses huge challenges. If the tacit knowledge of people within an organization can be made explicit, this is known as externalization. Such knowledge might be translated into manuals or incorporated into new products and processes. Internalization is the process of taking explicit knowledge and using it to develop tacit knowledge. Socialization is the process of sharing tacit knowledge, while combination is about the dissemination of codified knowledge. This model considers the processes as part of a continual spiral.

Managers often rely on what is known as narrative knowledge or experiential knowledge, which is to do with a history of practice within organizations. Such knowledge is invaluable, but cannot easily (if at all) be tabulated or codified in a form that would be familiar to a physical scientist, such as a chemist. There is no formula. There are guidelines and "rules of thumb," but using the same approach in a similar situation to one that had been successfully addressed previously may not achieve the same result.

Organizational learning must be more than simply adding together the learning of individuals within an organization. A learning organization extends the concept of organizational learning. While organizational learning may occur in any organization, a learning organization is one that actively supports and helps create knowledge capture and transfer. In this context, mistakes are perceived as opportunities to learn, rather than opportunities to cast blame. It is therefore interactions between individuals and the culture they create that fosters organizational learning. The more this is actively and explicitly facilitated, the more the concept of the learning organization is manifested.

Capturing individual knowledge assists in developing organizational learning. This may be by means of talking with others, publications, reports, training sessions, presentations, intranet and internet postings, video conferencing or any other means that enables knowledge to be accessed. Ideally, knowledge needs to be organized in forms that provide ease of access and ease of understanding. It can include storage in knowledge repositories, databases and libraries. Knowledge transfer in today's digital world typically involves browsers, search engines and the use of available technology. It is important not to confuse the technology with the transfer of knowledge. The former is simply a tool in the process.

Learning to learn is key for individuals, groups and organizations. If an individual gains knowledge, it is available for their immediate use, but to share that knowledge with others and to share how the knowledge was gained, requires systematic and systemic processes to help create, capture, transfer and assess knowledge. Considering culture is vital in this, considering technology is also helpful.

Linked to the foregoing discussions, the term "knowledge organization" is used to describe a situation in which people use systems and processes to create, manage and use knowledge-based products and services to achieve organizational goals. A knowledge organization learns from the past and adapts to sustain competitive advantage. From organizational learning, knowledge organizations have collective intelligence. Objects, data, information and knowledge are generated by knowledge workers, with content captured, organized and stored, preserved to enable its reuse and leveraging by people and groups other than those who generated it.

This requires an infrastructure to enable sharing of content across all elements of an organization and even with customers and suppliers. In addition, process needs to exist to integrate content from multiple sources and utilize it to achieve organizational goals. A learning culture will help promote both individual learning and shared understanding, and will facilitate the organization to deal with continual change.

To achieve true (and valuable) iterative knowledge, double loop learning encompasses both experimentation and feedback. If the learning organization's culture is strong, new behaviors can be instilled which embrace learning. Argyris (1991) provides an excellent analogy to distinguish between single and double loop learning:

> To give a simple analogy: a thermostat that automatically turns on the heat whenever the temperature in the room drops below 68 degrees is a good example of single loop learning. A thermostat that could ask "Why am I set at 68 degrees?" and then explore whether or not some other temperature might more economically achieve the goal of heating the room would be engaging in double loop learning.
>
> (Argyris, 1991: 100)

The schematic (Figure 5.9) depicts the concept of single, double (and even triple) loop learning.

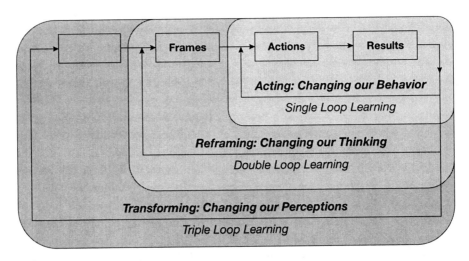

Figure 5.9 *Single, Double and Triple Loop Learning.*

Reproduced with kind permission of Doctrina Applied Research and Consulting LLC—www.consultdoctrina.com

CASE EXERCISE: A KNOWLEDGE-BASED HEALTHCARE RESOURCE BALANCING SYSTEM[10]

by Aapo Immonen

Introduction

IT has enabled new possibilities in providing and distributing public services, which includes the renewal of processes in the healthcare sector. Consideration of patient requirements remains of the highest importance when improving the quality and cost-effectiveness of healthcare services. State-of-the art eHealth applications, electronic patient records and secure broadband networks will improve the quality of delivered healthcare services equally, regardless of distance between the healthcare provider and the patient. Several countries within the EU have become robust in the specific area of health informatics, combining challenging research and educational activities with active development work involving small and medium-sized enterprises (SMEs) and healthcare professionals.

Ongoing research, led by a consortium of EU-based partners (the U.K., Finland and Germany), has the ability to generate new, innovative and user-friendly eHealth applications, monitoring and diagnostic devices to support the distribution of healthcare in a new holistic way. One of the specific regional characteristics of the Finnish partners in this consortium is the sparse population in a large geographical area. This aspect, in conjunction with increasing healthcare costs and the growing problem of healthcare professionals emigrating, creates a conflict between the legislation that defines equal healthcare services to all citizens. It has led to a situation where healthcare policy makers, researchers and healthcare professionals have been compelled to deliver healthcare services using new, even radical, methods.

The primary aim of these facts led us to postulate the efficacy of a secure, usable and effective clinical information network for the development of a suitable grid methodology to support humanitarian aid work. The basis for the work are open standards, interoperability and reliability with the aim of the wide exploitation of grid networking technology to ensure that industry, governments and citizens make the best use of ICT in order to improve industrial competitiveness, support growth and the creation of jobs, as well as aiming to address key societal challenges.

The hypothesis of the work is based on the conception that special healthcare services can be provided equally to developing countries alike in industrial countries. By utilizing new information and communication technology it is possible to distribute and deliver the best knowledge available provided by different specialists acting in the healthcare sector. This proposed approach can be seen as a generic model for the existing phenomena to provide humanitarian aid. Medical imaging has been chosen as a specific special healthcare sector in order to validate the new service model. The work aims to provide proven evidence of the best ways for humanitarian aid organizations to utilize grid methods to support the operative work. This work for humanitarian organizations, besides its high necessity for mankind, will prefigure what could be deployed in Europe for daily clinical practice.

Aims

This research aims to generate well-defined and theoretically proven methods and guidelines to utilize GRID methods in supporting humanitarian aid work. The conclusion will mainly deal with the following issues: impact, feasibility and validation of the new service model. The research will face the upcoming challenges of interoperability from the service oriented architecture point of view. The outcomes of the work will generate research results to support a new clinical services model based on the knowledge generated out of the interface layer, application layer, security layer and GRID layer. These outcomes will be measured by technical and usability studies in order to provide evidence of the efficacy and effectiveness of resource balancing of medical experts, information sharing as well as sharing archiving capacity to support humanitarian aid. Humanitarian aid organizations can utilize a new holistic way of providing healthcare service to areas most in need, which will fabricate new organization models in the context of grid and data-based infrastructure. This strives to produce added value, quality and cost-efficiency for the healthcare sector.

Objectives

The objective is to co-ordinate and support research activities in order to establish a secure infrastructure-based service. This service would ultimately aim to:

- overcome the lack of qualified healthcare specialists;
- establish trustworthy cross-border data transmission;
- improve patient treatment and optimize existing healthcare resources;
- use existing healthcare resources for humanitarian aid purposes; and
- provide a powerful tool for the development of expert databases relating to specific disease areas particularly for rare disorders, where clinical data sharing will expand and enhance knowledge relating to diagnosis and treatment.

This research will further investigate grid techniques to enable the effective management of resources across different time zones, and the availability of healthcare personnel for rapid diagnosis in large scale incidences. The combination of increased critical mass of clinical data in particular disease areas, and the use of new intelligent prognostic techniques, will potentially lead to improved diagnosis and increased quality of care.

The chief outcome from research will be an increase in the quality and efficiency of humanitarian healthcare delivery through the secure outsourcing of clinical data. Other outcomes include the definition and dissemination of the necessary organizational and technological changes required to deliver these improvements, with a view to continually extending the technology to include an increasing range of clinical applications. These outcomes are envisaged in order to provide a high-profile focus that can bring together the various multidisciplinary aspects of work. The results would also raise the profile of new ways of working for organizations in the field of providing humanitarian aid and inform the end users of issues concerning secure, cross-border and cross-cultural transfer of clinical knowledge (and bring interdisciplinary expertise to bear upon key and fundamental issues), as well as developing a deeper understanding of the efficacy of using ICTs in clinical and healthcare environments and to learn from previous experiences.

The study would also enable the provision of evidence for a high-quality and equitable method of clinical knowledge exchange supported by ICT. Additionally, the outcomes would include the production of a summary of relevant technical standards within a legal and ethical framework with due consideration to privacy and confidentiality issues, as well as develop organizational standards and protocols for the clinical sector.

The Technologies

The research will adopt a four pillar research and governance strategy: (1) interoperability; (2) legal and ethical issues; (3) research and KM; and (4) service-oriented architecture. This strategy will be underpinned by four project instruments: (1) interface layer; (2) security layer; (3) applications layer; and (4) grid layer. The combined output of these instruments generates knowledge. Monitoring and evaluation will be carried out by three metrics: (1) impact; (2) feasibility; and (3) validation.

By creating a secure information society, the development of eHealth and the usability of health informatics will increase. The aim is to provide a higher quality of healthcare in a more efficient way. The objective is to follow previously disseminated EU objectives and provide a demonstration and testing environment to:

- improve the quality of life;
- ensure interoperable digital rights;
- ensure management of patient data in a secure information society; and
- introduce actions to overcome the geographic and social digital divide among all citizens.

Once an environment of trust has been created, cross-border patient data transmission will allow consultation from one region to the other. This will enable the balancing of medical resources, and could be applied, for example, in the consultation of MRI images.

Medical Imaging and Resource Balancing

The research would foster the possibilities of a new GRID-based service model to support the distribution of healthcare services more efficiently and more equally than before. The goal is to combine GRID methods, Information Security Management Systems, medical applications and a network of experts to become one holistic entity. The model will support distribution of healthcare services in a new way, supporting and consolidating humanitarian work.

The target and objectives is to study the usability and effectiveness of GRID technology within the global healthcare service. The objective of the research is to study the usability and effectiveness of the theoretical model as well as validate the state-of-the-art technology from the humanitarian aid point of view. The research will be carried out by using the existing networks, ensuring that the model will match up with existing standards and guidelines and by end-users rating the model. From the Information Security Management Systems point of view in medical applications, the goal is to understand the demands of privacy and fulfill confidentiality (by way of authorization, strong authentication, role-based access controls and identity management).

The core of the method is the GRID resource broker with the real-time balancing and allocation of resources, which will knit together the separate partners into a network of trust. This model will enable more effective management of resources across different time zones. At the same time, the expectation is that the data collected from the field will be archived in a structured manner in order to get the maximum benefits out of the information from the research and educational point of view. The sharing of resources is not primarily file exchanges but rather direct access to databases, software, professional resources, as required by a range of emerging collaborative problem-solving and resource brokering strategies. This sharing is necessarily highly controlled, with resource providers and rules defining clearly and carefully what is shared, who is allowed to share and the conditions under which sharing occurs.

The second goal examines the imbalance between clinical demands and available resources in a crisis situation. Historically, the healthcare sector has been unable to effectively address the imbalance; however, with modern ICT (Information and Communication Technologies) systems, it is possible to share expert knowledge, use sophisticated data manipulation software, archive data in servers and share information (and storage capacity) across geographical borders in a secure internet environment. Within future initiatives, we will be seeking to investigate other areas of healthcare where this model may be applied.

Future Work

The future initiatives will seek to investigate other potential areas of healthcare where this model may be applied. One option under consideration is the use of digital pen and PDA technology to encourage increased reporting of clinical/anesthetic outcomes and adverse incidents. Project objectives include improving healthcare risk management and achieving consistent clinical outcomes based on improved reporting methods. A successful pilot has been conducted in Australia, creating an opportunity for technology transfer to the U.K. and Finland to evaluate and improve the product. This involvement would expose the technology to a wider professional audience and different healthcare systems, with a strong emphasis on usability and effectiveness. Other potential application areas include the mapping of drug trial patients and development of healthcare search engines.

TRENDS IN HEALTHCARE

Healthcare has been shaped by each nation's own set of cultures, traditions, payment mechanisms and patient expectations. Given the common problem facing healthcare globally, i.e. exponentially increasing costs, no matter which particular health system one examines, the future of the healthcare industry will be shaped by commonalities based on this key unifying problem and the common solution; namely, the embracing of new technologies to stem escalating costs and improve quality healthcare delivery. Currently, the key future trends that will perhaps significantly impact healthcare include:

■ empowered consumers;
■ e-health adaptability; and
■ a shift to focus on healthcare prevention.

Key implications of these future trends include:

■ health insurance changes;
■ workforce changes as well as changes in the roles of stakeholders within the health system;
■ organizational changes and standardization; and
■ the need for healthcare delivery organizations and administrators to make difficult choices regarding practice management.

(Wickramasinghe, 2000)

In order to be well positioned to meet and manage these challenges within the U.S. and elsewhere in the world, healthcare organizations are turning to KM techniques and technologies (Bali *et al.*, 2005; Quinn *et al.*, 2005; Baskaran *et al.*, 2006). Thus, as the role of KM in healthcare increases in importance, it becomes crucial to understand the process of adoption and implementation of KM systems.

CONCEPTUALIZING KNOWLEDGE WITHIN HEALTHCARE

Knowledge is a critical resource in any organization and is also crucial in the provision of healthcare. Access to the latest medical research knowledge is often the difference between life and death, between accurate or erroneous diagnosis, and between early intervention or a prolonged and costly hospital stay.

KM deals with the process of creating value from an organization's intangible assets (Wickramasinghe and Mills, 2001; Edwards *et al.*, 2005). It is an amalgamation of concepts borrowed from the artificial intelligence/knowledge based systems, software engineering, BPR (business process re-engineering), human resources management and organizational behavior (Purvis *et al.*, 2001). KM deals with conceptualization, review, consolidation and action phases of creating, securing, storing, combing, co-ordinating and retrieving knowledge. In essence, then, KM is a process by which organizations collect, preserve and utilize what their employees and members know about their jobs and about activities and procedures in their organization (Xu and Quaddus, 2005).

KM is a still relatively new phenomenon and a somewhat nebulous topic that needs to be explored. However, organizations in all industries, both large and small, are racing to integrate this new management tool into their infrastructure. KM caters to the critical issues of organizational adaptation, survival and competence in the face of increasingly discontinuous environmental change (Rubenstein and Geisler, 2003). Essentially, it embodies organizational processes that seek synergistic combination of data and information processing capacity of information technologies, and the creative and innovative capacity of human beings.

The KM system is extremely helpful in internal and external sectors of an organization. Internally, KM is designed to enhance the maintenance and organization of the databases. Externally, it aims to make a better impact on the customer and external partners. The healthcare sector is characterized by its diversity and the distributiveness of its component organizations. There is a continuous process of generation of knowledge within each of these components (such as providers, patients, suppliers, payers and regulators), as well as an immense volume of knowledge created at the interfaces among these organizations (Jadad *et al.*, 2000; Pavia, 2001).

Healthcare provider organizations are special types of organizations in that they are for the most part motivated by topics such as quality and service, but without the profit drivers that animate private industry. At the same time they are highly professional institutions, populated by people with specialized knowledge that needs to be constantly updated, shared and leveraged (van Beveren, 2003). This phenomenon creates even more pressure on healthcare providers and others in the sector to manage the knowledge that flows through the sector.

The role of KM in healthcare organizations would be important in both clinical and administrative practices. Clinical care would be much more effective with increased sharing of medical knowledge and "evidence-based" experience within and among healthcare delivery organizations (Nykanen and Karimaa, 2006). Administrative practices in healthcare organizations will benefit from the systemic interfaces of knowledge about technology, costs, "best-practices," efficiencies and the value of co-operation. Such effects of knowledge creation and sharing would make it easier and more effective to manage the healthcare organization.

Finally, the role of KM is especially crucial in the interface between the clinical and administrative functions. By and large these two categories of activities are separated by differentiations such as professional specializations, role in the organization, and goals and standards of practice. Hence, there is a tendency to avoid sharing knowledge and exchanging experience-based lessons so as not to upset the existing balance of power of the organization.

WORKED EXAMPLE: PERSONALIZED HEALTHCARE

As KM deals with the tacit and contextual aspects of information, it allows an organization to know what is important for it in particular circumstances, in the process maximizing the value of that information and creating competitive advantages and wealth. A KM solution would allow healthcare institutions to give clinical data context, so as to allow knowledge derivation for more effective clinical diagnoses. KM can enable the healthcare sector to successfully overcome the information and knowledge explosion, made possible by adopting a KM framework that is specially customized in light of their ICT implementation level.

Personalized healthcare (which includes such items as smart wearable and implantable systems) has come about mainly because of the public's desire to become more active in their healthcare decisions and well-being. Healthcare providers are exploring new ways of delivering care that are tailored to each person's unique needs. In order for personalized healthcare to become a reality, we need to consider several necessary components. These include inputs from healthcare professionals, regulations and standards, perspectives from the general public and views from fashion clothing manufacturers. These seemingly disparate inputs can be conceptualized in Figure 5.10.

This schematic, which we have termed the "carpet tile" approach, sees eight essential concepts ("tiles"), each one of which revolves a central concept of KM. In this conceptualization, we view KM as being both the central tenet as well as the "glue" that holds personalized healthcare together. A critical success factor would include the development of a logical design

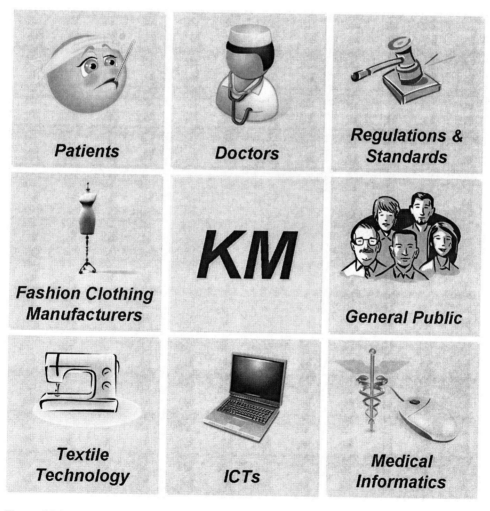

Figure 5.10 The "carpet tile" conceptualization.

Source: Wickramasinghe and Bali (2008)

that supported the ubiquitous transfer of pertinent information and germane knowledge to aid the decision maker. Without such a knowledge architecture in place, the automation of any (and all) information would very rapidly create information overload and result in chaos. In this example, we would advocate following a systems-based approach and would develop a gestalt perspective to ensure that the whole was indeed greater than the sum of the parts.

Gödel's theorem tells us that, in order to find a solution within a system, one must look outside the system. We contend that KM provides the solution to the current and prospective challenges for personalized healthcare as it provides the tools, techniques and strategies to facilitate the necessary paradigm shift for making our healthcare system truly functional in the twenty-first century. We acknowledge that the "carpet tile" analogy may be overly simplistic to conceptualize the varied and various challenges for contemporary healthcare institutions. In Chapter 7, we discuss in greater detail the fact that critical technologies for supporting healthcare (network-centric) operations are not new, but rather reconfigurations of existing technologies including web and internet technologies. We introduce a "healthcare information grid" that consists of distinct domains, each made up of multiple, interconnected grids to enable complete and seamless information and data exchange throughout the system.

The 3D (three dimensional) nature of the "healthcare information grid" is perhaps a better way to examine ICT-enabled and knowledge-based healthcare. The resulting 3D "Healthcare

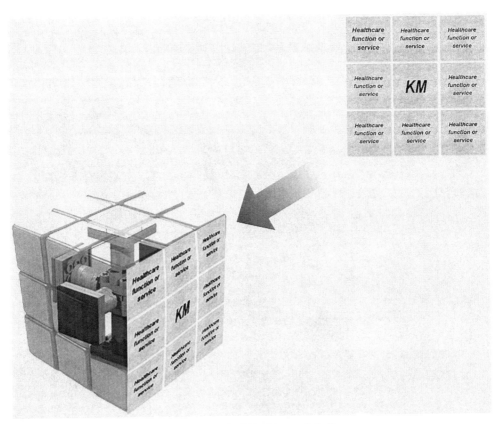

Figure 5.11 *Mapping the Carpet Tile onto the "Healthcare Cube".*

Reproduced with kind permission of Doctrina Applied Research and Consulting LLC—www.consultdoctrina.com

Cube" is not wholly unlike a *Rubik's Cube*. The central pivot mechanism within the Cube (visible in Figure 5.11) enables each face to turn. As healthcare processes evolve, the Healthcare Cube can be adjusted to meet new requirements.

Figure 5.11 depicts how the "carpet tile" can be mapped onto one face of the Healthcare Cube. For clarity, only one of the faces has been mapped; it is entirely possible that the remaining faces could also be mapped with additional healthcare services and functions. To conclude the analogy, the central pivot mechanism represents "KM" and is what holds contemporary healthcare together as well as enabling seemingly disparate healthcare services and functions to interact in a seamless and continuous manner.

CONCLUSIONS

This chapter has concentrated on the organizational issues of KM. The importance of the organization and its culture have been described in detail as successful organization-wide KM implementation depends on the correct culture being in place. The concept of the learning organization (LO) is of paramount importance to those organizations claiming to be knowledge-empowered.

SUMMARY

This chapter introduced the concept of the learning organization (LO) and the importance of this concept to contemporary KM. The importance of organizational culture and how this relates to both the learning organization and contemporary KMt was described. The socio-technical issues around KM were also introduced.

REVIEW QUESTIONS

1 What is a Learning Organization?

2 Describe Senge's five disciplines.

3 What is organizational culture?

4 What is double loop learning?

DISCUSSION QUESTIONS

1 Why is an organization's culture so important when incorporating KM?

2 Why can it be so hard to achieve an effective organizational culture?

CASE EXERCISE: KM FOR URBAN HEALTH

Key Concepts in Urban Health

For the better part of the twentieth century, and now into the twenty-first century, the U.S. has been recognized as having one of the world's leading healthcare systems in terms of its use of leading edge techniques, technologies and application of latest medical findings to healthcare delivery (Starr, 1982; Kongstvedt, 1994). Looking at the miraculous cures, incredible surgical feats, control of infectious disease and other aspects of American medicine, it is difficult to dispute the claim. But there is another story when one looks at the health of the nation's urban poor. The healthcare system in the U.S. seems to hardly touch many of the most vulnerable individuals and communities. Additionally, when medical care is delivered, it is often inadequate to meet the complex health, social, economic, educational and environmental needs of inner-city urban residents.

The paradox of the modern American medical system is that, although it has an unparalleled capacity to treat and repair (particularly with regard to trauma and infectious disease), it is often ill-prepared to prevent illness, especially within the complex context of the urban environment. Although this contradiction has implications for the entire American population, its impact is greatest for those with the fewest resources, including the urban poor. For inner-city residents who often live close to large academic health centers, the paradox is all the more acute. Even though the "best care in the world" may literally be right next door, poor urban residents experience some of the worst health conditions, live in some of the least-healthy environments, and have some of the worst health indices of any population group in the nation—in some instances comparable to those found in developing nations.

It is important to stress that such problems are not restricted to the U.S. as the issues are replicated in countries throughout the world. Quality care of patients requires the evaluation of considerable amounts of data at the right time and right place and in the correct context. These clinical, administrative and operational sources of data are typically kept in separate and disparate operational repositories. With the advent of the electronic health record, these data warehouses will provide data and information at the point of care and provide for a continuous learning environment in which lessons learned can provide updates to clinical, administrative and financial processes. What becomes critical in such a context is the identification of relevant data, pertinent information and germane knowledge to support rapid and superior healthcare decision making. Given the advancement of the information tools and techniques of today's knowledge economy, it is imperative that these tools and techniques be appropriately utilized to enable and facilitate the identification and evaluation of these knowledge assets. To do this effectively and efficiently it is imperative that healthcare incorporates the principles of KM.

Several features of the urban environment distinguish it in character or degree from other settings. These differences constitute the foundation for a consideration of those elements of teaching about urban health that are distinct from teaching about health in general. These include complexity, diversity, economies of scale, contextual factors and unique organizational and political requirements. Also it is clear that several features of life and living exist on a rural–urban continuum. These differences may be qualitative, quantitative or both. Attempting to understand the *interrelationships* between factors and the mechanisms by which these factors impact each other and health may enhance our understanding of health in the urban environment. The major factors impacting the health of urban populations are outlined here.

Economics

The association between higher levels of economic resources and more optimal health is widely documented and economic aspects of local areas have been among the most frequently analyzed contextual factors with regard to mortality and other outcomes. Significant associations have been shown between health status and community economic characteristics, including income and inequality in income distribution, wealth and poverty, and the geographic concentration of poverty (Hillemeier et al., 2003). Generally the associations are linear and positive in the case of income and wealth while inverse in the case of income inequality and poverty.

Stress and Health

Stress has short-term and long-term effects on the body. Given the right balance of factors the effect is positive. It is beginning to be realized that social and psychological circumstances may damage health over the long term (Wilkinson, 1996; Marmot and Wilkinson, 2006). Chronic anxiety, insecurity and social isolation appear to undermine health (Marmot and Wilkinson, 2006). The ability of psychological factors such as stress to affect health is biologically plausible (Berkman and Kawachi, 2000). The excessive or prolonged activation of biologic stress responses within the body may enhance the risk of depression, diabetes, high blood pressure, heart attack and increase disease susceptibility (Marmot and Wilkinson, 2006). The poor and minorities are at increased risk for many of these health problems. The clustering and accumulation of psychological disadvantage, perhaps beginning as early as childhood, is being investigated as a potential contributor to these disparities (Marmot, 1986; Marmot et al., 1997; Marmot and Wilkinson, 2006).

Early Life Experiences and the Life Course

Social experiences can exert a significant effect on health from in utero development of the fetus through infancy and childhood. At discrete points early in embryological development of the fetus unique periods of time exist, in which an insult could exert detrimental effects that evidence themselves at some point later in the process of growth and development (Marmot and Wilkinson; 2006). As such, the origins of adult health and health inequity may begin in early childhood and perhaps even prior to birth. It has been estimated that over 200 million children worldwide are not reaching their development potential (WHO Commission, 2007). A child's early environment has a vital impact on the way the brain develops. The more stimulating the environment, the more connections are formed in the brain and the better the child thrives in all aspects of life: physical development, emotional and social development, and the ability to express himself or herself and acquire knowledge. While physical health and nutrition are important, a young child needs to spend their time in caring, responsive environments that protect from inappropriate disapproval and punishment. Children need opportunities to explore their world, to play and to learn how to speak and listen to others (WHO Commission, 2007). Discreet poor adult health consequences that have been associated with poor growth and development in early life include high blood pressure, cardiovascular disease and diabetes (Cheung et al., 2000; Miura et al., 2001; Smith et al., 2001) and breast cancer (De Stavola et al., 2004).

Education and Literacy

One key factor that may mitigate adverse child development is education. Education and the associated high social standing in adult life may protect against health-damaging early life exposures. It is possible that inadequate education plays a key role in generating health inequities because it has a profound influence on income, employment status and living conditions (WHO Commission, 2007). The importance of education is not limited to primary education nor to low-income countries. A key measure of social stratification is education. The influence of education on health is seen not only as a difference between those with some and those with none but it is a gradient that runs to the highest level (WHO Commission, 2007).

Many health literacy studies rely on the number of school years completed as the sole measure of literacy (Baker, 1999). However, many factors including language proficiency and age are associated with health literacy. Measuring the number of years of school measures education completed. Health literacy, on the other hand, reflects what was learned during those years and an individual's ability to comprehend new material (Baker, 1999). Individuals with low literacy skills have poorer health, higher rates of hospitalizations, and incur higher healthcare costs than those patients with adequate literacy. Finally, in the U.S. low literacy is more frequent among persons of lower socioeconomic status, the poorly educated, the elderly, racial and ethnic minorities, immigrants and the disabled (Smedley *et al.*, 2003).

Social Support

There has been longstanding scientific interest in the organization of social life, and the implications of interpersonal and group interactions for emotional and physical health status. As far back as the 1970s, research on social support suggested a health-enhancing role for social relationships in buffering the ill effects of stress while subsequent studies confirmed an inverse relationship between social relationships and mortality risk (Hillemeier *et al.*, 2003). More recently, aspects of social interactions and relationships have been increasingly conceptualized as forms of social capital that Putnam defines as "features of social organization, such as trust, norms and networks that can improve the efficiency of society by facilitating co-ordinated actions." Social capital has been operationalized in several ways, including per capita membership in groups and associations th' has been used to assess civic engagement or political participation. Greater levels of mistrust been related to lower levels of social capital. Perceived helpfulness/reciprocity has also bee' as a gauge of social capital, and even crime levels have been seen as indicators of collect' being that is influenced by the degree of cohesiveness in social relations or social capital (' *et al.*, 2003).

Food Availability

A good diet and adequate food supply are central for promoting health and v of food and lack of variety increase the risk of poor health. On the other hand certain foods contributes to cardiovascular diseases, diabetes, cancer, degenerative obesity and dental caries (Marmot and Wilkinson, 2006). The important public health issue availability and cost of healthy, nutritious food. Access to good, affordable food makes more difference to what people eat than health education (Marmot and Wilkinson, 2006). Several studies have documented that the types of food and grocery store establishments differ in white versus minority communities. In general, the white communities have the larger national chain grocery stores while the minority communities tend to have the small corner store food stores with much more limited selection of foods, particularly fresh fruits and vegetables (Morland *et al.*, 2002; Moore and Diez Roux, 2006). In addition, it has been shown that the costs of food differs by as much as 30 percent between these types of food stores. The higher costs tend to be found in the minority grocery stores where the patrons have lower financial resources at baseline (Diez Roux, 2001; Morland *et al.*, 2002; Moore and Diez Roux, 2006). In the case of liquor establishments, store location and number of stores in a given community were shown to be associated with amount of alcohol ingested per capita in the local community and associated with dietary nutrient intake by local community residents (LaVeist and Wallace, 2000).

Community and Neighborhood

The physical environmental characteristics exert important effects on communities and the health of its population (Amick *et al.*, 1995). The most important factors include air, water pollution, geographic location (urban vs. rural), noise level, housing, transportation patterns and issues. The quality of a community's air and water resources are among the most visible aspects of the physical environment (Amick *et al.*, 1995). For example, in the U.S. environmental, behavioral and occupational exposures to well-known pulmonary carcinogens, including tobacco, asbestos, radon, polycyclic aromatic hydrocarbons (PAHs) and heterocyclic amines are well documented (Franceschi and Bidoli, 1999; Pitot, 2002; Alberg and Samet, 2003). Individuals living in housing units located close to a factory spewing carcinogenic emissions from its smoke stack might be expected to experience higher carcinogenic exposure levels over time compared to ambient air exposures in individuals who live in rural areas. In fact, location of urban residence has been associated with increased personal exposure and an increased lifetime risk of cancer (Kinney *et al.*, 2002; Morello-Frosch *et al.*, 2002). In addition, carcinogenic exposures from other sources such as automobile exhaust fumes may be significantly higher in urban communities than exposures to these same carcinogens in rural environments.

Work Environment

A major challenge to health is the working environment: working conditions, the nature of employment contracts and the availability of work itself (WHO Commission, 2007). In high-income countries, much action has been taken on physical and chemical hazards in the workplace. Now, however, the labor market is mainly segmented and precarious employment has become more prevalent. These labor market changes pose major health risks from the psychosocial and economic hazards associated with less job control, insecurity, lack of work time flexibility and access to paid family leave, and unemployment (WHO Commission, 2007). In low-income countries these risks are in addition to major persisting physical and chemical hazards. In many countries the majority of workers are excluded from labor protection. Other workers are deprived of effective protection because of weaknesses in labor law enforcement. The price of "cheap" consumer goods for people in high-income countries should not be poor health in low-income countries (WHO Commission, 2007).

Healthcare

Given the high burden of illness, particularly among the socially disadvantaged, it is urgent that health systems become more responsive to population needs. International, national and local systems of disease control and health services provision are both a determinant of health inequities and a powerful mechanism for empowerment (WHO Commission, 2007) In both the U.S. and the U.K. growing proportions of the population are living with chronic diseases. Approximately 60 percent of U.K. citizens and 50 percent of U.S. citizens report having at least one chronic disease (IOM, 2001; NHS, 2004). These numbers are expected to rise further in the near future. Fragmented healthcare delivery systems and significant proportions of individuals with multiple comorbid conditions contribute directly to poor quality care, unnecessary medical errors and poor patient outcomes (IOM, 2001; NHS, 2004). In addition, the healthcare systems of both countries have historically been oriented toward acute episodic inpatient treatment, and as such, have only limited ability in their current configurations to respond adequately to these growing concerns. Indeed, the World Health Organization has suggested that healthcare systems worldwide are struggling to meet the needs of populations suffering from chronic diseases (NHS, 2004). Healthcare quality and health inequalities are related to each other, efforts to eliminate inequalities and those to improve the quality of contemporary medical care represent two inseparable components of high-quality healthcare systems (Fiscella et al., 2000).

Elective chronic care, unlike acute treatment care, is a much more collaborative process between patients and providers. It involves a much larger reliance on provider directed self care and community-based health risk management, disease management, care co-ordination and care facilitation. Increasingly in the future, much of this community-based care will be provided by non-physician healthcare professionals, family members, friends and associates (IOM, 2001; NHS, 2004). Electively addressing inequalities will require innovative collaborative approaches that address patient factors, provider factors, healthcare system factors and relevant environmental factors (Health Inequalities, 1997; Acheson, 1998; Smedley et al., 2003). Development of a robust population perspective in addition to the more traditional medical model of individualized medicine is needed. While individual genetic factors exert substantial influence on the risk of developing disease and or disability among individuals, most people with increased risk do not actually become ill until one or more environmental, cultural or socially determined behavioral factors come into play. Healthcare systems of the future must recognize and respond to shifts in the very nature of medical care away from individualized care to that of care that not only predominantly occurs in communities, and also recognize the neighborhood and community contributions to health outcomes that exist beyond individual and genetic factors (Gibbons, 2006).

Transportation

Cycling, walking and the use of public transport provide exercise, reduce pedestrian-motor vehicle accidents, increase social contact and reduce air pollution. Because mechanization has reduced the exercise involved in jobs and housework, and added to the growing epidemic of obesity, people need to find new ways of building exercise into their lives. Transport policy can play a key role in combating sedentary lifestyles by reducing reliance on cars, increasing walking and cycling, and expanding public transport (Marmot and Wilkinson, 2006). Regular exercise protects against heart disease and, by limiting obesity, reduces the onset of diabetes. It promotes a sense of well-being and protects older people from depression. In contrast to cars, which insulate people from each other, cycling, walking and public transport stimulate social interaction on the streets. Road traffic often divides communities. With fewer pedestrians, streets cease to be social spaces and isolated pedestrians may fear personal violence (Marmot and Wilkinson, 2006). Reduced road traffic decreases harmful pollution from exhaust. Walking and cycling make minimal use of non-renewable fuels and do not lead to global warming. They do not create disease from air pollution, make little noise and are preferable for the ecologically compact cities of the future (Marmot and Wilkinson, 2006).

Political/Governance

Since the beginning of time, in every culture across the globe, those who provide protection from ill health or treatment of ill health, stand to gain the gratitude and good will of those who are sick and their families (Starr, 1982). The prospect of these tangible and intangible returns on investments in health, often create powerful motives for governments to intervene and at times control the processes. Political leaders since Bismarck seeking to strengthen the state or advance their own agendas have used issues of health and care as a means of turning benevolence into power (Starr, 1982). Indeed, from the Roman sewers and public water systems, to the eradication of smallpox, the health of populations depends upon the power of the state (Public Health and Preventive Medicine, 1998). At times it is necessary for government authorities to seize property, close businesses, destroy animals, treat and even confine involuntary individuals. In the absence of these powers the health of populations could be compromised (Public Health and Preventive Medicine, 1998). On the other hand, the lack of exerting these powers or the inequitable execution and enforcement of these responsibilities can leave individuals and populations vulnerable. Robust oversight, management and accountability measures are critically important to ensure that every individual has the maximum opportunity to achieve and maintain good health.

Alternatively, aspects of community political participation have been found to be associated with population health status. In England and Wales, areas with better material circumstances and more optimal health, voters were more likely to support leadership that favors reducing public assistance programs. In the U.S., individuals living in states with the highest voting inequality were shown to have increased odds of fair or poor self-rated health relative to those in other states, which may be related to disproportionate political participation by the more economically well-off that skews subsequent policymaking toward their interests (Hillemeier et al., 2003). More broadly, political participation it is considered to be a reflection of social capital within a community. Social capital, measured in several different ways, has been associated with positive health outcomes (Hillemeier et al., 2003).

The Environment

The environmental dimension includes physical and chemical components that have known associations with adverse health outcomes: air pollutants, water pollutants and environmental hazards including hazardous waste, heavy metals, climatic extremes and excessive noise. These exposures are known to vary by area and to be disproportionately concentrated among disadvantaged populations (Hillemeier et al., 2003). In addition, this contextual dimension encompasses structural features of communities such as physical design of streets, sidewalks and safety structures that are associated with level of injury risk. Aspects of land usage are also considered, such as public spaces and parks that may facilitate greater physical activity levels, as are services related to environmental quality like waste disposal and recycling programs (Hillemeier *et al.*, 2003).

Housing

Physical characteristics of housing have been linked to adverse outcomes. For example, the presence of dampness and mold lead to increased risk of respiratory and other illnesses. Dilapidated and abandoned housing in the local area increases the risk of accidental injury among residents, is associated with increased emotional stress and may provide situational opportunities for high-risk behaviors (Cohen *et al.*, 2000). Population density and overcrowding have also been associated with increased chances of contracting infections and sustaining injury (Hillemeier *et al.*, 2003)

Homelessness has known associations with differentially poorer health. In addition, racial segregation has been associated with adverse health outcomes. Similarly, concentration of poverty has been found to be associated with elevated mortality risk. Zoning policy can also affect the degree to which residential areas are exposed to industrial pollution and other health threats such as increased traffic (Hillemeier *et al.*, 2003).

Public Health Services

Adequate functioning of the core public health services of assessment, policy development and assurance at the local level are critical to urban health. There are a variety of programs aimed at prevention, early detection and optimal management of a range of health problems that may be provided by local public health agencies or departments (Hillemeier *et al.*, 2003).

Behavior

There has been increasing recognition that aspects of social, physical and cultural context can affect health status in a community by facilitating or inhibiting behaviors that impact well-being. In the U.S., tobacco use, physical activity, diet/obesity, alcohol and illicit drug use, and violence are among the nation's major determinants of premature morbidity and mortality. These behaviors though are socially patterned and significantly impacted by several environmental factors. In the case of tobacco use, current community smoking rates, the presence of cessation and preventive education programs, workplace smoking restrictions, the cost and accessibility of cigarettes, and targeted advertising all impact smoking behaviors of individuals. In terms of physical activity, physical education requirements in schools, participation in local sports and recreational activities, as well as availability of exercise facilities in the workplace and in the area more generally, all influence activity levels of individuals. In addition, television viewing patterns and video game sales and use will also influence activity levels.

Regarding diet and obesity, the quality, availability and cost of a range of different foods impacts intake as does the community availability of generally less-nutritious ''fast food.'' Similarly aspects of nutrition in schools, such as the prevalence of subcontracting to vendors of non-nutritious items and the presence of nutrition education programs, may affect the dietary intakes of children. In the area of alcohol and illicit drug use, the number of liquor stores in the community, the local marketing laws as well as the nature of public advertising have all be shown to affect intake. Also drug and alcohol treatment service availability and the presence of syringe laws and exchange programs impacts behavior. Finally, violence in the community will impact the behaviors of residents and is related to the availability of guns in the community and the level of exposure to violence occurring in the neighborhood.

As can be readily seen from the above outline, the major factors impacting health outcomes among persons living in urban populations are extremely diverse. It is a challenge for any health practitioner or researcher to quantitatively consider the impact of all factors in an attempt to understand health status or in designing the most effective intervention strategies. Thus, conventional wisdom would suggest taking a more narrow and focused approach.

While conceptually and practically such an approach has merit, because it necessarily leads us to consider one or more factors in isolation of potentially important contextual variables, the inevitable results are attenuated understandings of disease pathogenesis and interventional strategies with limited efficacy. KM offers promise for enabling scientists and practitioners to consider diverse forms of knowledge in a replicable and scientifically defensible manner. In so doing, we will likely improve our understanding of health and disease as it exists, not in test tubes, but in communities and society. In turn we may also uncover novel opportunities for treatment, therapeutics and public health interventions.

Case Exercise References

Acheson, D. (1998) *Independent Inquiry into Inequalities in Health.* London: Department of Health.

Alberg, A.J. and Samet, J.M. (2003) Epidemiology of Lung Cancer, *Chest*, 123: 21S–49S.

Amick, B.C., Levine, S., Tarlov, A.R., and Walsh, D.C. (1995) *Society and Health.* New York: Oxford University Press.

Baker, D.W. (1999) Reading Between the Lines: Deciphering the Connections Between Literacy and Health, *Journal of General Internal Medicine,* 14: 315–317.

Berkman, L.F. and Kawachi, I. (2000) *Social Epidemiology.* New York: Oxford University Press.

Cheung, Y.B., Low, L., Osmond, C., Barker, D., and Karlberg, J. (2000) Fetal Growth and Early Postnatal Growth are Related to Blood Pressure in Adults, *Hypertension*, 36: 795–800.

Cohen, D., Spear, S., Scribner, R., Kissinger, P., Mason K., and Wildgen, J. (2000) Broken Windows and the Risk of Gonorrhea, *American Journal of Public Health*, 90: 230–236.

De Stavola, B.L., Dos, Santos Silva, I., McCormack, V., Hardy, R.J., Kuh, D.J., and Wadsworth, M.E. (2004) Childhood Growth and Breast Cancer, *American Journal of Epidemiology*, 159: 671–682.

Diez Roux, A.V. (2001) Investigating Neighborhood and Area Effects on Health, *American Journal of Public Health*, 91: 1783–1789.

Fiscella, K., Franks, P., Gold, M.R., and Clancy, C.M. (2000) Inequality in Quality: Addressing Socioeconomic, Racial, and Ethnic Disparities in Health Care, *Journal of the American Medical Association*, 283: 2579–2584.

Franceschi, S. and Bidoli, E. (1999) The Epidemiology of Lung Cancer, *Annals of Oncology*, 10 (supp. 5): S3–S6.

Gazmararian, J.A., Baker, D.W., Williams, M.V., Parker, R.M., Scott, T.L., Green, D.C., Fehrenbach, S.N., Ren, J., and Koplan, J.P. (1999) Health Literacy Among Medicare Enrollees in a Managed Care Organization, *Journal of the American Medical Association*, 281: 545–551.

Gibbons, M.C. (2006) Health Inequalities and Emerging Themes in Compunetics, *Studies in Health Technology and Informatics*, 121: 62–69.

Health Inequalities (1997) *Decennial Supplement* (F. Drever and M. Whitehead, Eds.), M. Series DS No. 15, London: London Stationery Office.

Hillemeier, M.M., Lynch, J., Harper, S., and Casper, M. (2003) Measuring Contextual Characteristics for Community Health, *Health Services Research*, 38: 1645–1717.

IOM Committee on Quality of Healthcare in America (2001) *Crossing the Quality Chasm: A New Health System for the 21st Century*, Washington, DC: National Academy Press.

Kinney, P., Chillrud, S., Ramstrom, S., Ross, J., and Stansfeld, S.A. (2002) Exposure to Multiple Air Toxics in New York City, *Environmental Health Perspective*, 110 (supp. 4): 539–546.

Kongstvedt, P. (2003) *Essentials of Managed Health Care with Study Guide* (4th Edition). Sudbury, MA: Jones & Bartlett.

LaVeist, T.A. and Wallace, J.M., Jr. (2000) Health Risk and Inequitable Distribution of Liquor Stores in African American Neighborhood, *Social Science and Medicine*, 51: 613–617.

Marmot, M. and Wilkinson R.G. (2006) *Social Determinants of Health*. Oxford: Oxford University Press.

Marmot, M.G. (1986) Does Stress Cause Heart Attacks?, *Postgraduate Medical Journal*, 62: 683–686.

Marmot, M., Ryff, C.D., Bumpass, L.L., Shipley, M., and Marks, N.F. (1997) Social Inequalities in Health: Next Questions and Converging Evidence, *Social Science and Medicine*, 44: 901–910.

Miura, K., Nakagawa, H., Tabata, M., Morikawa, Y., Nishijo, M., and Kagamimori, S. (2001) Birth Weight, Childhood Growth, and Cardiovascular Disease Risk Factors in Japanese Aged 20 Years, *American Journal of Epidemiology*, 153: 783–789.

Moore, L. and Diez Roux, A. (2006) Associations of Neighborhood Characteristics with the Location and Type of Food Stores, *American Journal of Public Health*, 96: 325–331.

Morello-Frosch, R., Pastor, M., Porras, C., and Sadd, J. (2002) Environmental Justice and Regional Inequality in Southern California: Implications for Future Research, *Environmental Health Perspectives*, 110 (supp. 2): 149–154.

Morland, K., Wing, S., Diez, R.A., and Poole, C. (2002) Neighborhood Characteristics Associated with the Location of Food Stores and Food Service Places, *American Journal of Preventive Medicine*, 22: 23–29.

National Health Service (2004) *Chronic Disease Management: A Compendium of Information*. London: Department of Health.

Pitot, H.C. (2002) The Host-Tumor Relationship, in H.C. Pitot (Ed.), *Fundamentals of Oncology*. New York: Marcel Dekker, pp. 743–781.

Smedley, B.D., Stith, A.Y., and Nelson, A.R. (2003) *Unequal Treatment; Confronting Racial and Ethnic Disparities in Healthcare*. Washington, DC: National Academies Press.

Smith, G.D., Greenwood, R., Gunnell, D., Sweetnam, P., Yarnell, J., and Elwood, P. (2001) Leg Length, Insulin Resistance, and Coronary Heart Disease Risk: The Caerphilly Study, *Journal of Epidemiology and Community Health*, 55: 867–872.

Starr, P. (1982) *The Social Transformation of American Medicine*. New York: Basic Books.

Vlahov, D., Gibble, E., Freudenberg, N., and Galea, S. (2004) Cities and Health: History, Approaches, and Key Questions, *Academic Medicine*, 79: 1133–1138.

Wallace, R.B. (Ed.) (1998) *Public Health and Preventive Medicine* (14th Edition). Stamford, CT: Appleton & Lange, p. 795.

Weiss, B.D. and Coyne, C. (1997) Communicating with Patients who Cannot Read, *New England Journal of Medicine*, 337: 272–274.

WHO Commission on Social Determinants of Health (2007), *Interim Statement*, Geneva, Switzerland: World Health Organization.

Wilkinson, R.G. (1996) *Unhealthy Societies: The Afflictions of Inequalities*. New York: Routledge.

Williams, M.V., Parker, R.M., Baker, D.W., Parikh, N.S., Pitkin, K., Coates, W.C., and Nurss, J.R. (1995) Inadequate Functional Health Literacy among Patients at Two Public Hospitals, *Journal of the American Medical Association*, 274: 1677–1682.

Case Exercise Questions

1 What are the cultural considerations that are highlighted in this case and how does KM facilitate reaching a superior healthcare outcome?

2   Identify examples of tacit and explicit knowledge in this scenario?

3   What are some general lessons?

FURTHER READING

Brown, A. (1995) *Organizational Culture*. London: Pitman Publishing.

Davenport, T.H. and Prusak, L. (1998) *Working Knowledge. How Organizations Manage What They Know.* Boston, MA: Harvard Business School Press.

REFERENCES

Alavi, M. and Leidner, D.E. (2001) Knowledge Management and Knowledge Management Systems: Conceptual Foundations and Research Issues, *MIS Quarterly*, 25(1): 107–136.

Anon (1997) *Managing Culture*. Available online at www.davjac.co.uk (accessed February 19, 1999).

Anthony, R. (1965) *Planning and Control Systems: A Framework for Analysis*. Cambridge, MA: Harvard University Press.

Argyris, C. (1991) Teaching Smart People How to Learn, *Harvard Business Review*, May–June: 99–109.

Argyris, C. and Schön, D. (1978) *Organizational Learning: A Theory of Action Perspective*. Reading, MA: Addison Wesley.

Bali, R.K., Feng, D.D., Burstein, F. and Dwivedi, A. (2005) Advances in Clinical and Health-Care Knowledge Management, *IEEE Transactions on Information Technology in Biomedicine*, 9(2): 157–161.

Bali, R.K. (1999) Successful Technology Management: Cultural and Organizational Dimensions of MIS Implementation in SMEs, unpublished Ph.D. thesis, Sheffield Hallam University, U.K.

Baskaran, V., Bali, R.K., Arochena, H., Naguib, R.N.G., Wheaton, M., and Wallis, M. (2006), Improving Uptake of a Breast Screening Programme: A Knowledge Management Approach for Opportunistic Intervention, in L. Bos *et al.* (Eds), *Medical and Care Compunetics 3*. Netherlands: IOS, pp. 191–197.

Bessant, J. and Cole, S. (1985) *Stacking the Chips: Information Technology and the Distribution of Income*. London: Frances Pinter.

Boddy, D. and Gunson, N. (1996) *Organizations in the Network Age*. London: Routledge.

Borman, W.C. (1983) Implications of Personality Theory and Research for the Rating of Work Performance in Organizations, in F.J. Landy, S. Zedeck, and J.N. Cleveland (Eds), *Performance Measurement and Theory*, Hillsdale, NJ: Lawrence Erlbaum Associates.

Bower, M. (1966) *The Will to Manage*. New York: McGraw-Hill.

Brown, A. (1995) *Organizational Culture*. London: Pitman Publishing.

Carnall, C. (1995) *Managing Change in Organizations*. Hemel Hempstead: Prentice-Hall.

Coakes, E. (2002) Knowledge Management: A Sociotechnical Perspective, in E. Coakes, D. Willis and S. Clarke (Eds), *Knowledge Management in the Sociotechnical World*. London: Springer-Verlag, pp. 4–14.

Davenport, T.H. and Prusak, L. (1998) *Working Knowledge. How Organizations Manage What They Know.* Boston, MA: Harvard Business School Press.

David Skyrme Associates (2008) Insights No. 3: The Learning Organization. Available online at www.skyrme.com/insights/3lrnorg.htm (accessed May 19, 2008).

Dudley, J. (1990) *1992: Strategies for the Single Market*. London: Kogan Page.

Earl, M. (1989) *Management Strategies for Information Technology*. Hemel Hempstead: Prentice-Hall.

Edwards, J., Shaw, D., and Collier, P. (2005) Knowledge Management Systems: Finding a Way with Technology, *Journal of Knowledge Management*, 9(1): 113–125.

Fiedler, K., Grover, V. and Teng, J.T.C. (1994) Information Technology-Enabled Change: The Risks and Rewards of Business Process Redesign and Automation, *Journal of Information Technology*, 9: 267–275.

Flood, R. and Romm, N. (1996) *Diversity Management: Triple Loop Learning*. Chichester: Wiley.

Garrity, J. and Barnes, V. (1968) The Payout in Computers: What Management has Learned about Planning and Control, *The Computer Sampler: Management Perspectives on the Computer*. New York: McGraw-Hill.

Gibson, J.L., Ivancevich, J.M., and Donnelly Jr., J.H. (1994) *Organizations: Behavior, Structure, Processes*. Homewood, IL: Richard D. Irwin.

Gray, P.H. and Meister, D.B. (2003) Introduction: Fragmentation and Integration in Knowledge Management Research, *Information, Technology & People*, 16(3): 259–265.

Gummesson, E. (1988) *Qualitative Methods in Management Research*. Sweden: Chartwell-Bratt.

Gupta, J.D. and Sharma, S.K. (2004) *Creating Knowledge Based Organizations*. Hershey, PA: Idea Group.

Hampden-Turner, C. (1990) *Creating Corporate Culture*. Reading, MA: Addison-Wesley.

Handy, C. (1985) *Understanding Organizations*. London: Penguin Business.

Harrison, R. (1972) Understanding Your Organization's Character, *Harvard Business Review*, 50(3): 119–128.

Hofstede, G. (1993) Cultural Constraints in Management Theories, *Academy of Management Executive*, 7(1): 81–94.

Hofstede, G. (1994) *Cultures and Organizations: Software of the Mind, Intercultural Cooperation and its Importance for Survival*. London: HarperCollins.

Huczynski, A. and Buchanan, D. (1991) *Organizational Behavior*. London: Prentice-Hall.

Hutchinson, C. and Rosenberg, D. (1994) The Organization of Organizations: Issues for Next Generation Office IT, *Journal of Information Technology*, 9: 99–117.

Jackson, T. (1995) *Virgin King*. London: HarperCollins.

Jadad, A., Haynes, R., Hunt, D., and Brondman, G. (2000) The Internet and Evidence-Based Decision Making: A Needed Synergy for Efficient Knowledge Management in Healthcare, *Canadian Medical Association Journal*, 162(3): 362–367.

Johnson, G. (1992) Managing Strategic Change—Strategy, Culture and Action, *Long Range Planning*, 25(1): 28–36.

Johnston, H. and Vitale, M. (1988) Creating Competitive Advantage with Interorganisational Information Systems, *MIS Quarterly*, June: 153–165.

Kroeber, A. and Kluckhohn, C. (1952) *Culture: A Critical Review of Concepts and Definitions*. Cambridge, MA: Vintage Books.

Laver, M. (1989) *Information Technology: Agent of Change*. Cambridge: Cambridge University Press.

Licker, P. (1997) *Management Information Systems: A Strategic Leadership Approach*. Orlando, FL: Dryden Press.

Long, L. (1989) *Management Information Systems*. Upper Saddle River, NJ: Prentice-Hall.

Lucas, H. (1990) *Information Systems Concepts for Management*. Singapore: McGraw-Hill.

Lucey, T. (1991) *Management Information Systems*. Guernsey: Guernsey Press.

March, J. and Simon, H. (1958) *Organizations*. New York: Wiley.

Mintzberg, H. (1989) *Mintzberg on Management: Inside Our World of Organizations*. New York: Free Press.

Nonaka, I. and Takeuchi, H. (1995) *The Knowledge-Creating Company*. New York: Oxford University Press.

Nykanen, P. and Karimaa, E. (2006) Success and Failure Factors in the Regional Health Information System Design Process—Results from a Constructive Evaluation Study, *Methods in Information Medicine*, 45(1): 89–124.

Pavia, L. (2001) The Era of Knowledge in Health Care, *Health Care Strategic Management*, 19(2): 12–13.

Pedler, M., Burgoyne, J., and Boydell, T. (1996) *The Learning Company. A Strategy for Sustainable Development.* London: McGraw-Hill.

Pennings, J. (1993) Executive Reward Systems: A Cross-Cultural Comparison, *Journal of Management Studies*, 30(2): 261–280.

Pheysey, D. (1993) *Organizational Cultures: Types and Transformations.* London: Routledge.

Polanyi, M. (1967) *The Tacit Dimension.* New York: Anchor Books.

Porter, M. (1985) *Competitive Advantage: Creating and Sustaining Superior Performance.* New York: Free Press.

Purvis, R., Samamburthy, V., and Zmud, R. (2001) The Assimilation of Knowledge Platforms in Organizations: An Empirical Investigation, *Organization Science*, 12(2): 117–132.

Quinn, T., Bali, R.K., and Shears, K. (2005) Managing Knowledge for the Emergency Care of Heart Attack Patients: Paramedics and Thrombolytic Treatment. *Proceedings of the 2005 IEEE Engineering in Medicine and Biology 27th Annual Conference*, Shanghai, China, September 1–4.

Reference for Business (2008) Management Information Systems (MIS). Available online at www.reference forbusiness.com/small/Mail-Op/Management-Information-Systems-MIS.html (accessed May 24, 2008).

Robbins, S. (1991) *Management.* Upper Saddle River, NJ: Prentice-Hall.

Schein, E. (1990) Organizational Culture, *American Psychologist*, 45(2): 109–119.

Schultheis, R. and Sumner, M. (1995) *Management Information Systems: The Manager's View.* New York: Richard D. Irwin.

Scott-Morton, M. (1995) Emerging Organizational Forms: Work and Organization in the 21st Century, *European Management Journal*, 13(4): 339–345.

Senge, P.M. (1992) *The Fifth Discipline—The Art & Practice of The Learning Organization.* London: Century Business.

Smircich, L. (1983) Concepts of Culture and Organizational Analysis, *Administrative Science Quarterly*, 28: 339–358.

Spender, J.C. (2006) Method, Philosophy and Empirics in KM and IC, *Journal of Intellectual Capital*, 7(1): 12–28.

Thornhill, A. (1993) Management Training Across Cultures: The Challenge for Trainers, *Journal of European Industrial Training*, 17(10): 43–51.

Tylor, E. (1971) *Primitive Culture: Researches into the Development of Mythology, Philosophy, Religion, Language, Art and Custom* (first published 1903). London: Murray (1871).

Van Beveren, J. (2003) Does Health Care for Knowledge Management?, *Journal of Knowledge Management*, 7(1): 90–97.

Vitell, S.J., Nwachukwu, S.L., and Barnes, J.H. (1993) The Effects of Culture on Ethical Decision Making: An Application of Hofstede's Typology, *Journal of Business Ethics*, 12: 753–760.

Ward, J. and Peppard, J. (1995) Reconciling the IT/Business Relationship: A Troubled Marriage in Need of Guidance, Working Paper Series, Cranfield School of Management, SWP2/95, Cranfield: Cranfield University.

Wickramasinghe, N. and Bali, R.K. (2008) Knowledge Management: The Key to Network-Centric Healthcare, *International Journal of Biomedical Engineering and Technology*, 1(3): 342–352.

Wickramasinghe, N. and Mills, G. (2002) Integrating e-Commerce and Knowledge Management—What Does the Kaiser Experience Really Tell Us, *International Journal of Accounting Information Systems*, 3(2): 83–98.

Wickramasinghe, N. (2000) IS/IT as a Tool to Achieve Goal Alignment: A Theoretical Framework, *International Journal of Healthcare Technology Management*, 2(1–4): 163–180.

Williams, A., Dobson, P. and Walters, M. (1993) *Changing Culture: New Organizational Approaches*. London: Institute of Personnel Management.

Wiseman, C. (1985) *Strategy and Computers*. Homewood, IL: Dow-Jones-Irwin.

Xu, J. and Quaddus, M. (2005) A Six-Stage Model for the Effective Diffusion of Knowledge Management Systems, *The Journal of Management Development*, 24(4): 362–374.

Zmud, R. (1984) Design Alternatives for Organizing Systems Activities, *MIS Quarterly*, 8(2): 79–93.

Chapter 6

Applying Knowledge

INTRODUCTION

As has been discussed in previous chapters, KM is essential for healthcare organizations to attain and/or maintain their value proposition and thereby affect superior healthcare delivery. What becomes of significance then, is how to apply the tools, techniques, technologies and tactics of KM in healthcare settings. This chapter serves to explore the key areas of creating value from KM, applications of KM, as well as succeeding with KM.

In so doing, two respective approaches: the OODA Loop by Boyd (Wickramasinghe and von Lubitz, 2007) and the intelligence continuum by Wickramasinghe and Schaffer (2006) are described and the paradigm of networkcentric healthcare is introduced. Finally the model of populomics is presented.

CREATING VALUE FROM KNOWLEDGE

In most healthcare activities, a critical function is decision making. More importantly, this decision making is typically complex and unstructured. Unstructured decision making requires the gathering of multi-spectral data and information if the decision maker is to make a prudent choice (Wickramasinghe and von Lubitz, 2007). Unstructured decision making in dynamic and complex environments is challenging and the decision maker is always at a point of information inferiority (von Lubitz and Wickramasinghe, 2006). It is in such situations that the need for germane knowledge, pertinent information and relevant data are critical (*ibid*) and hence the value of knowledge and the tools, techniques, technologies and tactics of KM are most beneficial.

Hierarchically, the gathering of information precedes the transformation of information into useable knowledge (Alavi and Leidner, 1999; Massey, 2002). Hence, the rate of information collection and the quality of the collected information will have a major impact on the quality (usefulness) of the generated knowledge (Award and Ghaziri, 2004).

In the dynamic and, to a large degree, unpredictable world of global healthcare, "action space awareness" (or synonymous "competitive space awareness") and information superiority

(Boyd, 1976; von Lubitz and Wickramasinghe, 2006a) have become the key factors to all successful operations. Such awareness, however, can only be enabled through the extraction of multi-spectral data.

Boyd's OODA Loop (Figure 6.1) provides a formalized analysis of the processes involved in the development of a superior strategy (Boyd, 1987; Cebrowski and Garstka, 1998; Alberts *et al.*, 2000; von Lubitz and Wickramasinghe, 2006a,b) and a suitable model to facilitate the organizing of germane knowledge.

The Loop is based on a cycle of four interrelated stages revolving in time and space: Observation followed by Orientation, then by Decision and finally Action. At the Observation and Orientation stages, multi-spectral implicit and explicit inputs are gathered (Observation) and converted into coherent information (Orientation). The latter determines the sequential Determination (knowledge generation) and Action (practical implementation of knowledge) steps.

The outcome of the latter affects, in turn, the character of the starting point (Observation) of the next revolution in the forward progression of the rolling loop. The Orientation stage specifies the characteristics and the nature of the "center of thrust" at which the effort is to concentrate during the Determination and Action stages. Hence, the Loop implicitly incorporates the rule of "economy of force," i.e. the requirement that only minimum but adequate (containment) effort is applied to insignificant aspects of competitive interaction.

The Loop exists as a network of simultaneous and intertwined events that characterize the multidimensional action space (competition space), and both influence and are influenced by the actor (e.g. an organization) at the center of the network. Moreover, the events provide the context and search criteria for extracting germane knowledge.

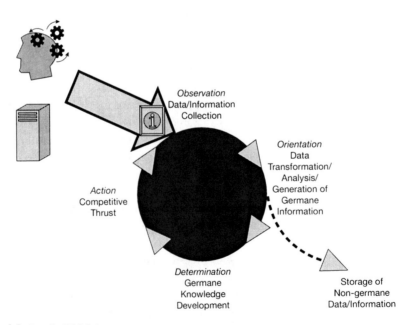

Figure 6.1 *Boyd's OODA Loop.*

Reproduced with kind permission of Doctrina Applied Research and Consulting LLC—www.consultdoctrina.com

THE INTELLIGENCE CONTINUUM

Currently, the healthcare industry is contending with relentless pressures to lower costs while maintaining and increasing the quality of service in a challenging environment (Pallarito, 1996; Wickramasinghe and von Lubitz, 2007). It is useful to think of the major challenges facing today's healthcare organizations in terms of the categories of demographics, technology and finance. Demographic challenges are reflected by longer life expectancy and an aging population; technology challenges include incorporating advances that keep people younger and healthier; and finance challenges are exacerbated by the escalating costs of treating everyone with the latest technologies.

Healthcare organizations can respond to these challenges by focusing on three key solution strategies; namely, 1) access—caring for anyone, anytime, anywhere; 2) quality—offering world-class care and establishing integrated information repositories; and 3) value—providing effective and efficient healthcare delivery. These three components are interconnected such that they continually impact on the other and all are necessary to meet the key challenges facing healthcare organizations today. Given the interdependent nature of these elements, the relationship can be defined as the AQV Möbius (see Figure 6.2).

In order to fully actualize the AQV Möbius and thus best meet the current healthcare challenges, it is imperative that healthcare organizations embrace the tools, techniques and processes of today's knowledge economy; namely, incorporate the intelligence continuum into the generic healthcare information system.

To understand the role of the intelligence continuum, an examination of a generic healthcare information system is necessary (Figure 6.3). The important aspects in this generic system include the socio-technical perspective, i.e. the people, processes and technology inputs required in conjunction with data as a key input. The combination of these elements comprises an information system and in any organization multiple such systems could exist.

To this generic system, we add the healthcare challenges, i.e. the challenges of demographics, technology and finance. As the baby boomers age, the incidence of people over the age of sixty-five is projected to be increased for the next forty years. Moreover, as people age, improved healthcare is providing those people over the age of sixty-five a longer lifespan and the ability to tell about it but also ultimately endure many complicated medical problems and diseases. Certainly technology is helping to keep everyone alive and younger and in better health, but the cost to do so is escalating exponentially (Wickramasinghe and Silvers, 2003).

In order to address these challenges and actualize the AQV Möbius, a closer examination of the data generated by the information systems and stored in the larger data warehouses and/or smaller data marts is necessary. In particular, it is important to make decisions and

Figure 6.2 *AQV Möbius.*

Source: adapted from Wickramasinghe and Schaffer (2006)

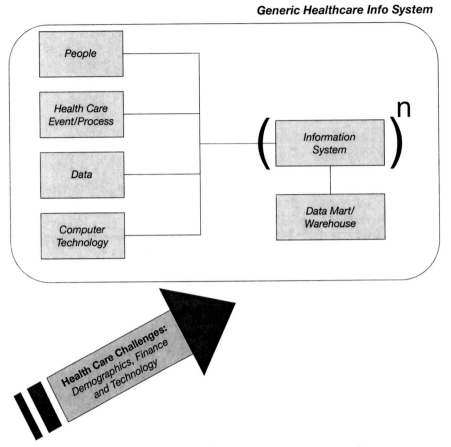

Figure 6.3 *Generic Healthcare Information System with Healthcare Challenges.*
Source: adapted from Wickramasinghe and Schaffer (2006)

invoke the intelligence continuum; apply the tools, techniques and processes of data mining, business intelligence/analytics and KM respectively. On applying these tools and techniques to the data generated from healthcare information systems, it is first possible to diagnose the "as is" or current state processes in order to make further decisions regarding how existing processes should be modified and thereby provide appropriate prescriptions to enable the achievement of a better future state, i.e. improve the respective inputs of the people, process, technology and data so that the system as a whole is significantly improved.

The intelligence continuum (Wickramasinghe and Schaffer, 2006) then, is a collection of key tools, techniques and processes of today's knowledge economy, i.e. including but not limited to data mining, business intelligence/analytics and KM. Taken together they represent a very powerful system for refining the data raw material stored in data marts and/or data warehouses and thereby maximizing the value and utility of these data assets for any organization. The first component is a generic information system, which generates data that is then captured in a data repository.

In order to maximize the value of the data and use it to improve processes, the techniques and tools of data mining, business intelligence and analytics and KM must be applied to the data warehouse. Once applied, the results become part of the data set that are reintroduced into the system and combined with the other inputs of people, processes and technology to develop an improvement continuum. Thus, the intelligence continuum includes the generation of data, the analysis of these data to provide a "diagnosis" and the reintroduction into the cycle as a "prescriptive" solution (Figure 6.4).

In today's context of escalating costs in healthcare, managed care in the U.S., regulations and a technology and health information savvy patient, the healthcare industry can no longer be complacent regarding embracing key processes and techniques to enable better, more effective and efficient practice management. The proliferation of databases in every quadrant of healthcare practice and research is evident in the large number of isolated claims databases, registries, electronic medical record data warehouses, disease surveillance systems and other ad hoc research database systems.

Not only does the number of databases grow daily, but even more importantly, so does the amount of data within them. Pattern-identification tasks such as detecting associations between certain risk factors and outcomes, ascertaining trends in healthcare utilization, or discovering new models of disease in populations of individuals rapidly become daunting even to the most experienced healthcare researcher or manager (Holmes *et al.*, 2002).

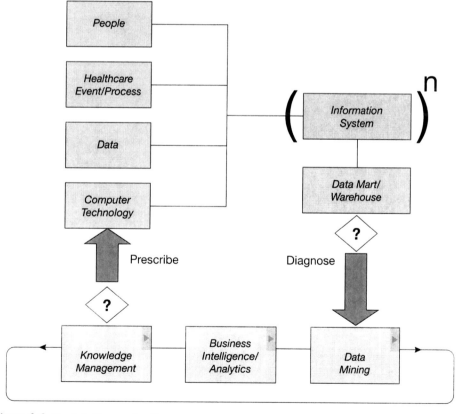

Figure 6.4 *The Intelligence Continuum.*

Source: adapted from Wickramasinghe and Schaffer (2006)

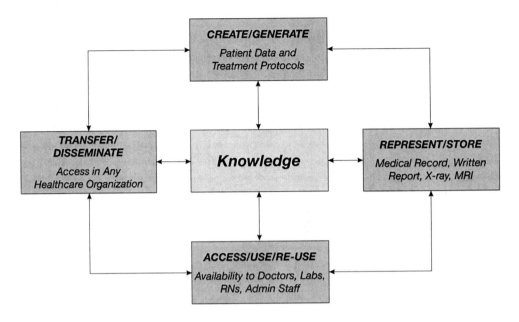

Figure 6.5 *The Key Steps of Knowledge Management.*

Yet these tasks may hold the answers to many clinical issues, such as treatment protocols or the identification across geographic areas of newly emerging pathogens and thus are important. Add to all of this, the daily volumes of data generated and then accumulated from a healthcare organization administrative system, clearly then, the gap between data collection and data comprehension and analysis becomes even more problematic. IT tools coupled with new business approaches such as data mining, business intelligence/analytics and KM should be embraced in an attempt to address such healthcare woes (McGee, 1997; Berinato, 2002). Figure 6.5 highlights important aspects of knowledge in essential healthcare operations.

CLINICAL EXAMPLE: OPERATING ROOM

The orthopedic operating room represents an ideal environment for the application of a continuous improvement cycle that is dependant on the intelligence continuum. For those patients with advanced degeneration of their hips and knees, arthroplasty of the knee and hip represent an opportunity to regain their function. Before the operation even begins in the operating room, there are a large number of interdependent individual processes that must be completed. Each process requires data input and produces a data output such as patient history, diagnostic test and consultations.

From the surgeon's and hospital's perspective, they are on a continuous cycle such as depicted by the AQV Möbius. The interaction between these data elements is not always maximized in terms of operating room scheduling and completion of the procedure. Moreover, as the population ages and patient's functional expectations continue to increase with their advanced knowledge of medical issues, reconstructive orthopedic surgeons are being presented with an increasing patient population requiring hip and knee arthroplasty. Simultaneously, the implants are becoming more sophisticated and thus more expensive.

In turn, the surgeons are experiencing little change in system capacity, but are being told to improve efficiency and output, improve procedure time and eliminate redundancy. However, the system legacy is for insufficient room designs that have not been updated with the introduction of new equipment, poor integration of the equipment, inefficient scheduling and time consuming procedure preparation. Although there are many barriers to re-engineering the operating room, such as the complex choreography of the perioperative processes, a dearth of data and the difficulty of aligning incentives, it is indeed possible to effect significant improvements through the application of the intelligence continuum.

The entire process of getting a patient to the operating room for a surgical procedure can be represented by three distinct phases: preoperative, intraopertive and postoperative. In turn, each of these phases can be further subdivided into the individual yet interdependent processes that represent each step on the surgical trajectory. As each of the individual processes are often dependant on a previous event, the capture of event and process data in a data warehouse is necessary. The diagnostic evaluation of this data, and the re-engineering of each of the deficient processes will then lead to increased efficiency.

For example, many patients are allergic to the penicillin family of antibiotics that are often administered preoperative in order to minimize the risk of infection. For those patients who are allergic, a preoperatively substitute drug requires a forty-five minute monitored administration time as opposed to the much shorter administration time of the default agent. Since the antibiotic is only effective when administered prior to starting the procedure, this often means that a delay is experienced. When identified in the preoperative phase, these patients should be prepared earlier on the day of surgery and the medication administered in sufficient time so that the schedule is not delayed.

This prescriptive reengineering has directly resulted from mining of the data in the information system in conjunction with an examination of the business processes and their flows. By scrutinizing the delivery of care and each individual process, increased efficiency and improved quality should be realized while maximizing value. For knee and hip arthroplasty, there are over 432 discrete processes that can be evaluated and re-engineered as necessary through the application of the intelligence continuum (Schaffer et al., 2004).

CASE EXERCISE: SUBSTANCE ABUSE PATIENT

Mr. S.B. is a 49 year old gentleman who has a previous history of cocaine and heroin addiction. He has not used these drugs since 1997. Since discontinuing the drug use, he began drinking socially and has now become a severe alcoholic, consuming fifteen to twenty-five drinks of alcohol every day. He has a past medical history of Hepatitis A and Hepatitis C and a sexually transmitted infection. Mr. S.B. has completed high school but not college. He was originally employed as a construction worker, but lost his job due to alcohol abuse. He is now unemployed and also has no medical insurance. In the past year, he has been to the Hospital Emergency Room (ER) seven times, been seen by a private MD four times, and been to a clinic four times. Additionally, he reports delaying seeking care at least five times in the last year because of inability to pay.

This patient was originally seen during a weekly free Hypertension screening event at a local open air market. The patient's blood pressure was without acute elevation. Twenty-four hours later, the patient came to the Center for Community Health seeking help with his alcohol abuse problem. The patient was acutely intoxicated and was urgently requesting placement in an alcohol detox program. The local academic Medical Center has a seventy-two hour detox unit for patients experiencing acute withdrawal symptoms (Intensive Treatment Unit or ITU). Entry into this unit is through the hospital ER. The patient was referred to the ER for admission to the ITU. The patient went to the ER and was seen by the ER physicians and staff. Because the patient was not in acute withdrawal at the time he presented to the ER, he was seen and then discharged to go home without admission to the ITU. Later that same day, the patient presented to the Center for Community Health still intoxicated, but now in significant emotional distress complaining that the "hospital would not help him."

He again was urgently requesting placement in a detox program. Additionally now the patient was complaining that he was tired of having an alcohol problem, tired of living with an alcohol problem and if the hospital would not help him he would rather kill himself than continue to live with this problem. Upon further evaluation by the Center for Community Health staff, and consultation with an MD, the patient was deemed to be at significant risk to himself. At this time there was no detox program available in the city. Because of the potential additional depressive/psychiatric components to this patient's condition, the patient was urgently transported back to the hospital ER via ambulance for comprehensive evaluation and treatment.

The patient was observed and monitored in the hospital ER for approximately sixteen hours. He was then transported to an inpatient detox program at the hospital. After a seventy-two hour stay in the detox program, Center for Community Health Staff assisted with the placement of the patient in a long-term substance and transitional housing program. The patient is now two weeks free of alcohol. He has identified several social triggers in his life that increase his likelihood of drinking and is developing a lifestyle plan to avoid these triggers. He has also begun to make significant progress towards obtaining employment, securing stable housing and transportation and redeveloping his positive social networks.

Case Analysis

The complexity of Urban Health is such that issues need to be considered from both a macro ("population") and micro ("individual") perspective. Regardless of which perspective we consider, KM can be beneficial to all stakeholders. In this "individual" example, the MD is actively attempting to place the patient in an appropriate treatment program. The MD's efforts are centered around improving the health of patients by perhaps thinking about the conventional and accepted healthcare protocol (e.g. insurance, treatment beds and so forth). It could be argued that this accepted approach would yield only limited results. The acute problem may be addressed and resolved but this patient, and many others like him, will keep coming back over and over again. The conventional wisdom in force in healthcare almost dictates that MDs are traditionally trained to ignore most factors that occur outside of a hospital or clinic.

This case may help point out how shortsighted this approach is and suggest a need for a more integrated, knowledge-centered approach that considers both the patient's acute medical needs and the more socially-oriented triggers that either reinforce his former drug-abusing behaviors, or those that are now supporting his recovery. Without considering these, the patient and many others like him may never have started using drugs in the first place or now may not be able to stay clean. This case goes some way in illustrating the complexity of issues and ultimately the need for KM. KM principles, if adopted by physicians at the clinical level, might enable them to come up with better, more comprehensive and more integrated clinical interventions for patients. As things currently stand, and as this case illustrates, the current healthcare system doesn't always deal as effectively as it perhaps could with such vulnerable patients.

NETWORKCENTRIC HEALTHCARE OPERATIONS

Healthcare is an information rich, knowledge intensive environment. In order to treat and diagnose even a simple condition a physician must combine many varied data elements and information. Such multi-spectral data must be carefully integrated and synthesized to allow medically appropriate management of the disease. Given the need to combine data and information into a coherent whole and then disseminate these findings to decision makers in a timely fashion, the benefits of information communication technologies (ICTs) to support decision making of the physician and other actors throughout the healthcare system are clear (Wickramasinghe et al., 2005a).

In fact, we see the proliferation of many technologies such as electronic health records (EHRs), picture archive computerized systems (PACS), clinical decision support systems (CDSS), etc. However, and paradoxically, the greater the investment in ICT by healthcare, the greater it is that global healthcare appears to be hampered by information chaos which, in turn, leads to inferior decision-making, ineffective and inefficient operations, exponentially increasing costs and even loss of life (Wickramasinghe et al., 2005a,b). We believe the reason for this lies in the essentially platformcentric application of ICT to date within healthcare, which at the micro level do indeed bring some benefits but at the macro level only add to the problem by creating islands of automation and information silos that hinder rather than enable and facilitate the smooth and seamless flow of relevant information to any decision maker when and where such information is required.

To remedy this problem and maximize the potential afforded by ICT and consequently alleviate the current problems faced by healthcare, von Lubitz and Wickramasinghe suggest the adoption of a networkcentric approach to healthcare operations (von Lubitz et al., 2006; von Lubitz and Wickramasinghe, 2006a; Wickramasinghe, 2006a,b). Such a networkcentric approach is grounded in a process oriented view of knowledge generation and the pioneering work of Boyd, specifically his OODA Loop (Boyd, 1987, 1976).

To capture this dynamic triad that continually impacts all healthcare operations, the doctrine of healthcare networkcentric operations is built around three entities that form mutually interconnected and functionally related domains. Specifically these domains include (von Lubitz and Wickramasinghe, 2006a; von Lubitz *et al.*, 2006; Figure 6.6):

A physical domain that:

- represents the current state of healthcare reality;
- encompasses the structure of the entire environment healthcare operations intend to influence directly or indirectly, e.g. elimination of disease, fiscal operations, political environment, patient and personnel education, etc.;
- has data within it that are the easiest to collect and analyze, especially that they relate to the *present* rather than future state; and
- is also the territory where all physical assets (platforms) such as hospitals, clinics, administrative entities, data management facilities, and all other physical subcomponents (including people) reside.

An information domain that:

- contains all elements required for generation, storage, manipulation, dissemination/sharing of information, and its transformation and dissemination/sharing as knowledge in all its forms;
- within the information domain, all aspects of command and control are communicated and all sensory inputs gathered;
- while the information existing within this domain may or may not adequately represent the current state of reality, all our knowledge about that state emerges, nonetheless, from and through the interaction with the information domain;
- all communications about the state of healthcare take place through interactions within this domain; and
- the information domain is particularly sensitive and must be protected against intrusions that may affect the quality of information contained within domain.

A cognitive domain that:

- constitutes all human factors that affect operations;
- is within the cognitive domain that deep situational awareness is created, judgments made, and decisions and their alternatives are formulated; and
- also contains elements of social attributes (e.g. behaviors, peer interactions, etc.) that further affect and complicate interaction with and among other actors within the operational sphere.

In essence, these domains cumulatively serve to capture and then process all data and information from the environment and given the dynamic nature of the environment new information and data must always be uploaded. Thus, the process is continuous in time and space captured by the "rolling nature" of Boyd's OODA Loop, i.e. is grounded in the process oriented perspective of knowledge generation.

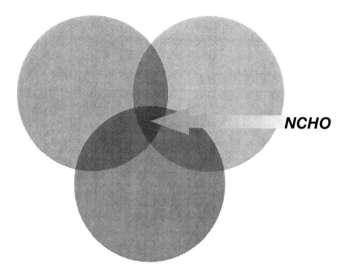

Figure 6.6 *Three Interconnecting Domains for Networkcentric Healthcare.*

Reproduced with kind permission of Doctrina Applied Research and Consulting LLC—www.consultdoctrina.com

ICT USE IN HEALTHCARE NETWORKCENTRIC OPERATIONS

The critical technologies for supporting healthcare networkcentric operations are not new, rather they are reconfigurations of existing technologies including web and internet technologies. The backbone of the network is provided by a healthcare information grid (von Lubitz and Wickramasinghe, 2006a; von Lubitz *et al.*, 2006). This grid consists of distinct domains that are each made up of multiple grids all interconnecting to enable complete and seamless information and data exchange throughout the system. Figures 6.7 and 6.8 depict the healthcare information grid with its distinct yet interconnected domains each made up of interconnecting grids.

The essential elements of the grid architecture are the smart portal that provides the entry point to the network, the analytic node with the intelligent sensors (von Lubitz and Wickramasinghe, 2006a; von Lubitz *et al.*, 2006; Figure 6.7). Taken together these elements make up the knowledge enabling technologies to support and affect critical data, information and knowledge exchanges that in turn serve to ensure effective and efficient healthcare operations.

In networkcentric healthcare operations the entry point or smart portal must provide the decision maker with pertinent information and germane knowledge constructed through the synthesis and integration of a multiplicity of data points, i.e. support and enable OODA thinking. Unlike current web pages in general and especially current medical web-portals and online databases such as MedLine, that provide the decision maker with large amounts of information that he/she must then synthesize and determine relative and general relevance, i.e. they are passive in nature, the smart portal enables the possibility to access the critical information required to formulate the Action (practical implementation) stage of Boyd's Loop.

145

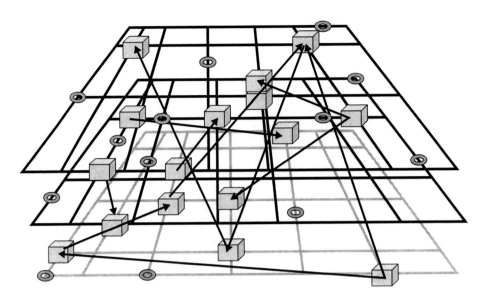

Figure 6.7 *Networkcentric Information/Knowledge Grid System.*

Source: adapted from von Lubitz and Wickramasighe (2006b)

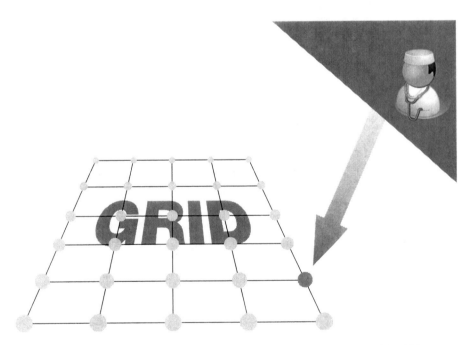

Figure 6.8 *"Knowledge Node" (e.g. Healthcare-IT System) Mapping onto Grid Architecture.*

Reproduced with kind permission of the Knowledge Management for Healthcare (KARMAH) research subgroup — www.coventry.ac.uk/karmah/

In addition, the smart portal includes the ability to navigate well through the grid system, i.e. the smart portal must have a well-structured grid map to identify what information is coming from where (or what information is being uploaded to where). In order to support the ability of the smart portal to bring all relevant information and knowledge located throughout the grid system to the decision maker, there must be universal standards and protocols that ensure the free flowing and seamless transfer of information and data throughout the healthcare information grid; the ultimate in shared services. Finally, given the total access to healthcare information grid provided by the smart portal to the decision maker it is vital that the highest level of security protocols are maintained at all times, thereby ensuring the integrity of the healthcare information grid.

The analytic nodes of the healthcare information grid perform all the major intelligence and analysis functions and must incorporate the many tools and technologies of artificial intelligence and business analytics, including OLAP (on-line analytic processing), genetic algorithms, neural networks and intelligent agents in order to continually assimilate and analyze critical data and information throughout the grid system and/or within a particular domain. The primary role of these analytic nodes is to enable the systematic and objective process of integrating and sorting information or to support the orientation stage of Boyd's Loop.

The final important technology element of the healthcare information grid is the intelligent sensor. These sensors are essentially expert systems or other intelligent detectors programmed to identify changes to the healthcare grid and data and/or information within a narrow and well-defined spectrum, such as, for example, an unusually high outbreak of anthrax in a localized geographic region, which would send a message of a possible bio-terrorism attack warning to the analytic node, or perhaps the possibility of spurious or corrupt data entering the system.

The doctrine of networkcentric healthcare operations offers several advantages. First, a similar concept is already implemented with significant success by the military establishment. Hence, the "lessons learned" can be readily adopted into the civilian environment. More importantly, however, by permitting free flow of information among currently disconnected entities and fields of healthcare operations, the networkcentric doctrine allows vast improvement in information management and use in all activities related to healthcare—from individual patient provider contact to massive, international relief operations as seen following the Tsunami of 2004.

Moreover, networkcentricity permits generation of the currently absent comprehensive, multifaceted and unified body of knowledge necessary to conduct healthcare activities in a manner addressing present inequalities through a consistent knowledge-based effort rather than, as it is presently done, through the erratic application of ever increasing funds. By the adoption of networkcentric operations for healthcare, the full potential of KM can be realized and thereby superior healthcare delivery will be effected.

The efficacy of KM within the contemporary healthcare environment encompasses improvements to clinical information availability and security. The promise of improved clinical workflows and the associated fiscal savings is now a reality due to properly organized and implemented KM programs. A relatively new modernization for U.S.-based healthcare organizations (one of which has radical consequences for healthcare transaction and administrative information systems) will now be discussed and considered.

THE HEALTH INSURANCE, PORTABILITY AND ACCOUNTABILITY ACT (HIPAA)

In the U.S., the Health Insurance, Portability and Accountability Act (HIPAA) focuses on three key elements for electronic submissions and exchange of healthcare information: security, privacy and standards (HIPAA Privacy Compliance Executive Summary, 2001; HIPAA Security Requirement Matrix, 2002; Moore and Wesson, 2002). It is useful to conceptualize this as a triangle (see Figure 6.9).

The three fundamental elements of the HIPAA regulation will now be discussed in greater detail.

Security

According to HIPAA, a number of security criteria must be met by all electronic healthcare transactions. Some of these criteria directly affect how healthcare systems can be accessed and interacted with by the users of healthcare information systems. Essentially, these security criteria fall into three main categories: administrative, physical and technical.

Transaction Standards

The standards for electronic health information transactions cover certain electronic health transactions, including claims, enrolment, eligibility, payment and co-ordination of benefits.

Figure 6.9 *The HIPAA Triangle.*

Reproduced with kind permission of Doctrina Applied Research and Consulting LLC—www.consultdoctrina.com

Privacy

The final element of the HIPAA triangle deals with ensuring the privacy of healthcare information. Specifically, the *Federal Register* (Vol. 67, No. 157) details all the rules that must be adhered to with respect to privacy. The purpose of these rules is to maintain strong protections for the privacy of individually identifiable health information, addressing the unintended negative effects of the privacy requirements on healthcare quality or access to healthcare, and relieving unintended administrative burdens created by the privacy requirements. Thus, these privacy requirements cover uses and disclosures of treatment and payment information, and create national standards to protect individuals' medical records and other personal health information.

INFORMATION PRODUCERS, CONSUMERS AND INFORMATION FLOWS WITHIN THE HEALTHCARE SYSTEM

In order to fully capture the flows of information, it is necessary to first identify the primary producers and consumers of data and information within the healthcare system. At the center of the information flows is the Health Care Information System (HCIS) because not only does it connect the key players within the healthcare system in an efficient and effective manner but also it forms the central repository for key information such as patient medical records, billing and treatment details. Hence, the HCIS provides the foundation for supporting the information flows and decision making throughout the healthcare system.

Healthcare procedures such as medical diagnostics, treatment decisions and consequent effecting of these decisions, prevention, communication and equipment usage can be thought of as iatric in nature (Perper, 1994). Integral to these iatric procedures is the generating and processing of information (Moore and Wesson, 2002). The patient naturally provides key information at the time of a clinical visit or other interaction with his/her provider.

Such a visit also generates other information including insurance information, medical history and treatment protocols (if applicable) that must satisfy regulatory requirements, payor directives and, obviously, the healthcare organization's informational needs. Thus, we see that from a single intervention many forms and types of information are captured, generated and then disseminated throughout the healthcare system. All this information and its flows must satisfy some common integrity characteristics such as accuracy, consistency, reliability, completeness, usefulness, usability and manipulability. Consequently, generating a level of trust and confidence in the information's content and processes. Since the information flows across various organizational boundaries, the challenge of ensuring information integrity is further compounded because any integrity problems will propagate with ripple effects following the same trajectory as the information itself. Given the high degree of inter-relatedness between the various players, the consequences of poor quality information (such as the cost of information integrity problems) are multiplied and far reaching. This highlights the need for robust, well-designed and well-managed HCIS (Applegate, Mason and Thorpe, 1986; Stegwee and Spil, 2001). Such a perspective should not be limited to new systems, but rather, equally and perhaps of even more importance, should be applied to existing systems as well.

INFORMATION INTEGRITY AND QUALITY (I*IQ)

Given the critical role of information both within and between the information producers and consumers in healthcare (Chandra *et al.*, 1995), it is imperative that the information flowing both within the HCIS and between the key participants in the healthcare system must exhibit both the attributes and dimensions of the information integrity construct as well as satisfy the healthcare quality aims. Specifically, the information should display the attributes of accuracy, consistency and reliability of content and processes as well as the dimensions of usefulness, completeness, manipulability and usability (Geisler *et al.*, 2003; Moore and Wesson, 2002).

INFORMATION INTEGRITY

Information integrity is an emerging area that is "not just about engineering the right properties of information but it also includes sensitivity to the context in which information is used and the purpose for its usage" (Geisler *et al.*, 2003: 5; Mandke *et al.*, 2003). More specifically, it encompasses the accuracy, consistency, and reliability of the information content, process and system. By focusing on the privacy, security and standards aspects of healthcare information, it would appear that HIPAA implicitly assumes certain characteristics of this information product such as its accuracy and reliability.

However, in practice this may not always be the case, and from the perspective of the healthcare organization it is not sufficient to be HIPAA compliant; rather it must also ensure the information product satisfies the principles of Information Integrity (I*I) standards. Implicit in taking an Information Integrity perspective is the shift from viewing information as a byproduct to viewing it as an essential product (Huang *et al.*, 1999). This requires following four key principles, namely that the information must:

- meet the consumers information needs;
- be the product of a well defined information production process;
- be managed by taking a lifecycle approach; and
- be managed and continually assessed vis-à-vis the integrity of the processes and the resultant information.

In order to actualize this Information Integrity perspective, healthcare organizations then need to implement specific protocols.

HEALTHCARE QUALITY AIMS

In the final report of the Committee on the Quality of Health Care in America (Crossing the Quality Chasm, 2001), it was noted that improving patient care is integrally linked to providing high-quality healthcare. Furthermore, in order to achieve a high quality of healthcare the committee identified six key quality aims:

1 Healthcare should be safe—avoiding injuries to patients from the care that is intended to help them.

2 Healthcare should be effective—providing services based on scientific knowledge to all who could benefit and refrain from providing services to those who will not benefit (i.e. avoiding under use and overuse).

3 Healthcare should be patient-centered—providing care that is respectful of and responsive to individual patient preferences, needs, and values and ensuring that patient values guide all clinical decisions.

4 Healthcare should be timely—reducing waiting and sometimes harmful delays for both those receiving care and those who give care.

5 Healthcare should be efficient —avoiding waste.

6 Healthcare should be equitable—providing care that doesn't vary in quality based on personal characteristics.

It is obvious that these quality aims can only be negatively impacted by poor information quality, flow and integrity. Conversely, a higher quality, flow and integrity of information will positively impact these quality aims by helping to reduce the large number of medical errors that currently permeate the healthcare system (Moore and Wesson, 2002; Geisler et al., 2003).

What becomes critical then is to incorporate these quality aims into the manufacturing of the information product so that the output is quality information. This requires the establishment of an information quality program, which serves to:

- articulate an information quality vision in healthcare business terms;
- establish central responsibilities for information quality within the information product manufacturing processes;
- educate the producers and consumers of information on information quality issues; and
- institutionalize and continuously evaluate and develop new information quality skills.

(Huang et al., 1999)

POPULOMICS

The term populomics has emerged from the synthesis of the population sciences, medicine and informatics (Gibbons, 2007; Abrams, 2006). Populomics is defined as an emerging discipline focused on population level, transdisciplinary, integrative disease/risk characterization, interdiction and mitigation that rely heavily on innovations in computer and information technologies. Populomics seeks to characterize the interplay of socio behavioral pathways and biophysiologic and molecular mechanisms that work across levels of existence, to impact health particularly, at the population level. Schematically, it can be portrayed as follows (Figure 6.10):

Increasingly, scientific evidence suggests that disease causation results from complex interactions of social, environmental, behavioral and biologic factors that simultaneously and often co-operatively act across more than one level of existence over time (Gibbons et al., 2007). Thus a comprehensive understanding of health and disease requires the integration of knowledge derived from the bench, sociobehavioral and population sciences. Most historic and contemporary conceptual models of health though, have often been derived either from

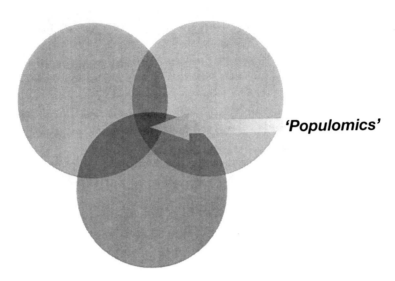

'Populomics'

Figure 6.10 *Depicting "Populomics".*

"Populomics" concept courtesy of M. Chris Gibbons, MD MPH. Schematic reproduced with kind permission of Doctrina Applied Research and Consulting LLC—www.consultdoctrina.com

the socio-behavioral sciences *or* the biomolecular sciences. With the exception of those pathways based on stress (neuro-immunological) mechanisms, the published frameworks in the behavioral sciences and epidemiological literature largely lack clearly stated, causal biologic connections to observed health outcomes (LaLonde, 1981; Evans and Stoddart, 1990; Macintyre, 1997; Acheson, 1998; Williams, 1999). On the other hand, most biologically oriented formulations poorly account for socio-environmental and behavioral effect modifiers that may profoundly influence the pathogenesis of disease and the development of health disparities (Meyer and Breitner, 1998; Sharma, 1998; Phillips and Belknap, 1999; Burger and Gimelfarb, 1999).

To complicate matters further, scientists and investigators trained in the clinical and bench sciences are generally taught to consider only discreet, quantitative exposures (viral, bacterial, toxicological, psychological, etc.) as etiologic agents of disease. Historically they have primarily studied these etiologic agents in isolation from the broader socio-behavioral contexts in which they exist. Social and behavioral scientists though, often consider more qualitative factors such as poverty, socioeconomic status and racial segregation as key determinants of health (Berkman and Kawachi, 2000; LaVeist, 2002). Usually most social scientists only consider other more quantitative exposures as factors that alter the nature of the association between a social factor and a given health outcome (Amick *et al.*, 1995). Most socio-behavioral scientists also study etiologic factors in isolation from the biophysiologic and/or molecular genetic mechanisms on which living organisms depend.

Because scientific investigation has historically progressed along these two largely parallel perspectives, the domain of clinical medicine, which largely derives from the biophysiologic and molecular genetic sciences, has been largely concerned with a hospital-based, individualized approach to health and disease. On the other hand, the domain of public health has historically been that of populations in communities. In the past, this dichotomy has indeed served science well and has rapidly led to many scientific advances in knowledge. Today however, healthcare challenges related to the burgeoning proportions of elderly citizens in the U.S. and the widespread documentation of racial and ethnic disparities in healthcare, are suggesting the need to reconsider the dichotomization of the role of sociobehavioral and community factors in healthcare research and clinical medicine. Elderly patients often suffer from multiple chronic diseases for which they are taking several medications. They may need home- and community-based health "support" services but may not need to be hospitalized.

Consequently, more family and community residents are becoming "caregivers" and "care providers." This shift is enhancing the impact of social, behavioral, community and economic realities on their therapeutic regimens and provider relationships. In short, the social and behavioral sciences, which traditionally had not been considered within the domain of healthcare, are increasingly recognized as fundamentally linked to illness, health and healthcare outcomes (Singer and Ryff, 2001) while the need for an integrated approach to health research and healthcare is gaining appreciation, thinking across disciplinary lines can be challenging.

Recently the Sociobiologic Integrative Model (SBIM) model has been proposed as a conceptual transdisicplinary research construct that provides for biologically driven conceptual integration of both sociobehavioral and biomolecular concepts known or hypothesized to influence disease pathogenesis in individuals and among populations (Gibbons *et al.*, 2007). As such, the SBIM facilitates organization of heterogeneous clinical, biological and socio-environmental data elements from and in relation to the biomolecular mechanisms through which they must operate, to impact health outcomes.

Finally, the growing realization of healthcare disparities is forcing clinical researchers to think about disease causation not only among individual patients, but also across entire groups or populations of people. Among patients who have vastly differing cultural beliefs and practices, diets, educational or literacy levels and socioeconomic resources, clinical practitioners and researchers developing interventions that ignore these sociocultural realities may struggle to demonstrate or maintain therapeutic efficacy across increasingly multicultural populations of patients.

TRANSDISCIPLINARITY AND THE ROLE OF HEALTH INFORMATION TECHNOLOGY

Disentangling the myriad determinants of disease and the biomolecular mechanisms through which they operate, especially within the context of healthcare disparities, cannot comprehensively be accomplished in the absence of a transdisciplinary approach nor without a significant reliance on the computational and information sciences. In the last decade, advances in computing and information sciences have been the catalyst for several methodological leaps in the biological and molecular sciences (e.g. DNA chip technology, and genome wide association studies), and speed the emergence of whole new fields of study (metabolomics, proteomics and regulomics) in the clinical and bench sciences.

Similarly, the potential also exists for similar ICT-based advances (Gibbons, 2005; Abrams, 2006) among public health physicians, those practicing in areas of social medicine and healthcare disparities researchers. In addition to improving the efficacy of current clinical interventions, new technology-based tools may facilitate the analysis and interpretation of population level data to enable the development of "community [population] arrays" or community-wide risk profiles based on clinical and socioenvironmental data. This population-level risk characterization could potentially go beyond the limitations of current analyses and yield insights distinctly different from those based on current epidemiologic or sociobehavioral methodologies (Gibbons, 2007).

Sociocultural and environmental realities are suggesting the need for integrated approaches within contemporary healthcare. Although overcoming the historic inertia towards dichotomization of the biomedical and social sciences may be challenging, informatics offers the promise of being a catalytic agent for scientific innovation in healthcare among populations. While in some ways similar to public health informatics, populomics is distinct in that it specifically focuses on the integration of medical and social sciences to foster the elucidation of the biophysicologic and molecular mechanisms that undergird socioenvironmentally determined outcomes among populations. In many ways, populomics research builds on the best of centuries of extraordinary scientific and clinical advances, and extends these by highlighting the need to focus on the *relationships* between groups of socioenvironmental factors and the underlying mechanisms that operate in communities and among populations.

In so doing it may lead to tools and methodologies to identify subpopulations that are superior to contemporary approaches of delineating subpopulations of people based on race, socioeconomic status, educational status or genetic mutations. Finally, in the future, therapeutics derived from populomics oriented research may significantly improve our ability to promote health, provide high-quality healthcare to every citizen and, in so doing, eliminate racial and ethnic disparities in healthcare.

POPULOMICS AND KNOWLEDGE MANAGEMENT

In essence, KM embodies organizational processes that seek synergistic combination of data and information processing capacity of information technologies, and the creative and innovative capacity of human beings. This confluence of three seemingly disparate concepts (population science, medicine and informatics) has parallels with the growing field of KM; the connection can be seen clearly in Figure 6.11.

It has been argued that such improvements and improvements in disciplines as supposedly diverse as organizational behavior, ICT, teamwork, artificial intelligence, leadership, training, motivation and strategy have been equally applicable and relevant in the clinical and healthcare sectors as they have been in others. Clinicians and managers have used many of these disciplines (in combination) many times before; they may have, inadvertently and partially, carried out KM *avant la lettre* (Bali *et al.*, 2005).

Having depicted the clear link between populomics and KM, we can extend this further by mapping the schematic to the concept of NCHO (described earlier). From Figure 6.12, we see that the key unifying component or common denominator is knowledge. KM principles and methodologies provide researchers and practitioners (concerned with health impacts associated with the urban environment) valuable analytic tools and a systematic approach to the integration of different types of data to enable novel knowledge-based insights and spur scientific advances in Urban Health.

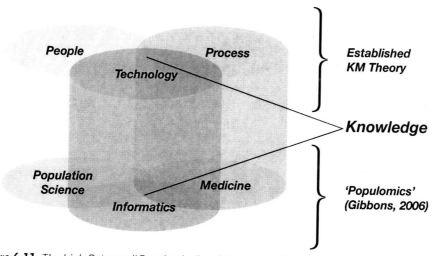

Figure 6.11 *The Link Between "Populomics" and Knowledge Management.*
Reproduced with kind permission of Doctrina Applied Research and Consulting LLC—www.consultdoctrina.com

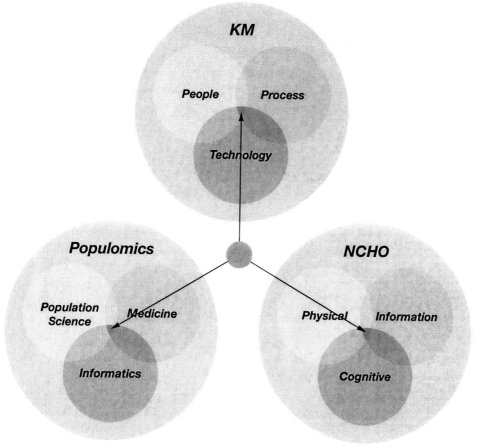

Figure 6.12 *Knowledge as a Unifier.*
Reproduced with kind permission of Doctrina Applied Research and Consulting LLC—www.consultdoctrina.com

SUMMARY AND CONCLUSIONS

In order to successfully incorporate KM, an organization must give careful consideration to how to extract germane knowledge pertinent information and relevant data if it is to truly derive the full value from KM. In this chapter, one systematic yet elegant method for ensuring that at all times germane knowledge is provided to the decision maker is via Boyd's OODA Loop and the consequent application of OODA thinking. In addition, the chapter presented a systematic and robust method for ensuring that an organization continues to succeed with KM; namely the intelligence continuum that is always focused on enhancing the current state and existing knowledge base. Finally, the chapter provided scenarios of applications of KM to underscore the universality of KM to all organizations, as well as presented a discussion on how it is relevant to industry.

REVIEW QUESTIONS

1 Describe the four stages of Boyd's OODA Loop.

2 Why is it essential to have germane knowledge?

3 Why do we say the business environment is dynamic and complex?

4 Why has intelligence gathering become so important?

5 Describe how the intelligence continuum enhances the extant knowledge base?

6 Describe scenarios where KM is useful?

DISCUSSION QUESTIONS

1 Why does the OODA Loop always enable an organization to have germane knowledge and stay ahead of its competition?

2 Can you think of a situation where KM would not be helpful and why?

CASE EXERCISE: KM AND THE SOCIOBIOLOGIC INTEGRATIVE MODEL (SBIM) [11]

Introduction

This case exercise briefly introduces a multidisciplinary conceptual model to assist understanding relevant issues in urban health and health disparities: the Sociobiologic Integrative Model (SBIM).

The model integrates the seemingly disparate areas of sociobehavioral science and biomolecular science. By adopting this holistic perspective, the model could enhance the nascent link between sociobehavioral investigation and biophysiologic or biomolecular mechanisms and enable novel insights and facilitate the development of better therapeutic interventions. Any model detailing all possible biologic pathways through which all possible social and behavioral factors impact all possible health outcomes would obviously be exceedingly complex. On the other hand, an overly simplistic model would likewise be of little value (Berkman and Kawachi, 2000). This case will provide an illustrative example that demonstrates how information from disparate fields might be integrated within a single biologically plausible, mechanistically driven, multilevel framework.

The SBIM

The SBIM depicts health and disease as existing on a two dimensional continuum from birth to death along the x axis and organized from cellular level systems to societal systems along the y axis. As such, this model can be used to depict health or disease among individuals and also among populations. In contrast to most classical medical bench scientific investigative models that seek to isolate the fundamental causes of illness which are often thought to exist within cellular, molecular or submolecular systems, the SBIM posits that causal factors exist across each of the depicted levels of organization. Some of these factors exert direct influence on DNA (direct inputs), others modify the activity, effect, dose or exposure of these direct inputs or otherwise themselves act indirectly on DNA (indirect inputs). All inputs then are acted upon by well-described, psychological and/or somatic homeostatic or regulatory systems.

If, however, one or more of these systems is unable to adequately surmount the challenge induced by the inputs, then a potentially health impacting outcome will occur. These outcomes themselves exist at the cellular/molecular level, individual and group (neighborhood, societal) levels. Implicit in this model is the notion that across a given population, not all individuals with a given health outcome will have obtained that health outcome via the same causal pathway or as a result of being impacted by the same set of direct/indirect inputs. Yet it is likely, that within populations there are one or more input/mechanism sets that are responsible for disease in larger proportions of people, while there are also one or more input/mechanism sets that cause disease in a minority of individuals in that population. These input/mechanism sets may be termed "causal profiles" or "community arrays."

The challenge then for science becomes that of thinking across systems of biologic and social organization to define the timing, scope, intensity and relevance of interactions between factors and to define those causal profiles that exist within a given population of individuals. Because this type of investigation seeks to understand not only isolated causal elements, but also the nature of interactions among elements remaining in the biologic and/or social contexts within which they exist, it is likely to facilitate a much better understanding of disease pathogenesis and outcomes, particularly at the population level (pandemics, epidemics, disparities) and lead to scientific insights that much more closely approximate reality, have much better predictive value and lend themselves better to the development of more efficacious multilevel health and healthcare interventions and therapies.

Lung Cancer and the SBIM

Current scientific evidence indicates that the development of lung cancer is preceded by one or more carcinogenic direct inputs (exposures), including tobacco, asbestos, radon and polycyclic aromatic hydrocarbons (PAHs) (Franceschi and Bidoli, 1999; Pitot, 2002a; Alberg and Samet, 2003). In addition, several other factors (indirect inputs) have the ability to modify these exposures. These may include physical proximity of housing to a source of ambient air particulate toxicants or individuals living in housing units located close to a factory spewing carcinogenic emissions from its smoke stack, DNA damage, abnormal methylation of tumor associated genes, and increased risk of lung cancer. Thus, both proximity of urban residence to a carcinogenic source (Morello-Frosch et al., 2002; Kinney et al., 2002), occupational exposures (Benowitz, 1997; Fielding et al., 1998; Hecht, 1999; Morello-Frosch et al., 2002) and ambient air toxicant concentrations likely influence cumulative individual and population PAH exposure (Zmirou et al., 2000; Belinsky et al., 2002; Kyle et al., 2002; Pope et al., 2002; Sorenson et al., 2003).

Dietary intake of fruits and vegetables has been linked to the activity of Cytochrome p. 450 and the Glutathione –S-Transferase enzymatic systems, thereby inhibiting phase I bioactivation of carcinogens and inducing phase II carcinogenic detoxification (Yang et al., 2001; Zhao et al., 2001; Weisburger and Chung, 2002). Thus, broccoli in the diet would be an individual-level indirect input, whereas the availability of broccoli at local grocery stores, the price of broccoli in those stores, or whether or not individuals would choose to eat broccoli would, on the other hand, represent societal (neighborhood), SES (market forces dictating prices), and cultural (certain cultures tend not to eat certain things) factors, which in the SBIM framework would all represent population-level indirect inputs. Local or national regulatory policy may also influence lung carcinogenesis at the population level by either indirectly influencing dietary food choices or by influencing carcinogenic exposures among populations.

Finally, many factors including genetic polymorphisms, can impact the carcinogenic potential of the PAHs and thus act as indirect inputs in this model (Kamataki et al., 1999; Shields, 1999; Haugen et al., 2000; Song et al., 2001; Alexandrov et al., 2002; Itoga et al., 2002; Lewis et al., 2002; Miller et al., 2002; Stucker et al., 2002; Sunaga et al., 2002). Researchers then could seek to elucidate the relationships between these multilevel phenomenon, which all operate along the lung cancer causal chain in individuals, to produce lung cancer or not and also among populations to produce a given lung cancer disparity.

While many others may be posited, especially at cellular and subcellular levels, the biomolecular experimental literature contains several excellent reviews that summarize the expansive current knowledge of biochemical and molecular genetic events involved in the metabolism of tobacco carcinogens (Pitot, 2002b). As such, these will not be detailed.

Finally, according to the SBIM, lung cancer will occur if the combined effects of all important carcinogenic direct and indirect inputs are sufficient to cause the accumulation of phenotypic and genotypic abnormalities, such that tumor initiation, promotion and progression will occur in individuals (disease) or populations (disparity). Thus, as can be seen from the preceding example, a single organizing framework such as the SBIM is needed to help organize the myriad of factors involved in lung cancer susceptibility and occurrence among individuals or to comprehensively explain differential outcomes between populations.

Health Disparities, Lung Cancer and the SBIM

Racial and ethnic disparities in lung cancer offer an illustrative case in point. According to Surveillance Epidemiology and End Results (SEER) data, African-American men have significantly elevated lung cancer incidence and mortality rates compared to white men. African-American women, on the other hand, have only a slightly elevated lung cancer incidence and essentially the same lung cancer mortality rate compared to white women (Cancer Facts and Figures, 2003).

The SBIM suggests that at a minimum, precise lung cancer risk characterization must include an assessment of tobacco-smoking patterns, geographic factors, occupational exposures and major potential indirect inputs. The evidence suggests that among working age individuals, overall smoking rates do not significantly differ between non-Hispanic African-Americans and non-Hispanic whites. Furthermore, only a small gender difference in smoking prevalence exists (men = 24.7, 95 percent confidence interval [CI] 23.9–25.6; women = 20.8, 95 percent CI 20.1–21.5; whites = 24.5 percent, 95 percent CI 23.8–25.2; and African-Americans = 2, 2.2 percent, 95 percent CI 22.1–23.3) (CDC, 2003). Smoking trends in the U.S. over the last three decades suggest that the prevalence of current smoking has consistently been highest among blacks and in black men in particular, with generally lower rates for women (Zang and Wynder, 1998; Garfinkel, 1997). Men generally smoked more cigarettes per day than women, but overall, whites smoke more cigarettes than blacks (Garfinkel, 1997; Zang and Wynder, 1998).

Recent increases in smoking by African-American women, however, have led to cigarette consumption rates on par with African-American men (Zang and Wynder, 1998). Despite the higher number of cigarettes smoked by Caucasians, most African-Americans smoke the brands with higher tar yields per cigarette (Zang and Wynder, 1998). Finally, in the 1960s and 1970s the age at smoking initiation for women was approximately four years later than men. By the 1990s, this difference had been reduced to two years (Zang and Wynder, 1998). Thus, although cigarette smoking is associated with the majority of lung cancer cases today, epidemiologic evaluation of historic smoking patterns in the U.S. do not easily help to explain racial differences in lung cancer incidence and mortality. Other potential factors, including occupation and place of residence, may be important in the genesis of observed lung cancer disparities.

Racial and ethnic minority workers are generally overrepresented in blue collar and service jobs while underrepresented in professional careers (Murray, 2003). In many of these jobs, minority workers are differentially exposed to occupational carcinogens, resulting in disproportionate disease (Murray, 2003). Also, significant proportions of racial and ethnic minority workers live in central cities, in close geographic proximity to industrial plants or factories. Finally, men comprise the majority of workers who work in exposure-prone industries (miners, steel workers and chemical industry workers). Individually, these findings do not suggest a unified causal pathway. However, by employing the SBIM to collectively understand how these contributing factors may collectively impact tumor biology, biologically plausible clues begin to emerge.

One possible pathway that is suggested by the SBIM is that differential exposures related to urban residence and occupation across racial and ethnic groups may act co-operatively to influence the genesis of lung cancer disparities. For example, at baseline, men smoke more than women and blacks smoke higher tar-yielding cigarettes compared to whites. In addition, this smoking-related risk elevation in African-Americans might be further heightened via ambient air carcinogenic exposures among African-Americans who live in the urban inner city. This could further elevate the risk of lung cancer in African-Americans above that of white Americans who are less likely to live

159

in neighborhoods with elevated baseline ambient air carcinogen levels or smoke high tar cigarettes. Among men, African-American incidence and mortality rates may still be further increased through occupational carcinogenic exposures, which biologically act synergistically with smoking patterns and geographic exposures. Women, both African-American and Caucasian American, who comprise a substantially smaller proportion of the workers in exposure-prone industries would not have this additional exposure and thus may not be expected to have lung cancer incidence and mortality rates at par with African-American men. Finally, indirect inputs including insurance status, healthcare access, dietary factors, genetic polymorphisms or regulatory policy may attenuate or potentiate this pathway as outlined in previous sections.

Discussion

Current scientific evidence suggests that disease causation in general and health disparities in particular result from complex interactions of many factors that simultaneously and often co-operatively act across more than one level of influence over time. An integrated understanding of disease or disparities causation would likely facilitate research and breakthroughs in treatments and interventions.

We will briefly introduce a multilevel, transdisciplinary integrative and systems oriented organizing model called the Sociobiologic Integrative Model. Then, using lung cancer as a case in point, we illustrate that this model provides a population-oriented, biologically grounded framework for understanding cancer etiology and pathogenesis. We also use the model to provide a mechanistic framework for understanding lung cancer disparities.

This model facilitates integrative cross-disciplinary investigation and communication by providing a common conceptual model and terminology while articulating a biologically driven construct employing both sociobehavioral and biologic variables that influence disease pathogenesis. We acknowledge that some investigators will favor further subdivisions at each of the proposed levels of organization presented in this model. For example, social scientists may prefer that the population level be subdivided into family, neighborhood and community levels. On the other hand, clinical scientists may want the individual level to be further subdivided into an "organ" level, whereas molecular scientists may seek a submolecular level to be added to the model.

Whereas each of these modifications may make sense to a given investigator, they also may have no meaning to an investigator who works largely on a different level. For example, social scientists may not see a reason or value of further subdividing the individual or cellular levels of the model whereas molecular scientists may see no need for multiple subdivisions at the population level. Indeed, further subdivisions of the basic model may increase confusion across disciplines. As such, this model presents a basic three-level framework. Yet, the authors vigorously encourage individual scientists and groups to further subdivide the model as deemed appropriate to facilitate their investigations. In this way, it is hoped that this model may help science to move beyond only attempting to identify isolated causes of disease or isolated causes of health disparities (be they behavioral, biologic or environmental), to also seeking to uncover patterns of behavior-biology interaction that positively or negatively affect individuals and populations. In so doing, we may then improve our understanding of health and disease at the interface of biology, behavior and the environment.

Case Exercise References

Alberg, A.J. and Samet, J.M. (2003) Epidemiology of Lung Cancer, *Chest*, 123: 21S–49S.

Alexandrov, K., Cascorbi, I., Rojas, M., Bouvier, G., Kriek, E., and Bartsch, H. (2002) CYP1A1 and GSTM1 Genotypes Affect Benzo[a]pyrene DNA Adducts in Smokers' Lung: Comparison with Aromatic/Hydrophobic Adduct Formation, *Carcinogenesis*, 23: 1969–1977.

Belinsky, S.A., Snow, S.S., Nikula, K.J., Finch, G.L., Tellez, C.S., and Palmisano, W.A. (2002) Aberrant CpG Island Methylation of the p16(INK4a) and Estrogen Receptor Genes in Rat Lung Tumors Induced by Particulate Carcinogens, *Carcinogenesis*, 23: 335–339.

Benowitz, N.L. (1997) Smoking and Occupational Health, in J. Ladou (Ed.), *Occupational and Environmental Medicine*. Stamford, CA: Appleton & Lange, pp. 713–722.

Berkman, L.F. and Kawachi, I. (2000) *Social Epidemiology*. New York: Oxford University Press.

Cancer Facts and Figures (2003) Washington DC: American Cancer Society.

CDC (2003) Early Release of Selected Estimates Based on Data from the 2001 National Health Interview Survey, CDC National Center for Health Statistics. Available online at www.cdc.gov/nchs/about/major/nhis/released200207.htm#early (accessed September 3, 2008).

Fielding, J.E., Husten, C.G., and Eriksen, M.P. (1998) Tobacco: Health Effects and Control, in R.B. Wallace (Ed.), *Public Health and Preventive Medicine*. Stamford, CA: Appleton & Lange, pp. 817–846.

Franceschi, S. and Bidoli, E. (1999) The Epidemiology of Lung Cancer, *Annals of Oncology*, 10 (supp. 5), S3–S6.

Garfinkel, L. (1997) Trends in Cigarette Smoking in the United States, *Preventive Medicine*, 26: 447–450.

Haugen, A., Ryberg, D., Mollerup, S., Zienolddiny, S., Skaug, V., and Svendsrud, D.H. (2000) Gene-Environment Interactions in Human Lung Cancer, *Toxicology Letters*, 112–113: 233–237.

Hecht, S.S. (1999) Tobacco Smoke Carcinogens and Lung Cancer, *Journal of National Cancer Institute*, 91: 1194–1210.

Itoga, S., Nomura, F., Makino, Y., Tomonaga, T., Shimada, H., Ochiai, T., Iizasa, T., Baba, M., Fujisawa, T., and Harada, S. (2002) Tandem Repeat Polymorphism of the CYP2E1 Gene: An Association Study with Esophageal Cancer and Lung Cancer, *Alcoholism: Clinical and Experimental Research*, 26: 15S–19S.

Kamataki, T., Nunoya, K., Sakai, Y., Kushida, H., and Fujita, K. (1999) Genetic Polymorphism of CYP2A6 in Relation to Cancer, *Mutation Research*, 428: 125–130.

Kinney, P., Chillrud, S., Ramstrom, S., Ross, J., and Stansfeld, S.A. (2002) Exposure to Multiple Air Toxics in New York City, *Environmental Health Perspectives*, 110 (supp. 4): 539–546.

Kyle, A.D., Woodruff, T.J., Buffler, P.A., and Davis, D.L. (2002) Use of an Index to Reflect the Aggregate Burden of Long-Term Exposure to Criteria Air Pollutants in the United States, *Environmental Health Perspectives*, 110 (supp. 1): 95–102.

Lewis, S.J., Cherry, N.M., Niven, R.M., Barber, P.V., and Povey, A.C. (2002) GSTM1, GSTT1 and GSTP1 Polymorphisms and Lung Cancer Risk, *Cancer Letters*, 180: 165–171.

Miller, D.P., Liu, G., De Vivo, I., Lynch, T.J., Wain, J.C., Su, L., and Christiani, D.C. (2002) Combinations of the Variant Genotypes of GSTP1, GSTM1, and p53 are Associated with an Increased Lung Cancer Risk, *Cancer Research*, 62: 2819–2823.

Morello-Frosch, R., Pastor, M., Porras, C., and Sadd, J. (2002) Environmental Justice and Regional Inequality in Southern California: Implications for Future Research, *Environmental Health Perspectives*, 110 (supp. 2): 149–154.

Murray, L.R. (2003) Sick and Tired of Being Sick and Tired: Scientific Evidence, Methods, and Research Implications for Racial and Ethnic Disparities in Occupational Health, *American Journal of Public Health*, 93: 221–226.

Pitot, H.C. (2002) *Fundamentals of Oncology*. New York: Marcel Dekker.

Pitot, H.C. (2002) The Host-Tumor Relationship, in H.C. Pitot (Ed.), *Fundamentals of Oncology*. New York: Marcel Dekker, pp. 743–781.

Pope, C., Burnett, R., Thun, M., Calle, E., Krewski, D., Ito, K., and Thurston, G. (2002) Lung Cancer, Cardio-pulmonary Mortality, and Long-Term Exposure to Fine Particulate Air Pollution, *Journal of the American Medical Association*, 287: 1141.

Shields, P.G. (1999) Molecular Epidemiology of Lung Cancer, *Annals of Oncology*, 10 (supp. 5): S7–11.

Song, N., Tan, W., Xing, D., and Lin, D. (2001) CYP 1A1 Polymorphism and Risk of Lung Cancer in Relation to Tobacco Smoking: A Case-Control Study in China, *Carcinogenesis*, 22: 11–16.

Sorenson, M., Autrup, H., Hertel, O., Wallin, H., Knudson, E., and Logan, R.A. (2003) Personal Exposure to PM2.5 and Biomarkers of DNA Damage, *Cancer Epidemiology Biomarkers & Prevention*, 12: 191–196h.

Stucker, I., Hirvonen, A., de Waziers, I., Cabelguenne, A., Mitrunen, K., Cénée, S., Koum-Besson, E., Hémon, D., Beaune, P., and Loriot, M.A. (2002) M.A. Genetic Polymorphisms of Glutathione S-Transferases as Modulators of Lung Cancer Susceptibility, *Carcinogenesis*, 23: 1475–1481.

Sunaga, N., Kohno, T., Yanagitani, N., Sugimura, H., Kunitoh, H., Tamura, T., Takei, Y., Tsuchiya, S., Saito, R., and Yokota, J. (2002) Contribution of the NQO1 and GSTT1 Polymorphisms to Lung Adenocarcinoma Susceptibility, *Cancer Epidemiology Biomarkers & Prevention*, 11: 730–738.

Weisburger, J.H. and Chung, F.L. (2002) Mechanisms of Chronic Disease Causation by Nutritional Factors and Tobacco Products and their Prevention by Tea Polyphenols, *Food & Chemical Toxicology*, 40: 1145–1154.

Yang, C.S., Chhabra, S.K., Hong, J.Y., and Smith, T.J. (2001) Mechanisms of Inhibition of Chemical Toxicity and Carcinogenesis by Diallyl Sulfide (DAS) and Related Compounds from Garlic, *Journal of Nutrition*, 131: 1041S–45S.

Zang, E.A. and Wynder, E.L. (1998) Smoking Trends in the United States between 1969 and 1995 based on Patients Hospitalized with Non-Smoking-Related Diseases, *Preventive Medicine*, 27: 854–861.

Zhao, B., Seow, A., Lee, E.J., Poh, W.T., Teh, M., Eng, P., Wang, Y.T., Tan, W.C., Yu, M.C., and Lee, H.P. (2001) Dietary Isothiocyanates, Glutathione S-Transferase -M1, -T1 Polymorphisms and Lung Cancer Risk among Chinese Women in Singapore, *Cancer Epidemiology Biomarkers & Prevention*, 10: 1063–1067.

Zmirou, D., Masclet, P., Boudet, C., Dor, F., and Dechenaux, J. (2000) Personal Exposure to Atmospheric Polycyclic Aromatic Hydrocarbons in a General Adult Population and Lung Cancer Risk Assessment, *Journal of Occupational & Environmental Medicine*, 42: 121–126.

Case Exercise Questions

1   Describe how incorporating the tools, techniques, technologies and tactics of KM can help in the context of SBIM?

2   The concept of KM and populomics are both relatively new—discuss, in the context of this case exercise, how introducing such new concepts impacts on the clinician, the patient and the delivery of healthcare. Specifically, what are the benefits? Are there any disadvantages?

FURTHER READING

Boyd, J.R. (1976, 2002) Destruction and Creation, in R. Coram (Ed.), *Boyd*. New York: Little, Brown & Co.

Davenport, T. and L. Prusak (1998) *Working Knowledge*. Boston, MA: Harvard Business School Press.

Liebowitz, J. (2008) *Making Cents Out of Knowledge Management*. Lanham, MD: The Scarecrow Press.

Wickramasinghe, N. and von Lubitz, D. (2007) *Knowledge-Based Enterprise Theories and Fundamentals*. Hershey, PA: IGI.

Wigg, K. (1993) *Knowledge Management Foundations*. Arlington, VA: Schema Press.

REFERENCES

Abrams, D.B. (2006) Applying Transdisciplinary Research Strategies to Understanding and Eliminating Health Disparities, *Health Education & Behaviour*, 33(4): 515–531.

Acheson, D. (1998) *Independent Inquiry into Inequalities in Health*. London: Department of Health.

Alavi, M. and Leidner, D. (1999) Knowledge Management Systems: Issues, Challenges and Benefits, *Communications of the Association for Information Systems*, 1 Paper #5.

Alberts, D., Garstka, J., and Stein, F. (2000) Network Centric Warfare: Developing and Leveraging Information Superiority, *CCRP Publication Series*, Washington, DC: Dept of Defense, pp. 1–284. Available online at www.dodccrp.org/publications/pdf/Alberts_NCW.pdf.

Amick, B.C., Levine, S., Tarlov, A.R., and Walsh, D.C. (1995) *Society and Health*. New York: Oxford University Press.

Applegate, L., Mason, R., and Thorpe, D. (1986) Design of a Management Support System for Hospital Strategic Planning, *Journal of Medical Systems*, 10(1): 79–94.

Award, E. and Ghaziri, H. (2004) *Knowledge Management*. Upper Saddle River, NJ: Prentice-Hall.

Bali, R.K., Dwivedi, A.N., and Naguib, R.N.G. (2005) Issues in Clinical Knowledge Management: Revisiting Healthcare Management, in R.K. Bali (Ed.), *Clinical Knowledge Management: Opportunities and Challenges*. Hershey, PA: Idea Group.

Berinato, S. (2002) CIOs at the Heart of Health-Care Change, *CIO Magazine*, June 15.

Berkman, L.F. and Kawachi, I. (2000) *Social Epidemiology*. New York: Oxford University Press.

Boyd, J. (1976, 2002) Destruction and Creation, in R. Coram (Ed.), *Boyd*. New York: Little, Brown & Co.

Boyd, J. (1987) Essence of Winning and Losing, in Patterns of Conflict, unpublished briefing. Available online at www.d-n-i.net.

Brown, J. and Duguid, P. (2002) *The Social Life of Information*. Boston, MA: Harvard Business School Press, pp. ix–328.

Burger, R. and Gimelfarb, A. (1999) Genetic Variation Maintained in Multilocus Models of Additive Quantitative Traits under Stabilizing Selection, *Genetics*, 152(2): 807–820.

Cebrowski, A. and Garstka, J. (1998) Network-Centric Warfare: Its Origin and Future, *U.S. Naval Institute Proceedings*, 1: 28–35.

Chandra, R., Knickrehm, M., and Miller, A. (1995) Healthcare's IT Mistake, *The McKinsey Quarterly* (5): 7–11.

Courtney, J. (2001) Decision Making and Knowledge Management in Inquiring Organizations: Toward a New Decision-Making Paradigm for DSS, *Decision Support Systems Special Issue on Knowledge Management*, 31: 17–38.

Crossing the Quality Chasm (2001) A New Health System for the 21st Century Committee on Quality of Health Care, in *America Institute of Medicine*. Washington, DC: National Academy Press.

Drucker, P. (1993). *Post-Capitalist Society*. New York: HarperCollins.

Drucker, P. (1999) Beyond the Information Revolution, *The Atlantic Monthly*, October: 47–57.

Evans, R.G. and Stoddart, G.L. (1990) Producing Health, Consuming Health Care, *Social Science & Medicine*, 31(12): 1347–1363.

Geisler, E., Lewis, D., Nayar, M., and Prabhaker, P. (2003) Information Integrity and Organizational Performance: A Model and Research Directions working paper.

Gibbons, M.C. (2005) A Historical Overview of Health Disparities and the Potential of eHealth Solutions, *Journal of Medical Internet Research*, 7(5): e50.

Gibbons, M.C. (2007) *eHealth Solutions for Health Care Disparities*. New York: Springer.

Gibbons, M.C., Brock, M., Alberg, A.J., Glass, T., LaVeist, T.A., Baylin, S.B. *et al.* (2007) The Socio-Biologic Integrative Model: Enhancing the Integration of Socio-Behavioral, Environmental and Bio-Molecular Knowledge in Urban Health and Disparities Research, *Journal of Urban Health*, 84(2): 198–211.

Health Insurance Portability and Accountability Act (HIPPA) (2001) *Privacy Compliance Executive Summary*. Stamford, CT: Protegrity.

HIPAA (2002) Security Requirement Matrix. Available online at www.hipaa.org.

Holmes, J., Abbott, P., Cullen, R., Moody, L. *et al.* (2002) Clinical Data Mining: Who Does It, and What Do They Do?, *AMIA 2002 Symposium*, November 9–13. Conference proceedings, San Francisco, CA.

Huang, K., Lee, Y., and Wang, R. (1999) *Quality Information and Knowledge*. Upper Saddle River, NJ: Prentice-Hall.

LaLonde, M. (1981) *A New Perspective on the Health of Canadians*. Government of Canada, working document, Ottawa: Government of Canada.

LaVeist, T.A. (2002) *Race and Health*. San Francisco, CA: Jossey-Bass.

McGee, M. (1997) High-Tech Healing, *Information Week*, September 22.

Macintyre, S. (1997) The Black Report and Beyond: What Are the Issues?, *Social Science & Medicine*, 44(6): 723–745.

Mandke, V., Bariff, M., and Nayar, M. (2003) Demand for Information Integrity in Healthcare Management, in *The Hospital of the Future Conference Proceedings*, 2nd International Conference on the Management of Healthcare and Medical Technology, Chicago, IL: August.

Massey, A., Montoya-Weiss, M., and O'Driscoll, T. (2002) Knowledge Management in Pursuit of Performance: Insights from Nortel Networks, *MIS Quarterly*, 26(3): 269–289.

Meyer, J.M. and Breitner, J.C. (1998) Multiple Threshold Model for the Onset of Alzheimer's Disease in the NAS-NRC Twin Panel, *American Journal of Medical Genetics*, 81(1): 92–97.

Moore, T. and Wesson, R. (2002) Issues Regarding Wireless Patient Monitoring Within and Outside the Hospital, in *The Second Hospital of the Future Conference Proceedings*, Chicago, U.S.

Newell, S., Robertson, M., Scarbrough, H., and Swan, J. (2002) *Managing Knowledge Work*. New York: Palgrave.

Nonaka, I. (1994) A Dynamic Theory of Organizational Knowledge Creation, *Organizational Science*, 5: 14–37.

Nonaka, I. and Nishiguchi, T. (2001) *Knowledge Emergence*. Oxford: Oxford University Press.

Pallarito, K. (1996) Virtual Healthcare, *Modern Healthcare*, March: 42–44.

Perper, J. (1994) Life Threatening and Fatal Therapeutic Misadventures, in M. Bogner (Ed.), *Human Error in Medicine*. Hillsdale, NJ: Lawrence Erlbaum Associates, pp. 27–52.

Phillips, T.J. and Belknap, J.K. (2002) Complex-Trait Genetics: Emergence of Multivariate Strategies, *Nature Reviews Neuroscience*, 3(6): 478–485.

Schaffer, J.L., Steiner, C., Krebs, V.E. and Hahn, J. (2004) Orthopedic Operating Room of the Future, unpublished data.

Schultze, U. and Leidner, D. (2002) Studying Knowledge Management in Information Systems Research: Discourses and Theoretical Assumptions, *MIS Quarterly*, 26(3): 212–242.

Sharma, A.M. (1998) The Thrifty-Genotype Hypothesis and Its Implications for the Study of Complex Genetic Disorders in Man, *Journal of Molecular Medicine*, 76(8): pp. 568–571.

Shin, M. (2004) A Framework for Evaluating Economies of Knowledge Management Systems, *Information & Management*, 42(1): 179–196.

Singer, B.H. and Ryff, C.D. (2001) *New Horizons in Health: An Integrative Approach*. Washington, DC: National Academy Press.

Stegwee, R. and Spil, T. (2001) *Strategies for Healthcare Information Systems*. Hershey, PA: Idea Group Publishing.

von Lubitz, D. and Wickramasinghe, N. (2006) Creating Germane Knowledge in Dynamic Environments, *International Journal of Innovation and Learning*, 3(3): 326–347.

von Lubitz, D. and Wickramasinghe, N. (2006a) Healthcare and Technology: The Doctrine of Networkcentric Healthcare, *International Journal of Electronic Healthcare*, 4: 322–344.

von Lubitz, D. and Wickramasinghe, N. (2006b) Dynamic Leadership in Unstable and Unpredictable Environments, *International Journal of Innovation Learning*, 4: 339–350.

Wickramasinghe, N. (2006a) Knowledge Creation: A Meta-Framework, *International Journal of Innovation and Learning*, 3(5): 558–573.

Wickramasinghe, N. (2006b) Healthcare Knowledge Management: Incorporating the Tools, Technologies, Strategies and Processes of KM to Effect Superior Healthcare Delivery, in R.K. Bali and A. Dwivedi (Eds), *Healthcare Knowledge Management*. Berlin: Springer, pp. 87–103.

Wickramasinghe, N. and von Lubitz, D. (2007) *Knowledge-Based Enterprise Theories and Fundamentals*. Hersey, PA: IGI.

Wickramasinghe, N. and Schaffer, J. (2006) Creating Knowledge Driven Healthcare Processes with the Intelligence Continuum, *International Journal of Electronic Healthcare*, 2(2): 164–174.

Wickramasinghe, N. and J.B. Silvers (2003) IS/IT: The Prescription to Enable Medical Group Practices to Manage Managed Care, *Health Care Management Science*, 6: 75–86.

Wickramasinghe, N., Geisler, E., and Schaffer, J. (2005a) Realizing the Value Proposition for Healthcare by Incorporating KM Strategies and Data Mining Techniques with the Use of Information Communication Technologies, *International Journal of Healthcare Technology and Management*, 7(3/4): 303–318.

Wickramasinghe, N., Bloomendal, H., de Bruin, A., and Krabbendam, K. (2005b) Enabling Innovative Healthcare Delivery through the Use of the Focused Factory Model: The Case of the Spine Clinic of the Future, *International Journal of Innovation and Learning*, 1: 90–110.

Williams, D.R. (1999) Race, Socioeconomic Status, and Health. The Added Effects of Racism and Discrimination, *Annals of the New York Academy of Sciences*, 896: 173–188.

Case Exercise

IMPLEMENTING THE NATIONAL LOCAL OWNERSHIP PROGRAMME (NLOP): INFORMATION SYSTEMS STRATEGY FOR CRANE CARE TRUST[12]

by Sushil Rai Patria

Background

This case summarizes local provider organization IM&T's plans for 2008/9. The contents are in line with the national requirements for local NHS organizations, specified in the following documents:

- Department of Health NHS Operating Framework for England 2008/9 (Department of Health, 2007a).
- Department of Health Guidance on Preparation of Local IM&T Plans (Department of Health, 2007b).

NHS IT Chronology

The use of IT systems in General Practice started many years ago, and has continually evolved—a brief chronology is as follows:

1970s	First General Practitioner clinical systems introduced
1993	RFA [Requirements for Accreditation] Accreditation systems reimbursed (NHS Information Management Centre, 1993)
1998	Information for Health (RCGP, 1998)
2000	The NHS Plan (Secretary of State for Health, 2000)
2002	The Wanless Report (Wanless, 2001)
2002	Delivering the NHS Plan (Secretary of State for Health, 2002)
2002	Delivering 21st Century IT Support for the NHS (Department of Health, 2002)

2002   National Programme for IT (NPfIT)
2005   NHS Connecting for Health (CfH)
2006   IM&T DES as part of the GMS/ PMS Contract.

NPfIT and NHS Connecting for Health (CfH)

NHS Connecting for Health (CfH) is the agency delivering key Department of Health (DH) priorities in the National Programme for Information Technology (NPfIT). The agency is tasked with providing new IT facilities for the NHS to improve patient care in all parts of the health service, by reducing risks, increasing efficiency and enabling more effective ways of working. As the NPfIT is developed and implemented, IT solutions for primary care will continue to evolve towards the NCRS (House of Commons Health Committee, 2007). There are many aspects of work in General Practice today that were previously manual and now use technology. Traditionally clinicians have recorded patient notes and correspondence on paper or on the computer without any requirements, ensuring that the terminology used provides a universal understanding. Many practices today would struggle to survive without the automated processes now using technology for pathology, registrations, appointments and many more daily workflows required in General Practices.

Crane Care Trust Commitment to IM&T

"The Care Trust's commitment to Connecting for Health and the IM&T Modernization agenda has been reflected in the investment of new resources across the directorate, leading to new opportunities for implementing innovative technology." Consequently, as those ICT projects started in 2008/09 (Crane Care Trust, 2008a) are completed in 2009/2010, a key challenge will be to realize the benefits of this investment and ensure that the technology is aligned to the Trust's key deliverables that are identified in the Crane Care Trust Performance Plan (Crane Care Trust, 2008b).

The Trust has historically been acknowledged as a high performing organization in the LHE, achieving best value in its procurements through the use of partnership arrangements increasing multi-agency working. To maintain the standard of a highly efficient provider of good quality services and cross economy benefits, the challenges are ahead to deliver what has been agreed in the plans and allocated resources.

The priorities for the year ahead are for improving health and the well being of the local population by achieving a set of outcomes that the people of the local population should see as a result from Crane establishing a Care Trust organization status from a Primary Care Trust on 1 October 2006. The establishment of a Care Trust has required the organization to change the way in which it provides its services impacting on the organizational culture. The key deliverables outlined are:

1 People will live longer healthier and happier lives
   − Develop information tools to improve data collection.
2 There will be less inequality across the borough
   − Improve access to improved core systems functionality.
3 More people will be able to care for themselves and to live independently
   − Develop user-centered assessment tools.

4 Easy and fast access to good specialist services will be available when needed
   – Develop patient record functionality.
5 There will be more involvement by people in local decisions, be it individually, as a community or more widely
   – Implement access to care record summary.
6 Services will be more joined up and there will be less bureaucracy
   – Integrated systems development.
7 Crane NHS Care Trust is a good place to work, staff are valued and good leadership is recognized
   – Further develop IM&T education and training development programs.
8 Decision-making is streamlined and based on good quality information
   – Deploy Connecting for Health programme.
9 Set an example for working with other employers to make Crane a healthy and thriving place to live and work
   – Implement national ICT standards.

The key deliverables identified are outlined in the Performance Plan, which supports the Business Plan and the Local Delivery Plans. Everyone in the organization has a role to play in the local town; a place where well-being, pride and quality of life is enjoyed by all (Serougi and Burton, 2008).

Implementation of NPfIT Products

A set of national IM&T expectations for 2008/09 is referred to in the Operating Framework (Department of Health, 2007a). A checklist within the Guidance document is addressed by the following headings, showing how the local IM&T plan meets national expectations and exploits the solutions available under NPfIT contracts.

Local Strategic Solutions

In line with the NHS implementation plans for Local Service Provider (LSP) strategic product sets providing clinical applications, all NHS providers need to include in their plans both deployment and the substantial business transformation and infrastructure readiness required to exploit these technologies. Implications for not providing these plans within timescales may impact on care provided to patients within the LHC.

Implementation Plans

There are no current implementation plans in place for the replacement of the Care Trust's community and social care systems (including child health). This is due to on going discussions with LSP and Strategic Health Authority (SHA) regarding the availability of The Phoenix Partnership's (TPP) "System One" application. An evaluation process is in place while the Trust will assess the business and service benefits as a pre-curser to introducing the key projects required to manage a successful technical deployment and change management programme. This will support overcoming barriers to change in the organization.

Business Preparedness

The Care Trust has capacity and capability both through its Organizational Development team and within the Information Management and Technology (IM&T) Directorate itself to ensure that all areas of engagement pertinent to business preparedness are identified and actioned. These will be materialized through a programme management structure that ensures high level ownership within the Trusts but additionally as part of the performance management framework agreed through the NLOP Board and the SRO.

Additionally, following the joint working agreements with BEN PCT as part of the LHE delivery model, Crane Care Trust will deploy the Business Change Team to address operational change management and clinical engagement in the light of their experience with the iSOFT "IPM" system recently deployed at BEN PCT. This will allow sharing of knowledge while identifying key problems with system migrations.

Local Technical Infrastructure

Currently the Trust's technical infrastructure has been developed using good practice standards in line with NPfIT but it recognizes that to deliver the full remit of benefits envisaged by CfH, it will be required to adopt the NHS Infrastructure Maturity Model (NIMM) at the appropriate time in order to align with other inter-dependent workstreams.

N3 Network

N3 is the name for the National NHS Network, which replaces the private NHS communications network NHSnet. N3 provides fast, broadband networking services to the NHS offering reliability and value-for-money. The N3 Service Provider is organizationally independent although the network is managed by British Telecom in a contract agreement with the NHS NPfIT.

N3 will be as important to the NHS as road and rail networks are to our daily lives. The new, high-speed network will make it possible to deliver the reforms and new services needed to improve patient care, such as those detailed above together with Picture Archiving and Communications (PACS) (the transfer of digital images such as x-rays and scans). N3 is vital to the delivery of the NPfIT, providing the essential technical infrastructure through which the benefits to patients, clinicians and the NHS from NPfIT can be realized.

In light of this, the Trust is part of a larger Community of Interest Network implementation (COIN) to replace a range of tactical wide area network solutions in place across the area. This network would be used to deliver CfH National Applications as well as local applications. There are significant advantages to utilizing a shared network to deliver local as well as National Applications rather than having a separate "overlay" network for National Applications. It will be easier to manage and represent better value for money for both the NHS nationally and for the locality.

GP Systems of Choice

In March 2006, NHS Connecting for Health published a proposal for GP Systems of Choice (GPSoC). The proposal is under consideration by the DH. GPSoC had input from GPs via the CfH primary care clinical leads (Connecting for Health 2006a). GPSoC will encourage GP system providers to upgrade their systems through a series of compliance levels in accordance with the GPSoC Maturity Model. The levels provide an objective basis on which to evaluate systems and set standards that GPSoC systems must achieve. The national standards become more stringent as higher compliance levels are achieved, and provide a roadmap along which practices can plan, aligned with the strategic objectives of the CfH. The Trust is in the process of upgrading the infrastructure within General Practitioners' premises to ensure compliance in the delivery of GPSoC. The Trust has systematically ensured that an IT infrastructure rolling replacement programme is in place that will assist in the delivery of care to patients.

Technical Infrastructure

The Trust is more dependent and reliant on technology than ever before. Modern hardware and software is essential in providing a robust infrastructure to support the Trust's business needs and the electronic patient record systems. This infrastructure includes equipment in four main areas— networks, distribution servers, personal computers and peripherals, e.g. printers and scanners.

The Trust operates a number of different hardware types (Dell, Compaq, Toshiba etc.) and software products (Microsoft 2000 and XP, SQL, MS Office 2000, XP, 2003, etc.) A team of technical specialists support the Trust's infrastructure, utilizing a wide range of knowledge and experience to meet the requirements of the organization and service users.

It is important to create a single Microsoft infrastructure. This should have no more than two concurrent operating systems and two Microsoft office versions for desktop and operational infrastructure to ensure resources are used effectively. This also allows in-house expertise to be developed to further support the Trust's business, offers greater workforce flexibility and will allow greater exploitation of existing and future technologies. This will also facilitate the introduction of automated maintenance tasks, which in turn provides greater project and development opportunities. The Trust is keen to exploit the use of the software Enterprise-Wide agreement (EWA) so it can benefit from this financial and best practice point of view while considering future directions.

Implementation of a rolling replacement programme for all equipment over three years old would provide continuity of the Trust's business and patient services. It would also be less likely that equipment would break down, providing a reliable operational environment.

In order to maintain an appropriate infrastructure and thereby meet service needs, there is a requirement to provide adequate ongoing investment both to support existing services and future development. Support of the IT infrastructure is essential and will require sufficient personnel with the relevant specialist training to fully exploit its capabilities.

It is important to keep up to date with new software releases and manage the training implications that these may bring. Additionally, over the next twelve months, the Trust will begin to introduce additional productivity tools to the end user, including MS Share Point. The potential benefits of utilizing MS Share Point are quite significant, although pilot testing is required for a thorough risk evaluation prior to procurement.

Networking

The Trust must provide a cost-effective, secure, independent, resilient and robust network, which will support all service needs, while acknowledging that this will not be provided solely by N3 as originally predicted. There is a requirement to incorporate business continuity in network planning; for example by providing alternate routes for network traffic so that if one fails the traffic is automatically rerouted to the other line.

The technical infrastructure is effectively the backbone that enables the Trust to function. Without this infrastructure in place, the Trust's ability to function would be severely compromised. With this in mind, it is important to ensure the health of this infrastructure is not compromised, as it is the key enabler to everything the IM&T department delivers to support the business of the organization. The Trust will therefore ensure that appropriate investment is maintained to keep the systems live, allowing business continuity.

Information Governance and Statement of Compliance

The Trust has been working in all areas of Information Governance (IG) and in 2007 completed the NHS CfH Information Governance Statement of Compliance migration process from the Code of Connection to the Statement of Compliance agreement (Connecting for Health, 2006b).

In addition, all thirty-one General Practices have completed the Information Governance Toolkit and have achieved compliance for the NHS CfH Information Governance Statement of Compliance migration process.

Patient Administration Systems (PAS) and Eighteen-week Referral to Treatment

In order to support the measurement of patients' waiting times, NHS providers will need to implement the appropriate changes to their PAS. Currently the Trust is implementing an upgrade to the Trust's community clinical system that will allow the recording and monitoring of eighteen-week waits. This is currently going through rigorous testing and will be implementing within the live system once testing is complete.

Information Governance and Data Quality

To meet the NHS commitment to maintain appropriate confidentiality of patient data, IG policy and practice should reflect the increases in the potential to share information afforded by the programme.

Care Record Guarantee

Part of the programme from CfH is to provide a Care Record Guarantee for the NHS in England that aims to provide to patients/clients the highest quality of healthcare. To enable the NHS to do this, all Trusts must keep records about patients/clients health and the care provided to them. Patients/clients records held by Crane NHS Care Trust are administered within a framework for handling information in a confidential and secure manner to appropriate ethical and quality standards, which is overseen by the IG Manager.

Information Sharing Protocols

IG has four fundamental aims and is measured using an electronic toolkit that can help organizations achieve the following:

1 Support of the provision of high quality care by promoting the effective and appropriate use of information.
2 A means for responsible staff to work closely together, preventing duplication of effort and enabling more efficient use of resources.
3 Development of support arrangements and providing staff with appropriate tools and support to enable them to discharge their responsibilities to consistently high standards.
4 To enable organizations to understand their own performance and manage improvement in a systematic and effective way.

The IG Framework and the IG Toolkit currently encompass a number of areas. These cover: The Data Protection Act 1998, The Freedom of Information Act 2000, The Confidentiality Code of Practice, Records Management, Information Quality Assurance, Information Security, Information Governance and Management Specific organizational views.

Information Governance

The Trust has recently completed an initial assessment identifying the area in which it needs to improve in order to reach an acceptable level. An action plan has been drafted to ensure that work is carried out to help the Trust achieve green status.

In 2007/2008 considerable changes have been made to the IG Toolkit and a new version (5) has been produced, which incorporates the evolving areas of CfH, and the requirements to support commercial third parties in respect of their Statement of Compliance application and additional requirements for PCTs to support Payment by Results and Secondary Uses.

Requirements	Results (based on requirements v4)
Management	66 percent
People	88 percent
Process	61 percent
Systems	66 percent

The Trust has a robust Freedom of Information system that has been in place since January 2005. It is compliant with legislation and the IG toolkit for responding to patient requests for non-personal information such as the Trust's data sharing policy.

Such requests are dealt within the Trust by information champions; there are thirty-two members of staff located in key areas of the Trust who have received training in all areas of Freedom of Information, and any information requests are logged onto the Trust's computerized handling system. A log of these members and requests are maintained by the IG Manager.

Requests for information are managed by the IG Manager in line with the Trust's Freedom of Information policy and guidelines, which clearly lay out the process for dealing with such requests. All requests are responded to within twenty working days. From October 2006, Crane Primary Care Trust merged with local authority Adult Social Services to become Crane Care Trust. Within the merger the Trust developed and instigated an overarching information sharing policy with the local authority that became part of the Partnership agreement between both authorities for the implementation of the new organization within the NHS, and this was ratified by both legal services, and was communicated as part of the Trust's communications strategy for the formation of the new organization.

The Trust and the local authority have reviewed aspects of the Partnership agreement; in particular ownership of information, and both legal services have determined that the ownership of Adult Social Service information should fall under the remit of the Trust. The respective Information Governance Managers from the Trust and the local authority have been tasked to facilitate the transfer, by developing detailed proposals and protocols.

Patient Identifiable Data

The Trust views patient identifiable data as a valuable asset that must be stored in a secure confidential manner, which it does in compliance with the following standards and legislation:

- Confidentiality
- Caldicott
- Data Protection.

Relevant Trust policies and procedures that are all available to staff on the intranet and patients on the publication scheme are:

- Code of Confidentiality
- Data Protection Policy
- Freedom of Information Policy + Guidelines
- Information Governance Policy
- Records Management Policy.

Considerations and Recommendations

The timing of deployment programs across the country will vary depending on the state of readiness of practices and the development of programs in various localities. Implementing a local IS strategy meeting requirements in line with the NPfIT has proved to be difficult, with much political debate and criticism publicized (Health Service Journal, 2006; eHealth Insider, 2007). Although the NPfIT has had many set backs with delivering objectives to original timescales, there are many benefits, as discussed throughout this document. To successfully implement the NLOP consideration to vital factors on organizational change, such as technical/ operational/ management issues, political/ social/ economical influences with identified risks must be considered. The use of effective clinical engagement and communications with timely and seamless delivery is vital while specialized training, allocated resources and learning from best practice will allow a strong strategic position that is essential for business continuity and improving workflow processes. Providing the best healthcare service to local patients will allow the Care Trust to ensure the organization is meeting its aims by "improving the health and well being of our population."

Case Exercise References

Connecting For Health (2006a) *GP Systems of Choice*. Available online at www.connectingforhealth.nhs.uk/systemsandservices/gpsupport/gpsoc/framework/planned (accessed May 2, 2008).

Connecting For Health (2006b) *Information Governance Statement of Compliance*. Available online at www.connectingforhealth.nhs.uk/systemsandservices/infogov/igsoc/faqs/about (accessed May 28, 2008).

Crane Care Trust (2008a) *Business Plan 2008/09*. Available online at www.xxxx.nhs.uk/foi/boardpapers/april 2008/2008-066%20SCT%20Business%20Plan.pdf (accessed May 27, 2008).

Crane Care Trust (2008b). Available from website anonymized (accessed May 28, 2008).

Department of Health (2007a) *The NHS in England: the Operating Framework for 2008/09*. London: Stationery Office. Available online at www.dh.gov.uk/en/Publicationsandstatistics/Publications/PublicationsPolicyAnd Guidance/DH_081094 (accessed May 27, 2008).

Department of Health (2007b) *Our NHS Our Future: NHS Next Stage Review Interim Report*. London: Stationery Office. Available online at www.dh.gov.uk/en/Publicationsandstatistics/Publications/PublicationsPolicyAnd Guidance/DH_079077 (accessed May 27, 2008).

eHealth Insider (2007) *MPs Say EPRs Essential But Delivery in Doubt*. Available online at www.e-health-insider.com/News/3024/mps_say_eprs_essential_but_delivery_in_doubt (accessed May 27, 2008).

Health Service Journal (2006) *Realizing the Benefits and Managing the Challenges of NHS IT: An Independent Analysis of National and Local Solutions*. Available online at www.hsj-nhsit.co.uk/homepage.asp?m_pid=0&m_nid=11398 (accessed April 22, 2008).

Langlands, A. (1998) *Health Service Circular: Information for Health: An Information Strategy for the Modern NHS*. Available online at www.dh.gov.uk/prod_consum_dh/groups/dh_digitalassets/@dh/@en/documents/digital asset/dh_4011790.pdf (accessed May 27, 2007).

NHS Information Management Centre (1993) *Requirements for Accreditation: Annex B*. Available online at www.redbook.i12.com/rb/Docs/rb605.htm (accessed May 26, 2008).

Royal College of General Practitioners (RCGP) (1998) *Information for Health: An Information Strategy for the Modern NHS 1998–2005*. Available online at www.rcgp.org.uk/docs/ISS_SUMM98_13.DOC (accessed May 27, 2008).

Secretary of State for Health (2000) *The NHS Plan*. London: The Stationery Office. Available online at www.dh.gov.uk/prod_consum_dh/groups/dh_digitalassets/@dh/@en/documents/digitalasset/dh_4055783.pdf (accessed April 22, 2008).

Secretary of State for Health (2002) *Delivering the NHS Plan*. London: The Stationery Office. Available online at www.dh.gov.uk/prod_consum_dh/groups/dh_digitalassets/@dh/@en/documents/digitalasset/dh_4059526.pdf (accessed April 22, 2008).

Sergoui, N. and Burton, S. (2008) *IM&T Performance Plan 2008/09*.

Wanless, D. (2001) *Securing Our Future Health: Taking a Long term View*. London: HM Treasury. Available online at www.hm-treasury.gov.uk/consultations_and_legislation/wanless/consult_wanless_final.cfm (accessed May 22, 2008).

Case Exercise Questions

1 Why and how can a KM approach facilitate the implementation process?

2 Outline a suitable KM driven success scenario. Be as specific as you can and be sure to address all people, process and technology issues.

Case Exercise

THE IMPACT OF ICT INITIATIVES WITHIN THE NHS MATERNITY SERVICES[13]

by Kim Davis

Introduction

At its conception in 1948, the NHS held three core principles: (a) that it meet the healthcare needs of everyone; (b) that it be free at the point of delivery; and (c) that it be based on clinical need, and not the ability to pay. The aim was to create a uniform service combining all hospitals under one central system with the ideal that healthcare should be available to all regardless of wealth or status. Sixty years on, the NHS is relatively uniform but with significant inequalities in service and quality of care with access to treatment. This report will focus and discuss the technical change management issues induced by the introduction of IT systems into the NHS with a particular focus on maternity services.

The NHS has undergone many reorganizations in its history; for example, the formation of twenty-eight Strategic Health Authorities (SHAs). Current restructuring is moving towards decentralization. Devolving delivery of service to local units allows greater innovation and freedom to meet the needs of the local population and improve quality of service and access to those services (The NHS Plan, 2000). The Government directed a review of the long-term trends affecting healthcare. The Wanless Report (2002) reviewed key factors that impacted on resources in healthcare and the projected expenditure, until 2022.

NHS Funding

The majority of the NHS is tax financed heathcare, while private healthcare is ultimately based on the patient's ability to pay. Additionally, income, political attitude and comparable qualities of services within the NHS and private sector, are factors that have had an impact on the purchase of private medical insurance (Besley *et al.*, 1999). Individual choice of either public funded or private healthcare has been influenced by a reduction in eligibility to access totally public funded treatments within certain services such as drug prescriptions, dentistry and ophthalmology (Propper, 2000).

Maternity services are not affected by these particularly changes in policy and NHS maternity care is given without charge at the point of delivery. However, in comparison to other European countries, the U.K. has contributed significantly less to healthcare (approximately 1–1.5 percent less on an annual basis). This has been a major factor in the inadequacies of healthcare provided by the NHS today (Wanless, 2002). The Wanless Report concluded that the U.K. must significantly increase national spending in the following twenty years to improve healthcare in terms of quality and levels of care, to gain equivalent standards with that of its European Union (EU) partners. However, it still remains that effective use of resources, income and education will still influence outcomes despite an increase in expenditure. The Report provides a detailed model on the projected costs of delivering a high-quality health service by 2022. In 2002–3 total expenditure on healthcare, including private healthcare, was approximately 7.7 percent of GDP. Calculating expenditure on a model used by the Report, three options were projected as follows:

Option 1 *Solid Progress*	Public engagement in relation to health using health care system appropriately Higher rise in life expectancy Health status improves Health service more responsive More efficient use of resources including extensive information communication technology
Option 2 *Slow Uptake*	No change in level of public engagement to health Minimal rise in life expectancy Health status is constant or deteriorates Relatively unresponsive health service low rates of productivity and IT
Option 3 *Fully Engaged*	High levels of public engagement to health Increased life expectancy beyond the anticipated Dramatic improvement in health status Responsive health service system with high rates of technology using resources more efficiently

Using these options, The Wanless Report estimated NHS spending would rise from between 9.4 and 11.3 percent of GDP by 2022–2023. However, each option is entirely dependent on projected public engagement in relation to health, improved health status and life expectancy, more efficient use of resources and extensive use of technology. It also assumes the premise that private health expenditure would remain constant at 1.2 percent of GDP. If different scenarios are used this would result in widely divergent estimates.

Organizational Structure

Today, the NHS has a multidivisional organizational structure. It remains a state-run organization with accountability through the Secretary of State with ultimate responsibility at Government level.

NHS reforms have, over the years, shifted from one of centralization to one of purchase and providers, and the introduction of an internal market. One of the major reforms, The NHS Plan (2000) focuses on the importance of quality issues. Clinicians and managers have greater independence to manage local services within a national framework.

Information and Communication Technology

The NHS organization consists of multiple layers of health service providers, each responsible for the procurement of their own IT systems. This has led to a vast amount of systems that have not been introduced in a coherent approach; therefore integration and sharing of information between providers and across the services has not been efficient or effective. In order to increase efficiency, effectiveness, equity and reduce risk, particularly at the point of care, The National Programme for Information and Technology (NPfIT) was introduced in 2002. Connecting for Health (CfH) is the Government agency responsible for the implementation of NPfIT. It is the largest civil technology programme undertaken and is intended to unite separate NHS organizations. This is a centrally driven mandate.

The aim is to electronically connect all 50 million plus patient records, allowing access by patients and health professionals in over 30,000 GP Practices and 300 hospitals. It was envisaged that during an incremental period of ten years, NPfIT will bring modern computer systems into the NHS, changing the way the NHS works to improve patient care and services. The new IT infrastructure is intended to unite multiple computer systems across the NHS to provide:

The NHS Care Records Service (NCRS)
delivering an individual electronic record for each NHS patient

Choose and Book
an electronic booking service for booking hospital appointments, which allows patients to choose the time and place of their appointment

Electronic Transmission of Prescriptions
e.g. prescriptions issued directly from a GP practice to a pharmacy

NHS (N3)
a national broadband IT network to support the programme

Picture Archiving and Communications Systems
enabling digital images to be captured, distributed, stored and displayed electronically

Quality Management and Analysis System and IT Supporting GP Payments Contact
a central email and directory service for the NHS

Although the procurement cost of the technology was initially set at £6.2 billion, the National Programme has incurred problems and is behind schedule. The Department of Health has not maintained detailed records of overall expenditure on the Programme; however, it has conceded that the estimated cost of the new service could be £20 billion over ten years; this excludes running costs (House of Commons, 2007). However, the formation of a single demographic database gives rise to many concerns. In particular, how this information will be used, by whom and how patient confidentiality and security will be maintained are common themes among those resistant to a national database. Many patients and clinicians are concerned that the system is not secure (Carvel, 2006). A number of clinicians are skeptical of the need for integrated records via a national database, as systems already exist for locality data sharing between relevant GP's and hospitals "without the need to leave a copy of the information on the nationally accessible database" (Leigh, 2006). In order to satisfy patient concerns and control access, the consequence of illegal misuse of data from the databases may require greater legal penalties than the current financial ones.

Proposed Changes Within Maternity Services

New Targets

Current NHS reforms aim "to develop a patient led NHS that uses available resources as effectively and fairly as possible to promote health, reduce health inequalities and deliver the best and safest healthcare" (Department of Health, 2006). Maternity organizations must therefore supply accessible, efficient, quality care. Services should provide care that is women focused, considering individual needs of health status, culture, religion, social needs and disabilities. High quality, efficient maternity services are essential in contributing to the attainment of the Department of Health's Public Service Agreement (PSA) targets (HM Treasury, 2004). In relation to maternity services, the PSA targets include:

- reduction by 10 percent of health inequalities, measurable by infant mortality and life expectancy at birth;
- a substantial reduction of mortality rates;
- reduction by 1 percent per annum of women who smoke in pregnancy;
- reduction in the under 18 year old conception rate; and
- increase in breastfeeding rates by 2 percent per annum.

(HM Treasury, 2004)

In addition, the Department of Health produced the Maternity Standard, National Service Framework (NSF) for Children Young People and Maternity Services (2004) identified as best practice guidance. The NSF is based on a care pathway approach. Care pathways place value on women-focused care rather than meeting the needs of the service. In doing so emphasis is placed on evidenced-based procedures and guidelines representing a method for continuous quality improvement. Maternity care pathways will provide a system through which services will be integrated between primary, secondary and social services to provide comparable high-quality effective clinical care. Identifying a clear pathway will establish definitive managerial and clinical responsibilities, with agreed administration of the process within local and national guidelines and protocols. It will also decrease duplication of workload and instigate an equitable quality of care.

Maternity Matters

The NSF in conjunction with the PSA targets accentuate the need that improved, accessible maternity services will not only provide for the safety and wellbeing of both mother and baby, but can be influential in improving family health. In April 2007, the Department of Health document "Maternity Matters" (2007) outlines the Government's commitment to providing high-quality maternity services with emphasis on accessibility, safety and choice to women and their partners, to be implemented by 2009. Women will be entitled to support from a named midwife during her pregnancy and following the birth, known as the post-natal period. In addition, women may also choose their maternity care to be delivered by non-local maternity facilities if it is within that provider's capacity.

Maternity Matters (2007) identifies four national choice guarantees that are to be implemented by 2009. The national choice guarantees are as follows:

- Choice of how to access maternity care.
- Choice of type of antenatal care.
- Choice of place of birth—depending on their circumstances, women and their partners will be able to choose between three different options. These are:
  - home birth;
  - birth in a local facility, including a hospital under the care of a Midwife; and
  - birth in a hospital supported by a local maternity care team including Midwives, Anaesthetists and Consultant Obstetricians. Women who are considered to have high risk pregnancies will be advised that this the safest option.
- Choice of place of postnatal care.

This strategy aims to identify future plans for the improvement of maternity services, developing policies on how to deliver the aims and objectives by engaging (a) the workforce; (b) finance; (c) commissioning; and (d) monitoring service activity and performance.

To comply with the four national guarantees depends on the capacity of the service to deliver patient choice. Currently there are considerable constraints concerning workforce and infrastructure. These constraints are crucial factors that limit choice. However, patient choice is unavoidably limited as a result of clinical need or finite resources.

Changes to Funding

At present, 80 percent of total NHS expenditure is calculated by using information generated from activity data and subsequently delivery of those units of activity (Wanless, 2002). Other costs could only be broken down by type of expenditure as there is insufficient data regarding unit activity and its delivery. Obstetric patients, community maternity services and screening fall into this 20 percent category. Therefore, the cost of supplying maternity care within the U.K. is inadequately calculated. To support the implementation of the Maternity Standard NSF, a national maternity dataset is being developed. The initial aim is a secondary purpose use for planning and commissioning of services. The intention is to identify historic under funding, allow activity to be separated, identified and calculated, and determine level of resources required to deliver maternity services.

Previous budgets were negotiated principally on historic budgets and the skilful bargaining of managers with commissioning through block agreements or "cost and volume" contracts. This process made inadequate attempts to specify the activity and payments. Treatments and interventions were grouped together under broadly similar Healthcare Resource Groups (HRG) and budgets were set by national tariffs based on the average cost of providing treatment in each HRG. Costs were then based on reference costs from two years previous. Adjustments were made dependent on market forces, for example, certain areas tended to place unique burdens on the NHS, such inner city areas with higher drug abuse dependency. There was no motivation to increase productivity or efficiency, as there was no additional reward dividend. Therefore, the NHS Plan (2000) introduced the Government objectives to associate the distribution of funds with activity. Payment by Results (PbR), a financial rule-based system, as a means for paying trusts, was introduced. By using a national price list, a "tariff," for units of activity, providers are paid according to activity. In most cases payment will be linked to activity and adjusted for types of patients and treatment episodes. This change in money flow also provides incentives to reward best use of capacity and performance and will also identify uneconomical units of activity.

Resource Management

Meeting targets and existing commitments as made by the NHS Plan and the implementation of National Service Frameworks will require additional skills and alteration in the current workforce. This will inflict managerial difficulties in the rate of service expansion. The rate of expansion of activity is determined by the capacity within the system. This not only involves infrastructure, but also information systems technology and a sufficiently skilled workforce. If capacity capability is not synchronized with the growth rates of activity, then costs will rise. But if improvements for change are to slow, then this would delay advancement in quality and access to healthcare.

The Workforce

The large scale and constituents of the workforce will have a major impact on change within the NHS. In comparison to other countries, the U.K. has a lower number of healthcare professional per population (Wanless, 2002). Recruitment and retention of staff in some services, particularly midwifery, create significant difficulties and can seriously affect patient care .The NHS Plan proposes new ways of working to reduce professional barriers resulting in a more flexible workforce between staff groups. In addition, it aims to increase the amount of skilled workforce. Nurse Practitioners/ Midwives could assume 20 percent of a doctor's work, while Health Care Assistants (HCAs) could perform duties of the Nurse/Midwife workload. This skill mix change would increase the workforce capacity. However, significant investment in IT would reduce administration time, allowing increased time for providing patient care.

Patient Expectations

Patients today are better informed with access to better information regarding treatment, management and prevention of illness and diseases. Patients have rights to informed consent but also demand informed choice of type and place of their care. Healthcare does not meet patient expectations, particularly regarding access of care and waiting times for treatment. In addition, the health service is not yet sufficiently patient centered. The Wanless Report included survey evidence showing that patients commonly feel that they have insufficient involvement in decisions, there is no one to talk to about anxieties and concerns, tests and treatment are not clearly explained, with insufficient written information provided. A survey by the Department of Health observed that women using NHS maternity services would have preferred more choice in type of care and place of delivery (Maternity Services Survey, 2005).

In addition, there is a commitment from the Department of Health to improve patient information; in particular, the areas of consent (NHS Plan, 2000). Moreover, the NHS Litigation Authority risk management standard, Healthcare Commission Standards, and the Department of Health Toolkit for producing patient information, provide national standards that Trusts must adhere to. Certain geographical locations have experienced an increase in European migrants. This has had impacts on maternity services, particularly with language difficulties. For local Trusts there are cost implications involving translators and written forms of communications that are not met centrally. With widening access to current maternity healthcare information, for example via the internet, the general public are more assertive and better informed to demand change within maternity services.

Data Handling Issues

Data Integrity

Patient clinical records when recorded in text format by health professionals will vary widely when describing the same subject matter. Codified information will ensure data integrity that is more easily exchanged between systems. Ultimately this will result in a reduction of errors, and in addition, improve patient care through clinical audit and best evidenced-based practice. However, this will require an agreed coding system and clinician compliance. The international division of the NHS CfH are currently partnering the College of American Pathologists who has developed SNOMED CT Systemized Nomenclature of Medicine Clinical Terms, which is a system of comprehensive standardized clinical terminology. To date, an absolute coding system is not yet in place.

Functionality

The delivery of Lorenzo software for clinical functionality will not be available as a solution for integration until probably 2011. Lorenzo is core for administration and for the installation of electronic patient records. Connecting for Health will have to consider a solution for the interim period. This may require Local Service Providers to extend contracts and will have implications for additional costs to local trusts for support and maintenance (Hoeskma, 2007).

There are increasing concerns regarding the capability of the Lorenzo software to meet the requirements of CfH while supplying a generic solution. This will result in delays, projects deadlines not being met and ultimately they may not be fit for purpose.

Information Governance

It is paramount that all patient identifiable data remains confidential and secure. Information governance provides the framework to support these values. This framework is formed around a number of concepts, such as: data integrity, the Caldicott Principles, the Data Protection Act 1998, and local and national standards and procedures. The NHS has approved the compliance of international standards for information security management systems IS027001 through the introduction of information governance. The use of recognized standards assures a level of quality and uniformity. All staff must comply with security procedures including the maintenance of data confidentiality and data integrity. Failure to do so carries strict penalties.

BARRIERS TO CHANGE

Modern Maternity Services

Maternity services within the U.K. are predominately provided by the NHS. Less than 1.2 percent of GDP is spent on all private heathcare (Wanless, 2002). However, all maternity providers are subject to both Government regulation and clinical professional legislation and codes of conducts. The working environment within a healthcare organization is very complicated in nature with multiple stakeholders. Change and innovation within the NHS maternity services will continue as a result of:

- new technology and research;
- greater understanding of changes in women and families needs and expectations;
- a need to improve infant and maternal mortality rates;
- a need to improve lifestyle challenges such as smoking and obesity;
- encouraging health seeking behavior;
- focusing on, and appropriately caring for the vulnerable for example domestic violence and teenage pregnancy;
- Government and public-driven initiatives to provide efficient, equitable, cost-effective, quality maternity care that is easily accessible.

Case Exercise References

Besley, T., Hall, J., and Preston, I. (1999) The Demand for Private Health Insurance: Do Waiting Lists Matter?, *Journal of Public Economics*, 72(2): 155–181.

Carvel, J. (2006) NHS Plan for Central Patient Database Alarms Doctors, *Guardian*, November 21, 2006.

Committee of Public Accounts (2007) *Department of Health: The National Programme for IT in the NHS Twentieth Report of Session 2006–2007 Report, Together with Formal Minutes, Oral and Written Evidence.* London: HMSO.

Department of Health (2000) *The NHS Plan.* London: HMSO.

Department of Health (2004) *National Services Framework for Children, Young People and Maternity Services.* London: HMSO.

Department of Health (2005) *Maternity Services Survey.* London: HMSO.

Department of Health (2006) *Health Reform in England: Update and Commissioning Framework,* London: HMSO.

Department of Health (2007) *Maternity Matters: Choice, Access and Continuity of Care in a Safe Service.* London: HMSO.

HM Treasury (2004) *Spending Review: Public Service Agreements 2005–2008.* London: HMSO.

Hoeskma, J. (2007) Lorenzo Delivery Plans Now Stretch past 2010. Available online at www.e-health-insider.com/news/3131/lorenzo_delivery_plans_now_stretch_past_2010 (accessed May 20, 2008).

House of Commons Health Committee (2007) The Electronic Patient Record no. 6. Available online at www.publications.parliament.uk/pa/cm200607/cmselect/cmhealth/422/422.pdf (accessed April 22, 2008).

Leigh D. (2006) What Health Professionals Say About the New NHS Database, *Guardian*, November 1, 2006.

Propper, C. (2000) The Demand for Private Health Care in the UK, *Journal of Health Economics*, 19: 855–876.

Wanless, D. (2002) *Securing Our Future Health: Taking a Long-Term View*. London: Stationery Office.

Case Exercise Questions

1 Describe how KM could assist the NHS Maternity Services.

2 Discuss how and why the "people issues" are as important as the technical overhaul described.

Epilogue

The aim of this book was to demystify the usefulness of KM in the healthcare environment. Healthcare is a dynamic and complex information rich, knowledge intensive environment. In order to treat and diagnose even a simple condition, a physician must combine many varied data elements and information. Such multi-spectral data must be carefully integrated and synthesized to allow medically appropriate management of the disease. Given the need to combine data and information into a coherent whole—and then disseminate these findings to decision makers in a timely fashion—the benefits of ICT to support decision making of the physician and other actors throughout the healthcare system are clear.

Despite the proliferation of many technologies, such as EHR (electronic health records), PACS (picture archive computerized systems), CDSS (clinical decision support systems) and so forth, paradoxically the more investment in ICT by healthcare, the more global healthcare appears to be hampered by information chaos which, in turn, leads to inferior decision making, ineffective and inefficient operations, exponentially increasing costs and even loss of life.

To remedy this problem and maximize the potential afforded by ICT and consequently alleviate the current problems faced by healthcare, we believe that the tools, techniques, tactics and technologies of KM hold the key. This book has attempted to present the healthcare professional with the fundamentals of KM so that he/she can apply these to healthcare settings and thereby ensure that, at all times, high quality healthcare solutions are delivered.

Glossary

Boyd's Loop (or OODA Loop)	A cycle of four interrelated stages revolving in time and space (observation, orientation, decision and action) aimed at trying to ensure action. The last stage is based on germane knowledge and relevance to the given context, thereby ensuring that it is superior to any other action that might have been contemplated.
BPR	Business process re-engineering – the radical redesign of processes in an organization to make them more effective and efficient.
Combination	The transformation of explicit knowledge into new explicit knowledge.
Community of Practice	Networks of people who work on similar processes or in similar disciplines, and who come together to develop and share their knowledge in that field for the benefit of both themselves and their organizations.
Competitive Advantage	The relative (against rivals) beneficial differentiation in the market of an organization, by means of cost, market position, product or service.
Critical Systems Thinking	Critical systems thinking attempts to bring together systems thinking, participatory methods and reflection to help address boundary judgements and complexity, with particular regard to power structures. Compare with Hard Systems Thinking and Soft Systems Thinking.
Data	A series of discrete events, observations, measurements or facts, which can take the form of numbers, words, sounds and/or images.
Data Analysis	Typically used to sort through data in order to identify patterns and establish relationships.
Data Sharing	Sharing and disseminating data with colleagues and collaborators, international entities, or making data available to the wider public.
Data Warehousing	A generic term for a system for storing, retrieving and managing large amounts of any type of data. Data warehouse software often includes

sophisticated compression and hashing techniques for fast searches, as well as advanced filtering.

Database	An organized body of related information.
Declarative Knowledge	Knowledge of what exists and what does not—knowing ''that.'' Declarative knowledge is about facts, concepts and inference. Compare with Procedural Knowledge.
Distributed Healthcare Environment	The Distributed Healthcare Environment is a middleware that constitutes the basic functional infrastructure of the healthcare center, independent from the technological requirements of the organization.
Double Loop Learning	The ability to challenge and rethink the assumptions, routines, standards and decisions within an organization.
Electronic Health Record	A secure, real-time, point-of-care, patient-centric information resource for clinicians. The EHR aids clinicians' decision-making by providing access to patient health record information where and when they need it and by incorporating evidence-based decision support.
Emergent Properties	The Emergent Property of a system is the thing that the system is able to do that its component parts cannot. A bicycle is a system of transport to enable travel from A to B. It has within it a braking system, a gear system, and so on. None of these systems enable, on their own, travel from A to B.
Epistemology	The study of how we know what we know.
Evidence-based Medicine	Evidence-based medicine (EBM) involves integrating individual clinical experience with the best available external clinical evidence from systematic research when making decisions about patient care.
Expert System	A computer program developed to simulate human decisions in a specific field or fields. A branch of artificial intelligence.
Explicit Knowledge	Knowledge that can be shared by way of discussion or by writing it down and putting it into documents, manuals or databases.
Externalization	The transformation of tacit knowledge into new explicit knowledge.
Hard Systems Thinking	This takes the approach of Reductionism and assumes that there are well-defined agreed technical problems that can be solved with a single optimal solution using a rigid scientific approach is the way to solve problems. Compare with Soft Systems Thinking and Critical Systems Thinking.
Health Care Infrastructure	Systematic provision of a society for the optimal well-being of its members.
Health Informatics	The understanding, skills and tools that enable the sharing and use of information to deliver healthcare and promote health.

Health Information Management	The planning, budgeting, control and exploitation of the information resources in a healthcare organization.
Healthcare	The prevention, treatment and management of illness and the preservation of mental and physical well-being through the services offered by the medical and allied health professions.
Healthcare Information System	System consisting of the network of all communication channels used within a healthcare organization.
Healthcare IS Research	Scientific investigation into systems and communication channels used within a healthcare organization.
Healthcare Standardization	Solving problems that are common across the healthcare communities.
Healthcare System	Organization by which an individual's healthcare is provided.
Healthcare Value Proposition	The effecting of superior access, quality and value in healthcare delivery.
Holism	Holism is about the concept of a system whole being greater than the sum of is parts. It encompasses the notion of Emergent Properties. Holism is sometimes viewed as the antithesis of Reductionism.
Hospital Information System	The aim of a HIS is to use a network of computers to collect, process and retrieve patient care and administrative information from various departments for all hospital activities to satisfy the functional requirement of the users.
Information	Data that has been arranged into meaningful patterns and thus has a recognizable shape.
Information Processing	Sciences concerned with gathering, manipulating, storing, retrieving and classifying recorded information.
Information Quality	Discerning which information sources are more useful and accurate than others.
Information Resource	Any entity, electronic or otherwise, capable of conveying or supporting intelligence or knowledge.
Information Systems	The general term for computer systems in an organization that provide information about its business operations.
Intellectual Capital	Knowledge (that can be converted into value or profit) and skills that lead to a competitive edge in the marketplace.
Intelligence	The systematic process of diagnosing any output from a system using the key

Continuum	tools, techniques, tactics and technologies of the knowledge economy, i.e. data mining , KM and business intelligence, to ensure that at all times the future state builds on the current state.
Internalization	The transformation of explicit knowledge into new tacit knowledge.
IT Management	The manner or practice of managing IT, specifically regarding handling, supervision or control.
IT Strategy	An elaborate and systematic IT plan of action.
Knowledge Architecture	The blueprints for identifying where subjective and objective knowledge and /or tacit and explicit knowledge reside in an organization.
Knowledge Assets	Knowledge regarding markets, products, technologies and organizations, owned by an entity allowing it to generate profits and add value.
Knowledge Capture	The process of acquiring and storing information, ideas and relationship links in the people, processes and technology within an organization.
Knowledge Creation	The creation of new ideas and thoughts.
Knowledge Delivery	The act of conveying knowledge.
Knowledge Infrastructure	The design of the socio-technical requirements for ensuring appropriate KM, i.e. the design of the necessary people and technology requirements for facilitating KM in a specific organization.
Knowledge Management	The creation and subsequent management of an environment that encourages knowledge to be created, shared, learnt, enhanced, organized and utilized for the benefit of the organization and its customers.
Knowledge Nugget	A small but important piece of knowledge.
Knowledge Retention	Keeping ideas and thoughts within an organization.
Knowledge Sharing	Mechanisms to communicate and disseminate knowledge throughout an organization.
Knowledge Spiral	The transformation of one type of knowledge to another.
Knowledge-based Systems	Computer programs designed to simulate the problem-solving behavior of human experts within very narrow domains or scientific disciplines—this discipline is a sub-set of Artificial Intelligence.
Learning Organization	An organization that views its success in the future as being based on continuous learning and adaptive behavior.

MIS	Information systems designed for structured flow of information and integration by business functions and generating reports from a database.
Narrative	A telling of some true or fictitious event or connected sequence of events.
Networkcentric Healthcare Operations	The paradigm shift in healthcare delivery (derived from the military application of the concept of networkcentric operations) that takes a holistic view of healthcare operations, recognizing that healthcare operations take place at the confluence of a physical domain, an information domain and a cognitive domain.
Objective perspective of knowledge	Following the Lokean/Leibnitzian forms of inquiry, such knowledge facilitates greater effectiveness and efficiency.
Ontology	The study of what exists; the categorization of things. Often used inter-changeably with Taxonomy.
OODA Loop	See Boyd's Loop.
Organizational Culture	Comprises the specific collection of values, norms, attitudes, experiences and beliefs that are shared by people and groups in an organization.
Organizational Learning	The ability of an organization to gain knowledge from experience through experimentation, observation, analysis and a willingness to examine both successes and failures, and to then use that knowledge to do things differently.
Procedural Knowledge	Knowing rules, methods and documented organizational norms. Procedures—"know what," "know where," "know who," "know how." Compare with Declarative Knowledge.
Reductionism	Reductionism is about the view that a system can be explained by science or an approach to understanding a complex system by consideration of its component parts. Reductionism is sometimes seen as the antithesis of Holism.
Socialization	The transformation of tacit knowledge into new tacit knowledge.
Social Capital	Represents the degree of social cohesion that exists in communities. It refers to the processes between people which establish networks, norms and social trust, and facilitate co-ordination and co-operation for mutual benefit.
Social Network	A social structure comprised of nodes, individuals or organizations that are tied together by one or more types of interdependency.
Social Networking Site	An online community of people who share interests and activities.
Soft Systems Thinking	Soft systems thinking is a Holistic approach that aims at understanding problem situations and agreeing what problems exist, with a view to resolving the problem situation. Organizations are viewed as complex social

systems in which resolution, as opposed to solution, is sought by debate. Compare with Critical Systems Thinking and Hard Systems Thinking.

Storytelling	Use of anecdotal examples to illustrate a point and effectively transfer knowledge.
Strategy	Strategy is about long-term planning to achieve competitive advantage.
Subjective Perspective of Knowledge	Following the Hegalian/Kantian schools of inquiry, such knowledge facilitates sense making and innovation.
System	A set of bounded activities, entities and their relationships that together comprise purposeful activity that has at least one Emergent Property not exhibited by the individual components within the set.
Systems Thinking	The study and organization of parts and their dynamic relationships, that comprise a whole, rather than the study of static organizational parts.
Tacit Knowledge	The knowledge or know-how that people carry in their heads. Compared with explicit knowledge, tacit knowledge is more difficult to articulate or write down and so it tends to be shared between people through discussion, stories and personal interactions.
Taxonomy	The categorization of things. Often used inter-changeably with Ontology (meaning 2).

Notes

1 Each entry explains how data mining enables the knowledge transfer from the type of knowledge in the cell row to the type of knowledge in the cell column.

2 This case has been adapted from a larger paper From Data To Decisions: A Knowledge Management Approach For Productivity Increase In A Radiology Department, *International Journal of Biomedical Engineering and Technology* by T. Goodfellow, R. Bali, R. Naguib, and N. Wickramasinghe, 1(3): 259–272.

3 This case was prepared by Ranveer Nagra as the basis for a class assignment rather than to illustrate either effective or ineffective handling of an administrative situation.

4 Case supplied by J.H.J. Choi, V.E. Krebs, T.M. Omilanowski, and J.L. Schaffer, Advanced Operative Technology Group, Orthopedic Research Center, Cleveland Clinic, U.S.

5 This case was prepared by Mohd Khanapi Abdul Ghani as part of his PhD research work and appears courtesy of the Knowledge Management for Healthcare (KARMAH) research subgroup (BIOCORE) at Coventry University (U.K.)—www.coventry.ac.uk/karmah.

6 This case was prepared by Vikram Baskaran as part of his PhD research work and appears courtesy of the Knowledge Management for Healthcare (KARMAH) research subgroup (BIOCORE) at Coventry University (U.K.)—www.coventry.ac.uk/karmah.

7 Robert (Buzz) Conn, (Project Manager, Scientific Technologies Corporation, U.S.), Frank J. Welch MD (Medical Director, Pandemic Preparedness Louisiana Office of Public Health, U.S.), Michael L. Popovich (CEO, Scientific Technologies Corporation, U.S.). Email address: Michael_Popovich@stchome.com, website: www.stchome.com.

8 This case appears courtesy of Michael L. Popovich (CEO, Scientific Technologies Corporation, U.S.), Dr Jeffery J. Aramini (Public/Animal Health Epidemiologist, Director of Canadian Operations, Scientific Technologies Corporation, Canada) and Michael Garcia (Vice President/COO, Scientific Technologies Corporation, U.S.). Email address: Michael_Popovich@stchome.com, website: www.stchome.com. [An extended version of this case appears in Popovich M.L., Aramini J.J., and Garcia M. (2008) Immunizations: The First Step in a Personal Health Record to Empower Patients, *Studies in Health Technology and Informatics*, 137: 286–295.

9 This case supplied by David Johnston (Director, Applied Network Solutions Ltd, U.K.) with special thanks to Barbara Harrell-Bond OBE, chairman of AMERA, for giving her permission to produce the AMERA case study.

10 This case was prepared by Aapo Immonen as part of his PhD research work and appears courtesy of the Knowledge Management for Healthcare (KARMAH) research subgroup, BIOCORE, at Coventry University (U.K.)—www.coventry.ac.uk/karmah.

11 This case has been adapted from a larger paper: Gibbons M.C., Brock, M., Alberg A.J., Glass T., LaVeist, T.A., Baylin, S., Levine, D., and Fox, C.E. (2007) The Sociobiologic Integrative Model (SBIM): Enhancing

the Integration of Sociobehavioral, Environmental, and Biomolecular Knowledge in Urban Health and Disparities Research, *Journal of Urban Health*, 84(2): 198–211.

12 This case was prepared by Sushil Patria as the basis for a class assignment rather than to illustrate either effective or ineffective handling of an administrative situation. The name of the NHS Trust has been changed to the pseudonym "Crane".

13 This case was prepared by Kim Davis as the basis for a class assignment rather than to illustrate either effective or ineffective handling of an administrative situation.

Index

Aas, I.H.M. 13, 19
Abrams, D.B. 151, 153, 163
Acheson, D. 126, 129, 152, 163
Ackoff, R.L. 69, 88
Adriaans, P. and Zantinge, D. 43, 63
AIRA 73, 77
Alavi, M. 2, 21
Alavi, M. and Leidner D. 110, 131, 135, 163
Alberg, A. J. and Samet, J. M. 125, 129, 158,
    161
Alberts D., Garstka, J., and Stein, F. 112,
    125
Alexandrov, K., Cascorbi, I., Rojas, M.,
    Bouvier, G., Krick, E., and Bartsch, H. 158,
    161
AMERA xix, 100, 103, 192
American Cancer Society Inc. 58–59, 62, 161
Amick, B.C., Levine, S., Tarlov, A.R., and
    Walsh, D.C. 125, 129, 152, 163
Anthony, R. 106, 131
Applegate, L., Mason, R., and Thorpe, D. 149,
    163
Argyris, C. 90, 112, 131
Argyris, C. and Schön, D. 110, 131
Award, E. and Ghaziri, H. 135, 163

Baker, D.W. 124, 129
Bali, R.K. 18, 19, 88, 94, 106, 109, 131
Bali, R.K., Dwivedi, A.N., and Naguib, R.N.G.
    154, 163
Bali, R.K., Feng, D.D., Burstein, F., and
    Dwivedi, A. 18–19, 117, 131, 154
Banathy, B. 66, 88
Bankhead, C., Austoker, J., Sharp, D., Peters,
    T., et al. 60, 62

Baskaran, V., Bali, R.K., Arochena, H.,
    Naguib, R.N.G., Wheaton, M., Wallis, M.
    117, 131
Becerra-Fernandez, I. and Sabherwal, R. 8, 21,
    43, 45, 63
Beem, C. 56, 64
Belinsky, S.A., Snow, S.S., Nikula, K.J., Finch,
    G.L., Tellez, C.S., and Palmisano, W.A. 158,
    161
Bendoly, E. 43, 64
Benowitz, N.L. 158, 161
Berinato, S. 8, 21, 140, 163
Berkman, L.F. and Kawachi, I. 123, 129, 152,
    157, 161, 163
Berners-Lee, T., Hendler, J., and Lassila, O. 30,
    39
Besley, T., Hall, J., and Preston, I. 177, 183
Bessant, J. and Cole, S. 106, 131
Blanks, R.G., Moss, S.M., McGahan, C.E., and
    Quinn, M.J. et al. 59, 62
Boddy, D. and Buchanan, D. 69, 88
Boddy, D. and Gunson, N. 106, 131
Boland, R. and Tenkasi, R. 3, 21
Borman, W.C 131
Bower, M. 93, 131
Boyd, J. 39, 135–136, 143–145, 147, 156,
    162–163
Boyd's Loop 145, 147
BPR 11, 117
breast cancer screening 58, 62–63
Brown, A. 92–93, 131
Brown, J. and Duguid, P. 163
Burger, R. and Gimelfarb, A. 152, 163
Burrell, G. and Morgan, G. 70, 78, 88
Burton, G. 59, 62

194

Cabena, P., Hadjinian, P., Stadler, R., Verhees, J., Zanasi, A. 43, 64
Carnall, C. 99–100, 131
"carpet tile" 119–121
Carvel, J. 179, 183
CDC 72, 77, 159, 161
Cebrowski, A. and Garstka, J. 136, 163
Chandra, R., Knickrehm, M., and Miller, A. 150, 163
Checkland, P. 67–71, 78, 88
Checkland, P.B. and Scholes, J. 71, 88
Cheung, Y. B., Low, L., Osmond, C., Barker, D., and Karlberg, J. 123, 129
Choi, B. and Lee, H. 43, 45, 64
Chung, M. and Gray, P. 45, 64
Churchman, C. 69, 88
Clandinin, D.J. and Connelly, F.M. 53, 64
Coakes, E. 109, 131
Cohen, D., Spear, S., Scribner, R., Kissinger, P., Mason K., and Wildgen, J. 128–129
Communities of Practice 50
competitive advantage 2, 3, 11–12, 21, 23, 28, 32, 42, 111, 132–133
Connecting for Health 12, 19, 167–168, 170–171, 174, 178, 182
Cothrel, J. and Williams, R. 18, 19
Courtney, J. 163
Crane Care Trust 166, 167, 169, 173, 174
Critical Systems Thinking 65, 79, 81, 83–84
Cross, M. 12–13, 19

Danish Agency for Trade and Industry 33–34, 40
data 1–12, 17–21, 25–27, 29–30, 36–38, 43–50, 52–53, 55, 57–58, 60–61, 73–77, 85–87, 101, 104, 107–108, 111, 114–116, 118, 120, 122, 135–141, 143–145, 147, 149, 153–154, 156, 159, 161, 164–165, 167, 171–173, 179–180, 182–183, 185
data warehousing 43
database 5, 8, 25, 29, 49, 74, 76, 86, 106, 139, 178–179
Davenport, T. and Prusak, L. 1–2, 5, 20–21, 110, 131, 162
David Skyrme Associates 91, 131
de Reuil, V. 72, 77
De Stavola, B. L. et al. 123, 129
declarative knowledge 26, 35
Department of Health 13, 30–31, 33, 59, 166–168, 178–180, 182
Dervin, B. 5
Diez Roux, A.V. 125, 129
double loop learning 110, 112, 121
Drucker, P. 1, 18–19, 21, 163

Dudley, J. 98, 132
Dupplaw, D., Dasmahapatra, S., Hu, B., Lewis, P., and Shadbolt, N. 19

Earl, M. 98, 108, 132
Edvinsson, L. and Malone, M. 34, 40
eHealth Insider 174
electronic health record xiii, 122
emergent properties 65, 70
epistemology 68
Evans, R.G. and Stoddart, G.L. 152, 163
explicit knowledge 4, 7–10, 12, 18, 24, 26, 31, 38–39, 63, 110–111, 131
externalization 4, 8, 111

Fayyad, U., Piatetsky-Shapiro, G., and Smyth, P. 9, 21, 43–45, 64
Fiedler, K. et al. 96, 132
Fielding, J.E., Husten C.G., and Eriksen, M.P. 158, 161
Fiscella, K., Franks, P., Gold, M.R., and Clancy, C.M. 126, 129
Flood, R. and Romm, N. 110, 132
Forrest, P. 59, 60, 63
Franceschi, S. and Bidoli, E. 125, 129, 158, 161

Garfinkel, L. 159, 161
Garrity, J. and Barnes, V. 106, 132
Gazmararian, J. A. et al. 129
Geisler, E., Lewis, D., Nayar, M., and Prabhaker, P. 118, 150, 151, 163, 165
Gibbons, M.C. 126, 129, 151, 153–155, 163–164
Gibbons, M.C. et al. 151, 153, 164
Gibson, J. et al. 94–95, 132
Gorry, G.A. and Scott Morton, M.S. 18–19
Grant, R. 2, 21
Gray, P.H. and Meister, D.B. 109, 132
Greenberger, M., Crenson, M., and Crissey, B. 69, 88
Greenhalgh, T. and Hurwitz, B. 53, 64
Guarino, N. 40
Gummesson, E. 95, 132
Gupta, J.D. and Sharma, S.K. 110, 132
Gurteen 39

Habermas, J. 78, 81, 88
Hampden-Turner, C. 95, 132
Handy, C. 100, 106, 132
hard systems thinking 66–67, 83
Harrison, R. 100, 132
Haugen, A. et al. 158, 161
health inequalities 126, 129, 179

health informatics 85, 113, 115, 154
Health Insurance Portability and Accountability
    Act (HIPAA) 148, 164
Healthcare Cube 120–121
healthcare information system 137, 138
healthcare resource balancing 113
healthcare system 12, 37, 46, 120, 122, 126,
    143, 149, 150–151, 185
healthcare value proposition 1
Hecht, S.S. 1, 158, 161
Hedlund, G. 3, 21
Helbig, H. 39
Hendy, J. et al. 12, 19
Hillemeier, M.M., Lynch, J., Harper, S., and
    Casper, M. 123–124, 127–129
Hoeskma, J. 182, 184
Hofstede, G. 93, 97, 103, 132
holism 65
Holmes, J., Abbott, P., Cullen, R., Moody, L.,
    et al. 8, 21, 139, 164
Holsapple, C. and Joshi K. 43, 45, 64
Huang, K, Lee, Y., and Wang, R. 150–151, 164
Huber, G. 8, 21
Huczynski, A. and Buchanan, D. 94, 132

information 1–9, 11–13, 17–23, 25–28, 30–34,
    42–45, 47–48, 58, 60–64, 67, 71, 73–79,
    84–88, 90, 93, 95–96, 100–104, 106–109,
    111, 113–116, 118, 120, 122, 130–139, 141,
    143–151, 153–157, 163–169, 171–174,
    177–183, 185
information systems 23, 45, 48–49, 67, 74–75,
    104, 107–108, 137–138, 147–148, 166, 181
intellectual Capital 28, 33–35, 57
intelligence continuum 38, 135, 137–141, 156
internalization 4, 8, 18, 111
Itoga, S. et al. 158, 161

Jackson, M. 68, 70, 82
Jackson, T. 94
Jadad, A., Haynes, R., Hunt, D., and Brondman,
    G. 118, 132
Johnson, D.W., Stringer, W.A., Marks, M.P.,
    Yonas, H., Good, W.F., and Gur, D. 17, 19
Johnson, G. 104
Johnson, G., Langley, A., Melin, L., and
    Whittington, R. 17, 69
Johnston, D.C.C. and Goldstein, L.B 17, 19
Johnston, H. and Vitale, M. 106, 132

Kamataki, T. et al. 158, 161
Kanter, J. 2, 21
Kaplan, R. and Norton, D. 34, 40

KARMAH research subgroup 51–52, 146, 192
Kinney, P. et al. 125, 130, 158, 161
knowledge architecture 3–4, 120
knowledge assets 3, 24, 43, 57, 122
knowledge capture 23–24, 26, 111
knowledge creation 24, 32, 45, 60, 63–64, 110,
    118, 164–165
knowledge infrastructure 4
knowledge management 1–22, 31, 40, 49, 52,
    60, 63–89, 100, 102, 109–110, 131–135,
    139–140, 146, 154–155, 162–165
knowledge nugget 57
knowledge sharing 4, 18, 23, 25–26, 31–33, 36,
    84
knowledge spiral 4–5, 7–12, 38
knowledge-based systems 26
Kongstvedt, P. 122, 130
Kroeber, A. and Kluckhohn, C. 92, 94, 132
Krzysztof, J.C. 21
Kyle, A.D. et al. 158, 161

LaLonde, M. 152, 164
Langlands, A. 174
LaVeist, T. A. and Wallace, J. M., Jr. 125, 130
LaVeist, T.A. 125, 130, 152, 164
Laver, M. 106, 132
learning organization 33, 90, 110–111, 121, 131,
    133
Lehaney, B., Clarke, S., and Paul, R.J. 65, 69,
    79, 88
Lehaney, B., Clarke, S., Coakes, E., and Jack, G.
    20, 33, 71, 88
Lehaney, B., Malindzak, D., and Khan, Z. 40
Lehaney, B., Warwick, S., and Wisniewski, M.
    79, 88
Leigh, D. 179, 184
Lemke, H.U. 19
Lewis, P. 68, 88
Lewis, S.J. et al. 68, 88, 158
Licker, P. 108, 132
Liebowitz, J. 20–21, 162
Liebowitz, J. and Beckman, T. 18, 20
Long, L. 108, 132
Louisiana mass immunization 72
Lucas, H. 108, 132
Lucey, T. 107–108, 132

McGee, M. 8–9, 21, 140, 164
Macintyre, S. 152, 164
Malhotra, Y. 3, 21, 33, 40
Mandke, V., Bariff, M., and Nayar, M. 150,
    164
March, J. and Simon, H. 94, 132

Marmot, M. and Wilkinson R.G. 123–124, 126–127, 130
Marmot, M. G. 123, 130
Marmot, M., Ryff, C. D., Bumpass, L. L., Shipley, M., and Marks, N. F. 123, 130
Massey, A., Montoya-Weiss, M., and O'Driscoll, T. 135, 164
medicine net 59, 63
Mehta, N. 28, 40
MERITUM Project 28, 39–40
Meyer, J.M. and Breitner, J.C. 152, 164
Miller, D.P. et al. 158, 161
Mingers, J. 81, 89
Mingers, J. and Taylor, S. 69, 89
Mintzberg, H. 98, 106, 132
MIS 107–109
Miura, K. et al. 123, 130
Moore, L. and Diez Roux, A. 125, 130
Moore, T. and Wesson, R. 148–149, 150–151, 164
Morello-Frosch, R., Pastor, M., Porras, C., and Sadd, J. 125, 130, 158, 161
Morland, K., Wing, S., Diez, R. A., and Poole, C. 125, 130
Murray, L.R. 159, 161

narrative 34, 52–53, 55, 57–58, 111
Networkcentric Healthcare Operations 143, 145, 147
Newell, S., Robertson, M., Scarbrough, H., and Swan, J. 164
NHS xx, 12–17, 30–33, 59–63, 79, 126, 166–174, 176–184
NHS maternity services 176, 182–184
NHS Review 59, 63
Nonaka, I. 3–4, 7, 8, 21, 164
Nonaka, I. and Takeuchi, H. 26, 40, 110, 132
Nykanen, P. and Karimaa, E. 118, 133

ontology 28, 42, 67
OODA Loop 39, 135–136, 143–144, 156
organizational culture 23, 35, 39, 50, 69, 90, 92–98, 121, 131, 133, 167
organizational learning 8, 50–51, 90, 110–111

Pallarito, K. 137, 164
Pavia, L. 118, 133
Pedler, M., Burgoyne, J., and Boydell, T. 90, 133
Pennings, J. 94, 133
Perper, J. 149, 164
personalized healthcare 118–120
Pheysey, D. 92, 100, 133

Phillips, T.J. and Belknap, J.K. 152, 164
Pitot, H.C. 125, 130, 158, 161
Polanyi, M. 3, 26, 40, 110, 133
Pope, C. et al. 158, 162
Popovich, M.L. xviii, 192
populomics 135, 151–152, 154–155, 162
Porter, M. 109, 133
Prince User Group 69, 89
Probst, G., Raub, S. and Romhardt, K. 26, 40
procedural knowledge 26, 35
Propper, C. 177, 184
Putnam, R.D., Feldstein, L.M., and Cohen, D. 56, 64

Quinn, T., Bali, R.K., and Shears, K. 117, 133

radiology 12–20, 48, 192
Redmond, O.M. et al. 17, 20
reductionism 65, 67
Reed, D.H., Herzog, D.G., and Reed, G. 13, 20
Robbins, S. 94–96, 100, 133
Roos, G., Pike, S., and Ferntröm, L. 35, 40
Roos, J., Roos, G., Edvinsson, L., and Dragonetti, N. 35, 40
Rosenhead, J. 68–69, 89

Sackman, H. 68, 89
Schein, E. 94, 133
Schellinger, P.D., Fiebach, J.B., and Hacke, W. 17, 20
Schultheis, R. and Sumner, M. 106–107, 133
Scientific Technologies Corporation xviii, 73, 192
Scott-Morton, M. 108, 133
Senge, P. M. 90–92, 110, 133
Sergoui, N. and Burton, S. 174
Sharma, A.M. 152, 164
Shields, P.G. 158, 162
Sieloff, C. 18, 20
Singer, B.H. and Ryff, C.D. 153, 164
Skyrme, D. 34, 40
Skyrme, D. and Amidon, D. 25, 40
Smedley, B.D., Stith, A.Y., and Nelson, A.R. 124, 126, 130
Smircich, L. 92, 133
Smith, E.M., Ruffel, J.D., and Fisher, M. 13, 20
Smith, G. D. et al. 123, 130
Snowden, D. 6, 21
social capital 50, 56–57, 124, 127
social network 56
socialization 4, 8, 18, 111
Sociobiologic Integrative Model (SBIM) 153, 156, 160, 192

soft systems thinking 65, 67–68, 79, 81, 83–84
Song, N. *et al.* 158, 162
Sorenson, M. *et al.* 158, 162
Spender, J.C. 109, 133
Starr, P. 122, 127, 130
Stegwee, R. and Spil, T. 149, 164
storytelling 52–55, 57–58
Stucker, I. *et al.* 158, 162
substance abuse 141
Sunaga, N. *et al.* 158, 162
Sveiby, K. 25, 35, 39–40
Swan, J., Scarbrough, H., and Preston, J. 1, 22
systems thinking 41, 65–69, 71, 79, 81, 83–84,
    88, 92

tacit knowledge 3–5, 7–12, 18, 20, 23–27,
    31–32, 35, 38, 50, 54, 58, 63, 111
taxonomy 41–43
Taylor, F. 66, 89
Taylor, P. 17, 20
Thornhill, A. 94, 133
Tylor, E. 92, 133

Ulrich, W. 81–83, 89
urban health 122, 128, 142, 154, 156, 164, 193
Urquhart, G., Williams, W., Tobias, J., and
    Welch, F. 73, 77

Van Beveren, J. 118, 133
Vanderwagen, W.C. 72, 77
Vlahov, D., Gibble, E., Freudenberg, N., and
    Galea, S. 130
von Lubitz, D. and Wickramasinghe, N. 22,
    135–136, 143–146, 164–165

Wallace, R.B. 130
Walter, L.C. and Covinsky, K.E. 17, 20
Wanless, D. 166, 175–177, 180–181, 183–184
Ward, J. and Peppard, J. 133

Weaver, C. 53, 64
Weick, K.E. 5, 22
Weisburger, J.H. and Chung, F.L. 158, 162
Weiss, B. D. and Coyne, C. 130,
Welch, F. 75, 77
Wenger, E. 50–51, 63–64
Wickramasinghe, N. 18, 20, 50, 63–64, 117,
    134, 165
Wickramasinghe, N. and von Lubitz, D. 1–5, 14,
    15, 35, 111, 124, 125
Wickramasinghe, N. and Mills, G. 7, 22, 117,
    134
Wickramasinghe, N. and Schaffer, J. 50, 64, 135,
    138, 165
Wickramasinghe, N. and Silvers, J.B. 137, 165
Wickramasinghe, N., Bloomendal, H., de Bruin,
    A., and Krabbendam, K. 143, 165
Wickramasinghe, N., Geisler, E., and Schaffer, J.
    143, 165
Wigg, K. 20, 22, 162
Wilkinson, R.G. 123, 130
Williams, A. *et al.* 96, 103, 134
Williams, D.R. 152, 165
Williams, M.V. *et al.* 130
Wilson, B. 69, 89
Wiseman, C. 103, 134
Wu, Y. *et al.* 17, 20

Xu, J. and Quaddus, M. 117, 134

Yang, C.S., Chhabra, S.K., Hong, J.Y., and
    Smith, T.J. 158, 162

Zack, M. 2, 22
Zang, E.A. and Wynder, E.L. 159, 162
Zhao, B. *et al.* 158, 162
Zmirou, D., Masclet, P., Boudet, C., Dor, F.,
    and Dechenaux, J. 158, 162
Zmud, R. 104, 134

9 780415 994446